What it all came down to, I realized, was the success of our infantry, tanks, and tactical air in pushing the Germans far back from the crossing. However, since the Ludendorff Bridge was still expected to collapse at any moment, *we* were in the best position to provide a lasting means for getting enough troops and tanks over to save ourselves and our effort. We would just have to take our beating, get the bridge done by one means or another, and support others who would be in a better position to settle our bridge's ultimate fate. The faster we built our bridge, the more troops, tanks, and artillery pieces our generals would be able to send into the attack that would ultimately provide the best security for the bridge.

In my mind that afternoon, everything—everything— depended on us.

FIRST ACROSS THE RHINE

The 291st Engineer Combat Battalion
in France, Belgium, and Germany

Colonel David E. Pergrin
with Eric Hammel

IVY BOOKS • NEW YORK

This book is for
Peggy
and for the Carmelite Sisters,
who, through their prayers, kept us alive to tell this story

CONTENTS

MAPS

ABBREVIATIONS IN MAPS

Abn.	Airborne
Bn.	Battalion
CP	Command Post
Co.	Company
Div.	Division
Engr.	Engineer
Grp.	Group
HQ	Headquarters
Inf.	Infantry
Pz	Panzer
Regt.	Regiment
VG	Volksgrenadier

INTRODUCTION

Anyone who studies "The Battle of the Bulge" will soon become aware that one unit in particular played a major part in halting what in Hitler's eyes was the main effort—the thrust by the 6th Panzer Army in the northern sector. That unit was the 291st Combat Engineer Battalion. It was commanded by the author of this book, Colonel Dave Pergrin. His unit was unique. Not only did it distinguish itself in the Ardennes, but it went on to play a vital part in the crossing of the Rhine at Remagen. It was constantly involved in action from 16 December 1944 until the end of the war in Europe. Few units have such a brilliant record in World War II. What made this unit different? What made this unit stand in the Ardennes in December 1944 when so many others decided "discretion was the better part of valor"? What made this unit continue to build a bridge across the Rhine under fire against what seemed impossible odds? Others of course stood and fought as well and others displayed great bravery, but few with such dramatic effects.

One only has to meet Dave Pergrin to realize that here is someone different. Highly professional in all he does, amusing, warm, approachable, and a true Christian. These were the qualities he imparted to his men. These were, and are, the qualities needed in all good soldiers. The 291st were highly trained and they trusted each other and their commanders—again essential factors in the makeup of any good unit in any army.

There are many lessons in this book—lessons that are as valid today as they were forty-three years ago. Modern soldiers will ignore them at their peril.

It is an honor to have known Dave Pergrin and some of his men. Their place in history is assured and today's generation owes them a huge debt. Their bravery and professionalism earned us our most precious asset—freedom.

MAJOR GENERAL MIKE REYNOLDS, CB. (Retd)
Sussex, England

GLOSSARY & GUIDE TO ABBREVIATIONS IN TEXT

1stLt	First Lieutenant
2ndLt	Second Lieutenant
Bazooka	U.S. 2.35-inch rocket launcher
Capt	Captain
CP	Command Post
Exec	Executive officer
GI	Government issue; U.S. soldier
H&S	Headquarters and Service
LST	Landing ship, tank
LtCol	Lieutenant Colonel
Maj	Major
M1	U.S. .30-caliber Garand rifle
M2	U.S. .30-caliber carbine
M-2	Steel treadway bridge
MP	Military Police
NCO	Noncommissioned officer
OCS	Officer Candidate School
S-1	Battalion/Group Adjutant
S-2	Battalion/Group Intelligence Officer
S-3	Battalion/Group Operations Officer
S-4	Battalion/Group Supply Officer
SHAEF	Supreme Headquarters, Allied Expeditionary Force
SS	Nazi Praetorian Guard
V-1	German rocket weapon
V-2	German rocket weapon
WO	Warrant Officer

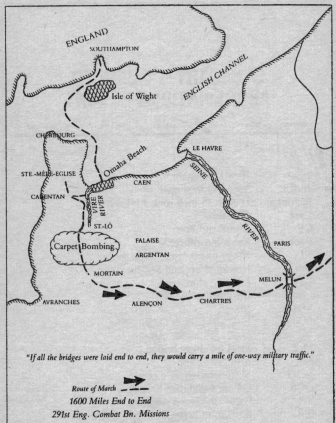

ENGLAND

SOUTHAMPTON

ENGLISH CHANNEL

Isle of Wight

CHERBOURG

LE HAVRE

Omaha Beach

STE.-MÈRE-EGLISE

SEINE

CAEN

CARENTAN

VIRE RIVER

ST-LÔ

FALAISE

RIVER

PARIS

Carpet Bombing

ARGENTAN

MORTAIN

MELUN

AVRANCHES

ALENÇON

CHARTRES

"If all the bridges were laid end to end, they would carry a mile of one-way military traffic."

Route of March

1600 Miles End to End

291st Eng. Combat Bn. Missions

23 Timber Bridges	6 Bridges Blown
44 Bailey Bridges	11 Bridges Under Fire
7 Treadway Bridges	7 Assault River Crossings
7000 Mines Cleared	235 Human Beings Rescued
8500 Prisoners Taken	15 Bombs Deactivated

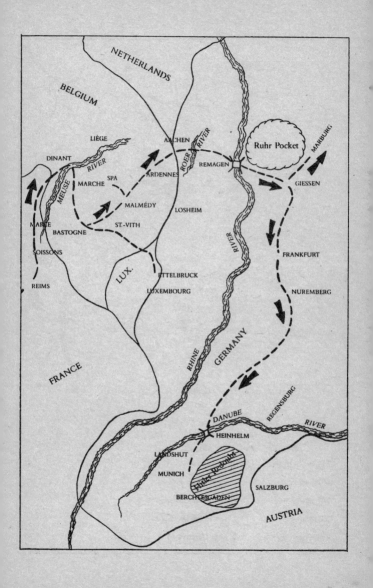

PROLOGUE

I would gladly have gone to West Point or Annapolis for my engineering education if there had been any appointments available in 1935. Fortunately, my high grades and football experience in high school sufficed to get me into Penn State *and* on the football team.

My freshman year at Penn State was busy, to put a good face on it. Most of the football players were physical education majors who were given ample time for practice. I was the only civil engineering major, and I had to attend many late afternoon science labs, which caused me to be routinely late for football practice. I also had to spend six hours a day working for my room and board as a dishwasher at a fraternity house, as a furnace attendant, as an engineering library librarian, and by delivering the college newspaper twice a week at midnight. Finally, I joined the Reserve Officers' Training Corps (ROTC), which was required of all male students at land grant colleges. My only time off from the grind was on Sundays, to attend church. Nevertheless, I wound up my freshman year on the dean's list and with an appointment to the varsity team.

Sophomore year was more of the same. My football season went well, but my grueling work load made me realize that my dream of making All-American probably would not come true.

My junior-year schooling was put off because of financial necessity; I spent the entire year surveying railroad tracks and laying out roads for a new U.S. Steel plant. I returned to Penn State in the Fall of 1938, made the football team, and rejoined the ROTC program. However, many of my junior-year engineering classes did not end until 4 P.M., and that made me late for most practices, so I wound up on the second string. The fall of 1938 proved to be Penn State's last losing season. I became

1

a ROTC cadet captain and commanded an engineer company. I was also elected president of my class. Despite the heavy load of responsibilities, my junior year ended in a blaze of glory when, among other academic honors, I was elected to the Tau Beta Phi and Chi Epsilon engineering honor societies.

Hitler's saber-rattling in Europe during the summer of 1939 added new impetus to my ROTC summer camp at Fort Belvoir, Virginia, where I progressed in my training as a future Army Corps of Engineers officer. Back at school that September, my duties as senior-class president, supervising a dormitory, and working at a bookstore completely eliminated football from my schedule. However, the loss of my football career left me free to pursue my major new interest—dating Peggy Cimahosky, whom I had first met when she worked as a tireless campaigner during my first run for class president. Peggy was kind enough to lend me the money for the honor society entrance fees. My senior-year ROTC training seemed particularly important, for the war in Europe had begun and seemed on the verge of spreading. Poland fell at the start of the school year, and our graduation in May was overshadowed by the fall of France. I was voted Outstanding Non-Fraternity Senior and, on Class Day, I presented the university with the Class of 1940 gift—the Nittany Lion Shrine, a fourteen-ton limestone monument symbolizing the Penn State tradition.

Upon graduation from college, I was commissioned a reserve second lieutenant in the Army Corps of Engineers and I was ordered straight to Fort Belvoir for my annual two-week training obligation. I spent the rest of the summer working as a junior engineer for the Pennsylvania Railroad maintenance department, which became a permanent full-time job. That Christmas, Peggy and I became engaged, but we decided to put off our marriage until the world situation changed for the better.

Early in April 1941 the Army called me up and ordered me to report to Fort Belvoir on May 22 for assignment at the Engineering Training School. The call to active duty was not unexpected and, to tell the truth, I was relieved that it had finally arrived. Until then, my life had been in a state of suspended animation.

Work began the day after I reported to Fort Belvoir. I was immediately assigned as a platoon commander with Company B of the Engineering Training Center. For the next thirteen weeks, I helped shepherd four thirteen-man squads of enlisted recruits through combat engineer basic training. The training was rigorous and without let-up: close-order drill and five- to twenty-mile marches; maintaining and firing rifles and machine guns; work with mines, demolitions, and fixed and floating bridges; map reading, scouting, and patroling in rugged terrain; physical fitness, athletics, and obstacle courses; night training in laying mines and demolitions; bridging in the assault of rivers; tactical engineer action in close support of infantry and armor in the offense and defense; and plenty of classroom time. My noncommissioned officers (NCOs) and I learned a lot ourselves and became superbly physically fit. In addition to broadening my experience in combat engineering, the first training cycle made me aware for the first time of all the different kinds of Americans there were living outside my native Pennsylvania. It slowly dawned on me that the war for which we were preparing would be a truly national effort.

During this period, my monthly paycheck amounted to all of $130, considerably less than I had been earning from the railroad. Nevertheless, on September 19, 1941, Peggy and I were married at the Catholic chapel on Fort Belvoir's main post. We found an apartment in nearby Alexandria, determined to have some time together during this uncertain era.

All talk among the officers at Fort Belvoir eventually turned to the progress of the war in Europe. We followed Hitler's dazzling blitzkrieg strategy through the Balkans and Yugoslavia and on into Russia. Far more than idle speculation was involved in after-hours discussions devoted to how German engineers cleared the way for tanks and mechanized infantry. Though we knew we would eventually be drawn in against the Wehrmacht, we were smart enough to begin thinking about how we might emulate the best lessons it had to offer.

Suddenly and startlingly, on December 7, we were at war with Japan. My indefinite tour of active duty had been indefinitely lengthened. Three days later, on December 10, we were also at war with Germany and Italy.

On February 2, 1942, after overseeing three recruit platoons through the basic-training cycle, I was appointed 1st Training Battalion adjutant. It was my job to develop a complete schedule for our four recruit training companies. The new job also provided me with an opportunity to study the performances of the various company commanders and their executive officers, all of whom had at least slightly more time in the Army than I. I was promoted to first lieutenant on March 3 and became the

Company C commander on June 4. On November 7, 1942, just as our forces were invading Morocco, I was promoted to captain and became executive officer of the 1st Training Battalion. The fact that we now had combat engineers in action in North Africa gave us incentive to deepen our already total commitment to turning out tough, savvy soldiers. Also, for the first time since being called to active duty, Peggy and I began talking openly about how soon I might be ordered to the Pacific, Europe, or North Africa. By then, younger officers with less experience than I had were filling company-commander billets in units bound for or already immersed in combat. I repeatedly requested transfer to the war zone, but nothing came of them.

Finally, on April 10, 1943, I was ordered to Camp Swift, Texas, for assignment to help train a new engineer combat battalion. Peggy and I packed our meager belongings and headed to my new station, fifty miles from Austin. We found an apartment on our first day in Austin, a Sunday, and I reported for duty the next day.

PART ONE

THE BATTALION

CHAPTER 1

Upon reporting in at Camp Swift, Texas, I was assigned to the 1115th Engineer Combat Group, a sort of regiment-size amalgam overseeing several newly created combat engineer battalions. After the briefest of welcomes, the group commander, a tough old bird colonel, assigned me to work as training officer for the 291st Engineer Combat Battalion. I was also designated an assistant division engineer. As I was leaving the colonel's office, he shouted after me that I better do what I had been brought there to do, which was to help shape the best combat engineer battalion in the Corps of Engineers.

Two weeks earlier, the 291st Engineer Combat Battalion had been created whole from a paper organization formerly designated the 2nd Battalion, 82nd Combat Engineer Regiment. The troops and all of the junior officers of this understrength new organization were raw newcomers. As an overseeing member of the group staff, my job was to be out with the troops while they underwent basic training and to pass on to the platoon commanders much of the expertise I had amassed during my time at Fort Belvoir. The training was intense, stressing physical fitness in the form of numerous forced marches and seemingly endless hours on the obstacle courses. As we introduced the troops to military discipline and inured them to the rigorous physical requirements of their work, we began introducing all the types of essential engineering training I had conducted or helped administer in Virginia. The only difference between the new and old assignments was that the 291st was a going tactical unit and not a manpower pool.

Among the many, many things we lacked was even one veteran of combat in the sixteen-month-old war. However, news from our units in combat had resulted in ongoing modifications

7

in combat engineering techniques and the identification of areas of expertise that had to be stressed.

The results were worth the grinding effort. On May 21, barely more than a month after the 291st was formed, 3rd Army inspectors rated the unit "very satisfactory" in its basic-training tests. I was particularly happy with the assessment, for I had been appointed executive officer of the 291st three days earlier.

The war on both fronts stood on the brink of expanding and intensifying in the late spring of 1943. Italy's and Germany's Tunisian bridgehead collapsed in early May, our forces in the Solomon Islands were preparing to jump off from Guadalcanal toward New Georgia, and several U.S. Army divisions in New Guinea were in a constant struggle. New Georgia was invaded by one U.S. Army division on June 30, and the British 8th and U.S. 7th armies invaded Sicily on July 10. On July 24, Mussolini was overthrown and, on August 17, our troops entered Messina, effectively putting an end to the fighting on Sicily.

As the 291st Engineer Combat Battalion entered its second phase of intense training, we all realized that we were going to be in the expanding war quite soon, perhaps within months. Emphasis was placed on small-unit problems coordinated from the company and battalion levels. Primarily, individual squads and platoons simulated close support of infantry companies and battalions in the attack and defense. We placed particular emphasis on radio and wire communications between units and with higher headquarters—a hallmark of the fluid blitzkrieg methods we sought to emulate. Despite Germany's almost incessant defeats in Russia, we were smart enough to perceive that the Germans were still winning when they could manage offensive armored and mechanized attacks, and that the Russians were doing the same. The highlight of the period was our assault crossing of the Colorado River using assault boats, footbridges, and pontoon bridges for supporting tanks.

At the time, the battalion commander and I—the only battalion officers who were not second lieutenants—were taking care to move many of the junior officers around, trying them out in billets for which their individual backgrounds and traits seemed best suited.

The battalion's officer cadre was an interesting mix. Less than half the lieutenants were college graduates, and only three had engineering degrees—one was a metallurgical engineer, one was a chemical engineer, and only one was a civil engineer (with a post-graduate year at Yale, no less). Several of the other officers had two or three years of college, but the majority were high-school graduates who, for one reason or another, had qualified for Officer Candidate School (OCS) and had been sent to the engineers because of some sort of civilian training or job experience. Nearly all had some sort of background in science, construction, or engineering. The average age of the junior officers was a bit over twenty-two, most had been athletes in high school or college, and 80 percent had been Boy Scouts. Several had served in the Civilian Conservation Corps.

We made a special effort to see that deserving junior enlisted men were given the opportunity to put on rank so we could move them up through positions of increasing responsibility. This factor and the constant movement of officers from job to job meant the battalion was in a state of self-imposed flux most of the time, but we felt it getting better and better with every change. Fortunately, we lost very few enlisted men and no officers through transfers we did not initiate.

On my twenty-sixth birthday, July 26, 1943, the 291st headed east to participate in large-scale maneuvers in Louisiana. Our job was to serve as an army-level engineering support asset for the newly formed 3rd Army. Here, we mainly constructed timber trestle bridges, as we had practiced time and again at Camp Swift. Also, for the first time in the field, our newly filled intelligence (S-2) section functioned as a key integral part of the matrix by acquiring information and feeding it to the decision makers and schedulers in the operations (S-3) section. In turn, S-3 assigned specific letter companies to complete multiple concurrent tasks suggested by the intelligence gleanings or assigned by higher headquarters.

Even at this early, rookie stage, it was gratifying to see the battalion functioning as a well-oiled machine. The only problem was that we remained well short of our full quota of officers and men. We knew that the unit would be brought to full authorized strength before we shipped out, but we had no idea how much time we would have to absorb and inculcate the last-minute flood of, we assumed, raw recruits and untested officers.

I missed most of the actual hands-on work the Louisiana maneuvers provided. As the battalion executive officer, I was considered sufficiently expendable to be detached temporarily for duty as a judge rating the engineer assault crossing of the Red River. However, on August 26, I was ordered by the 3rd Army senior engineer to report back to the 291st. As soon as I reached the command post tent, the battalion commander advised me

that the battalion had been ordered back to Camp Swift to prepare to move overseas. He also told me that he had severely
injured his back and thus would be spending a long time recu-
perating at the Camp Swift base hospital.

The trip back to Texas was not the least joyful for me. First,
I faced having to tell Peggy that her long-dreaded moment was
about to arrive; I would be leaving the country soon. Second, I
was genuinely concerned about the health of my battalion commander, an experienced engineer who had seen us through the
difficult formative months. Lastly, I was concerned that the loss
of a good, respected commander might be followed by the assignment of a less qualified, less caring outsider.

As soon as the troops were back in the barracks, I reported
to headquarters to face the group commander. The leathery old
colonel told me that the battalion had passed the unit-training
test with a very high "excellent" rating and the physical-fitness
test with a score of 94.7. This great news was followed by a
pause, then, "Young man, you are now the battalion commander. Prepare your unit for immediate overseas movement."

So, there I was, a well-trained but unblooded twenty-six-year-
old major in command of a combat engineer battalion on its way
to war. Since we would be on our way in a very short time, I
set multiple balls rolling to assure our readiness to enter combat
on the run, if it came to that.

I knew in my bones that the war in Europe—to which we
learned we were bound—was going to be highly mobile. Everything we had observed gave me the impression that combat engineers would be used in commandolike hit-and-run missions
with our lethal weapons, mines, and demolitions. To stand the
rigors of that type of warfare, the men had to be in top physical
condition, well trained to move into rugged terrain in close
proximity to the enemy to blow bridges or close defiles. Forced
marches and heavy physical training became daily routines.

As if it was not difficult enough just getting your old hands
up to peak physical condition, we had to absorb, train, and
harden the scores of recruits who were joining us from engineer
training commands throughout the United States. Fortunately,
the Corps of Engineers had a high priority for getting the best
and brightest recruits available. Our personnel people told me
that, even with all the new blood, the 291st was holding steady
at about 85 percent high-school graduates in the enlisted ranks.
The average age of all our enlisted men was nineteen, three or

four years younger than the average age of all soldiers in the U.S. Army that year. As a result of youth and intelligence, our recruits were able to come along fast as we threw literally everything in the book at them during those last frenetic weeks in the States; they quickly absorbed all they needed to learn, and they kept pace with the intense physical training. My experience with smart recruits from my earliest days on active duty obliged me to lay down the policy that everyone in the battalion, no matter how humble his rank, was to be kept as well informed as possible on all developments affecting the battalion. I had found that officers and men who knew the score put more effort into their duties than men who were kept in the dark. Besides, smart men needed an opportunity to apply their own capacity to reason to their situations.

What a mix! We had among our six hundred men and thirty-two officers born gentlemen and youngsters from the wrong side of every situation our society fostered. There were thinkers, and men who rarely imagined beyond the next meal. There were men who felt helplessly hemmed in by the strictures of communal living and the Army's often senseless rules and regulations. And there were men whose first real taste of freedom was provided by what, for them, was a lifting of personal responsibility provided by that same social order and by those same rules. There were men capable of committing unimaginable crimes, and men capable of bringing such moral outcasts back within the sphere of humanity, or at least of forgiving any human crime. There were eightballs, oddballs, and screwballs whose whole mission in life was to stretch the credulity and leadership skills of their appointed overseers to unimagined limits of tolerance. We had strong men, weak men, rough men and soft men. The Army had put them in uniform, called them "soldiers," scrambled them together, and unloaded them on my doorstep. Initially, it was up to me, about thirty raw second lieutenants, and a handful of seasoned, professional NCOs to refine the mixture in the crucible of training, to transform the human mixture into a palatable, useful 291st Engineer Combat Battalion we could all be proud of.

In addition to the hundreds of privates, we were joined by three officers during our final weeks at Camp Swift, two captains and a second lieutenant. The challenge was to find jobs for the captains that were commensurate with their rank but not at the expense of proven capable but junior incumbents holding captain's or even major's billets.

For starters, my old slot as battalion executive officer had not been filled; that would absorb one of the captains. Captain Ed Lampp was an academic high-school graduate with two years training as a civil engineer at Florida University. His records revealed superior evaluations at OCS. Most important among Ed's qualifications were his deep voice and noticeable command presence. I decided that he should be the battalion executive officer.

Captain John Brautovich had a two-year background in fine arts at the University of California before being commissioned and trained as a camouflage specialist at Camp Swift. I needed a senior S-3, but John's training helped me decide to appoint him S-2, in charge of intelligence and reconnaissance.

The third new officer, 2nd Lieutenant Frank Rhea, was unique, the only West Point graduate in the battalion. Possessed of a Military Engineering degree and a high scholastic record, Frank was a natural for eventual important duties, but he was also the battalion's junior lieutenant. I decided to give him one of the letter-company platoons, a perfect place for him to prove himself.

As always, some of the young officers continued to be moved around through the battalion to achieve their highest potential. I also did my best to identify the very best enlisted men deserving of quick promotion and maximum responsibility. The state of flux never really abated.

CHAPTER 2

Finally, on September 24, 1943, the 291st Engineer Combat Battalion set off from Camp Swift in a troop train bound for a destination undisclosed to most of the officers and none of the men. Hundreds of wives and children saw us off when we left Camp Swift, but only a handful of the wives knew that we were bound for England via Boston. Three of them, including Peggy—who was undertaking her first cross-country auto trip since learning to drive weeks earlier—set off together in time to deliver a round of last good-byes in Boston.

As soon as we arrived at Camp Miles Standish, outside the city, we got to work attending orientation lectures, abandon-ship demonstrations, and showdown inspections. Two days before we were due to sail, I turned the entire battalion loose on a twenty-four hour pass.

On the evening of October 6, Ed Lampp and his wife, also named Peggy, joined us at a Boston hotel to share a two-pound lobster. Then we all retired to our rooms for our last farewells. We boarded ship on October 8 and sailed for England on October 9.

Our last look at the United States was limited because most of the troops were otherwise engaged trying to hold themselves upright under individual pack loads better left to elephants. The result was pure slapstick of a variety only the Army can provide. Whole companies of overburdened engineers straggled from deck to deck in search of their assigned berthing areas. The confusion gradually subsided, though one hard-core loser finally found Company B when we had been three days at sea.

As the junior of four engineer battalion commanders, I was named sanitation officer. It was not a good choice. If seasickness is purely mental, as some experts contend, then our ship, a Grace liner hijacked for the duration, had more than a normal share of mental cases, myself among them. My poor stomach never mastered the incessant up-and-down-side-to-side-front-to-back roll of the ship.

Meals were served twice a day to those GIs lucky enough to be able to hold down their food. The usual procedure for those able to rise in the morning was to fall in the chow line for the average two or three hours it took to get served. As soon as the last breakfast had been dispensed, the line reformed for an afternoon meal. As time passed, fewer and fewer men found it worthwhile to stand in line for tasteless steamed food they were only going to throw up later. The lines got shorter and shorter at each meal. Partly as a means to get the troops up and around and keep them occupied, the ship's company offered seemingly continuous abandon-ship drills, which we were obliged to attend bearing full field packs. After a few days, two of my men threw their packs into the ocean. The ship rocked and rolled so violently at times that, one day, the denizens of one of the perpetual poker games slid across the deck in time to join a prayer service. I did not spend a moment aboard the ship when I was not bone-chilled and nauseous.

Finally, on October 19, a bedraggled, unshaven, filthy 291st was cast ashore at Liverpool. As ordered, I organized the dispirited troops for a grueling three-mile march to the nearest train station. There we boarded a long, overcrowded troop train that carried us to Devizes. When we formed up for inspection by our British landlords, we looked like a battalion of derelicts and drifters. The British colonel gave us an "unsatisfactory" and told me that I had nothing to be proud of except the American flag carried by our color guard.

We quickly got down to the business at hand, namely shaping up the battalion and drawing gear. Everyone was ordered to the barber for a haircut. As soon as we were looking and feeling good again, we traveled by train to Camp Stapley, in Taunton. There, I was told that we were to be part of the BOLERO operation, but no one told me what that was.

I continued to move my officers through the various billets within the battalion, first to find out who fit what job the best, but also to cross-train company officers and battalion staffers. I moved Captain John Brautovich out of S-2 to become my exec and made Captain Ed Lampp the battalion S-3. Two new captains were assigned in England, a doctor and a dentist.

We were in England for an entire month before we received even a hint as to how we might ultimately be employed. On November 19, 1943, Company B was suddenly ordered out after dark and dispatched to Truro, in Cornwall, to participate in a practice invasion landing exercise, our first amphibious drill ever. I followed the company to see what was going on and, for the first time, I gained the feeling that we might be in the forefront of the inevitable invasion of France. The engineers who participated in what was called the Duck Problem had to clear underwater obstacles and mines between ship and shore, overcome pillboxes, and support amphibian tanks in the attack. To me, the scariest realization was that we could be called upon to clear underwater mines under enemy fire and in advance of the infantry.

Finally, we lost our orphan status and were attached to the 1111th Engineer Combat Group. The group commander, Colonel H. Wallis Anderson, was the most picturesque character I had met in the Army until then—which is *really* saying something. He was a veteran of General Black Jack Pershing's pursuit of Pancho Villa into Mexico in 1915, and he had seen combat again in World War I. Between the wars, he had served in the 28th Infantry Division—Pennsylvania National Guard—while holding down a job as a civil engineer with the Pennsylvania Railroad. It was amazing to me how much we had in common—except for his age and combat experience.

Our training cycle was interrupted as soon as we were attached to 1111th Group. While Companies A and C were building two tent camps for large infantry units on their way to England, Company B rushed to construct a paved route to the future embarkation facilities for units that were slated to move to France. The work pressed our abilities to the limit, for the tasks were huge and the deadlines close. Only dedicated work by all hands got all three jobs done in time.

On March 1, 1944, the 291st moved to Highnam Court, in Gloucester, where we stopped building things and started training in earnest for what we all called the Big Show.

CHAPTER 3

I was *in* the Army Corps of Engineer hierarchy, but I was not *of* it. Like tens of thousands of fellow wartime officers, I had no direct stake in the Army's past or future. My stake was in the present, in winning the war. Hindsight has proven that this was the greatest strength of the U.S. military services in World War II. Most of us did not want to enhance our professional standing or even hone our professional skills beyond what was needed to win the war so we could all go home. Once I began thinking along those lines, I found that I was liberated from the "by-the-book" sort of conservative thinking that in so many ways hobbled the war effort. I found that I was obliged to follow the Army line only up to a point. Beyond that point, I was free to use my own mind, to form my own solutions, to conduct my own experiments.

For starters, I had some grave reservations about the formal organization of my standard, off-the-shelf engineer combat battalion. Mainly, these reservations came about when I started thinking about how inevitable combat losses might pluck key people with essential skills or unique training from our ranks. Once embarked upon this line of thought, I was quickly struck by an obvious solution: cross-train as many of my officers and troops as I could in whatever time we had left. The formal tables of organization stipulated how many specialists of a type we were permitted to carry on our roster, and how that cadre of specialists was to be apportioned through our line companies, platoons, and squads. However, there was no regulation I could find that prevented us from training specialist communicators, for example, to operate machine guns or arcane engineering tools. The training directives established minimum, not maximum, standards.

16

To be on the safe side, before embarking on my envisioned vigorous cross-training program, I visited the 1st Army Engineer, Colonel Bill Carter. After outlining my deep concerns about potential casualties and their inevitable results—a worry, it turned out, that the colonel shared—I briefed him on the details of my solution. He readily agreed to my proposal that I put the cross-training plan into immediate effect.

Shortly after we settled in at Highnam Court, we were given our first experience with the tactical assault bridge "erector set" designed by and named for Sir Donald Bailey. Depending on the length of the bridge, this engineering marvel was built by hoisting various scientifically determined combinations of prefabricated five-by-ten-foot vertical panels, each weighing five hundred pounds, into position across an obstacle such as a stream or ravine and then installing a tank-bearing roadway. "Panels up!" became our battle cry as we worked to delirium trying to shave seconds from the time it took our platoons to place their panels. We had no details, but it was pretty obvious that our primary mission in France would come down to emplacing Bailey bridges under fire. (See Appendix C, p. 329)

In addition to expanding, improving, and speeding our bridge-building technique, we were called upon to perfect our mine-detecting, -laying, and -clearing abilities. Then, when we had mastered those two vital combat engineering functions, we set about perfecting them in grueling night exercises. About the only condition we were not able and did not attempt to re-create was building bridges and clearing mines under fire.

My ongoing close study of engineer units in combat revealed a critical need to keep all elements of the battalion within the battalion's own communications network—no matter how much trouble the requirement demanded. Thus far, the war in Europe had been nothing if not fluid, and the engineering aspects placed enormous strains upon the organizational integrity of the combat engineer battalions, which were often doled out piecemeal to combat commands across a wide, ever-changing front. The absolute requirement to maintain cohesion via uninterrupted communications links was stressed throughout our training. The payoff to this admittedly rather rigid demand would be well beyond my wildest expectations.

The long hours of grueling labor and training was leavened by a moderately less grueling sports and athletics schedule—football and softball games, track-and-field meets, and Friday night boxing matches. Our arch rivals were our sister battalions in 1111th Group, the 296th and 51st Engineer Combat battalions. Our Company C swept the softball title, and four of our pugilists consistently won ring victories.

One of the most important factors resulting in the 291st's eventually outstanding combat record was that combat engineer units generally had the pick of the finest enlisted men entering the U.S. Army. Generally speaking, the average enlisted combat engineer was smarter, better educated, younger, and more physically fit than his infantryman counterpart. Brains and education equate directly with self-reliance, adaptability, and resourcefulness—precisely the traits we knew we would need to bank on the anticipated fluid, high-speed campaign through Western Europe.

The basic building block of the combat engineer line company was the thirteen-man squad. Each squad was composed of the squad leader, two riggers, one bridge carpenter, one assistant foreman, two carpenters, one demolitions man, one electrician, one jackhammer operator, two utility repairmen, and a driver. At least three of the thirteen had basic combat-engineering skills—the squad leader and two potential replacements.

By the time my cross-training syllabus was completed, every member of every squad was a qualified rifleman (.30-caliber M2 carbines for NCOs and .30-caliber M1 Garand rifles for all others). Every member of every squad was also qualified to operate the squad's .30-caliber machine gun and bazooka (2.35-inch rocket launcher). All knew how to lay, detect, and clear mines, and all knew how to prepare a demolitions charge. Each man could operate bulldozers, dump trucks, chain saws, picks, shovels, jackhammers, and all the other large and small tools assigned to the squad or its parent platoon. Most of the men could read maps. The squad leader and his assistant were trained to use radio and field-telephone equipment, and each carried manuals on the three main types of bridges with which we expected to work—Bailey, timber trestle, and pontoon.

While the thrust of our squad indoctrination and training emphasized working among advancing infantry and armored units, we had to train for our possible role in delaying enemy advances. It was safe to imagine that individual squads would be called upon to patrol in the enemy's rear or even act as quick-hitting commando units, laying mines, demolishing bridges, or damaging roadbeds. Thus, squad leaders in the 291st were selected and trained to be decision makers who could use proper combat engineer tactics to stop or delay the enemy. Emphasis was placed upon hit-and-run tactics in order to avoid directly engaging enemy units which would certainly be able to bring greater firepower to bear than our squads could possibly return. These requirements placed a heavy burden upon our noncommissioned troop leaders, for they went far beyond the mere technical expertise commonly expected of engineer NCOs. A huge amount of our line officers' time went into developing the combat leadership traits of their subordinates.

There were three squads in each platoon, and three platoons in each of the three letter companies. The platoon commander was a lieutenant and the platoon sergeant was a staff sergeant. During training in the States, I had had a good look at the 291st officer material and had begun categorizing line and staff functions. I realized from my experience at Fort Belvoir that each letter company (A, B, and C) would need at least one engineer with college training who could lay out the line and level for the different types of assault bridges with which we would have to work. I selected Lieutenant Al Edelstein for Company A, Lieutenant Wade Colbeck and Lieutenant Frank Rhea for Company B, and Lieutenant Warren Rombaugh and Lieutenant Don Davis for Company C. Eventually, we trained all our line officers and NCOs to undertake this vital task.

Each line platoon was equipped with a bulldozer, a weapons carrier, a four-ton man-hauling truck with a .50-caliber machine gun, and a number of two-and-a-half-ton dump trucks for hauling equipment and material. The platoons, companies, and battalion each had their own motor pool staffed by mechanics charged with maintaining all the wheeled and tracked equipment and vehicles. Each platoon had a weapons sergeant and each company had a supply sergeant, each overseeing a small section of specialists.

In addition to providing a perfect opportunity for our hard-paced troop training, our stay in England afforded me the time and ample opportunity to continually reevaluate the battalion's leadership and to cut and paste my thin complement of officers. We were joined by several new officers and NCOs in England, including a captain, but none of the new arrivals had any combat experience. By then, also, my original crew of second lieutenants had been promoted, some twice.

After rotating all my officers through all possible billets for their respective ranks, I finally felt comfortable with making permanent staff and line-command assignments. I selected my company commanders from among those who showed strong leadership and fairness traits, and my staff officers were selected from among those who displayed the very best available qualities for their respective and widely differing staff assignments. Even then, it took some readjusting before I was finally able to count myself satisfied that the 291st would be going to war with the very best person filling each and every vital command and staff billet.

By early May, my company commanders were Captain Jim Gamble (Company A), Captain John Conlin (Company B), Captain Larry Moyer (Company C), and Captain Max Schmidt (Headquarters and Service, or H&S Company). Captain Ed Lampp, a tough, demanding, resourceful farm boy was my operations officer (S-3), and Captain Bill McKinsey, a quick-thinking, quizzical, dedicated Missourian, was my intelligence officer (S-2). Captain Lloyd Sheetz, an intellectual fellow Pennsylvanian, was our liaison officer with 1111th Group. Our supply officer (S-4) was Captain Jim Walton, a highly resourceful, detail-oriented officer who developed a fine staff while we were in England. The personnel officer (S-1) was 1st Lieutenant Don Gerrity, who had to maintain the battalion's field phone and radio communications network as well as oversee troop assignments and the battalion's personnel records.

We were well trained and physically hard as the D-Day jitters began to grip the battalion in early May. All signs pointed to the Big Show's getting underway within the month. Finally, in mid May, the battalion was officially alerted for the move. I spent hours poring over *Stars and Stripes* editions in search of information about Hitler's intentions and the movement to France of large Wehrmacht forces. As the days ground away, I, along with most others, attended religious services whenever they were held and took every opportunity to write what might be last letters to loved ones in the States.

We knew we had been had on June 6, as soon as we heard that Normandy had been invaded by U.S., Canadian, and British divisions that morning. As it turned out, the BOLERO build up in southern England was a ruse that fooled us as much as it fooled Hitler. For days and then weeks after the OVERLORD landings in Normandy, our dissemblers kept the Germans—and us—convinced that the *major* assault was still pending and that it would take place well to the south of Normandy. If the uncertainty drove us crazy, there is no telling what it did to the German General Staff. We do know now that Hitler himself withheld forces that could have delivered a crippling blow against our forces in Normandy. The fact is, most of us were quietly relieved that we remained at Highnam Court on June 6. Frankly, the mere thought of clearing mines and underwater obstacles in front of the beach was my worst nightmare.

Finally, on June 18, we were ordered to Southampton to board ships. As soon as we reached the marshaling area, the battalion was broken down into company components and loaded aboard two transports and two landing ship tanks (LSTs). One of the numerous storms that had been plaguing cross-Channel traffic since June 5 delayed our departure and another delayed our landing. Finally, on June 23, H&S Company and Company A landed on Omaha Beach. Companies B and C remained in shipborne misery for three more days before staggering ashore on Utah Beach.

No stirring thoughts, no memories of stirring martial phrases disturbed my deeply held concern. The lives of every man in my battalion and countless soldiers we would be called upon to support rested in the concept of preparedness I had maintained during my eleven-month incumbency. Only when I first set foot on Omaha Beach did it dawn on me that I might not have known enough, might not have done enough.

PART TWO

BREAKOUT FROM NORMANDY

CHAPTER 4

Omaha Beach was still a mess when H&S and A companies landed there on June 23, over two weeks after the invasion; steel hedgehogs still remained in the water and, on land, it was obvious that engineer units had cut through minefields, blasted pillboxes, and cleared sunken obstacles that had threatened instant destruction of assault landing craft. On each side of the wide, tape-defined roadways we could see the debris of a bitter fight to secure the beachhead.

It was obvious that combat engineers had led the way ashore in front of the infantry on these savagely contested beaches. Our friends of the 299th Engineer Combat Battalion had sustained a very high rate of casualties doing so. Some of their men were killed even before they came ashore, when their landing craft were shelled about five hundred yards out in the English Channel. We also learned that two assault companies of the 29th Infantry Division's 116th Infantry Regiment had been virtually wiped out at the edge of the beach we crossed before they could even fire a shot.

As we penetrated farther onto dry ground toward our battalion assembly point at Vierville, we could see smashed gliders and green parachutes hanging from trees. All along the way were roped-off minefields surrounding smashed pillboxes. In the swamps, bodies of our paratroopers were still being removed by engineers wielding mine detectors.

Vierville was a shell-smashed village close to the sea. The individually landed companies of the 291st were to reassemble there in order to begin our first wartime mission, the clearance of mines along and maintenance of the road between Carentan and Ste.-Mère-Eglise. The stretch of road that was to come

under our care was the only hard-surfaced highway connecting
the two American invasion beaches, Omaha and Utah, and it
was the 1st U.S. Army's only lateral roadway across the slowly
expanding beachhead.

I was briefed on June 25 by the 1111th Group commander, Colonel H. Wallis Anderson, and received the 291st's assignments
within the beachhead. Thus, when B and C companies landed
and we finally became fully operational on June 26, I called all
my senior line and staff officers in for a full situation and mission
briefing. In our operations tent, Captain Bill McKinsey, our S-
2, and Captain Ed Lampp, our S-3, had set up a map which
showed the invasion army's progress from D-Day, June 6, to
the previous evening. The map showed that by the evening of
June 25 the 1st U.S. Army had fought its way out of Omaha and
Utah beaches against stiff German opposition. Three of our infantry divisions were fighting their way north up the Cotentin
Peninsula and were poised to capture the strategically important
port at Cherbourg. Meanwhile the 82nd Airborne Division had
sealed the peninsula against possible reinforcement of the German garrison at Cherbourg by driving west to the Gulf of St.-
Malo from Ste.-Mère-Eglise.
    The 291st's zone of responsibility was in the center of the 1st
Army effort, in general support of the VII Corps' drive south
out of Omaha Beach. Initially, we were to provide engineer
support directly behind the 9th and 83rd Infantry divisions and
maintain the 1st Army main supply route (MSR) between Carentan and Ste.-Mère-Eglise and south out of Carentan toward
Périers. Our wide-ranging missions would place us directly behind the VII Corps' four infantry divisions as they conducted
vigorous offensive and possible defensive operations. Our entire
zone would be subject to heavy German artillery fire and ag-
gressive bombing raids conducted by the Luftwaffe. We also
would be facing heavily mined and booby-trapped fields, villages, and buildings throughout our zone as well as numerous
bridges blown by the retreating Germans.
    Our main job was maintaining the exceptionally heavily trav-
eled thirty-mile-long MSR between Carentan and Ste.-Mère-
Eglise. According to Bill McKinsey, traffic along the single
narrow roadway was at a virtual crawl because of the sheer
volume of vehicles as well as frequent German air and artillery
strikes.
    After McKinsey completed his intelligence briefing, Ed

Lampp began laying out the battalion's mission and company assignments. In gross terms, Company A was charged with maintaining the first ten-mile stretch west of Carentan, Company B had the center ten-mile stretch, and Company C had the ten-mile stretch east of Ste.-Mère-Eglise. However, we would also be obliged to provide task-oriented engineer detachments as and when they were requested by 1111th Group or the combat units we were charged with supporting.

After Lampp and McKinsey completed their briefings, and the S-1 and S-4 added their comments, I rose to stress to the assembled officers that our mission was to service the infantry and armor units within our zone of responsibility by always keeping the supporting road net open for their munitions and supplies as well as for ambulances bringing back their wounded. I also stressed that we were not in France to confront the Germans as infantry and that we would not become embroiled in direct combat unless we had to in support of our engineering mission. Our main purpose was to save lives in the battle areas by using our many skills and the fruits of our rigorous training. I advised the officers to stress small-unit operations employing our excellent combat-engineering equipment, to facilitate the movement of tanks in support of the attacking infantry, to clear mines rapidly, and to constantly police and patrol our area up to the front in order to provide vital information to decision makers up the chain of command. I discussed the casualties we would inevitably sustain and indicated that our anticipated missions would not place our men under enemy fire for protracted periods. I stressed again and again the need to conduct our missions with utmost speed in order to conserve our own lives and especially to help save the lives of the combat troops we supported. I told the line officers that we would be able to consider ourselves good leaders only if we accomplished our missions at the lowest possible human cost to our well-trained battalion.

McKinsey ended the meeting with news that the adjacent British 2nd Army was preparing to make an all-out assault against Caen, which was to the southeast, just outside their beachhead line. As Bill closed, he was at pains to point out that the Wehrmacht and Waffen SS officers and soldiers hemming us into Normandy remained among the finest combat troops in the world and that they remained imbued with the notion that they could still win the war.

* * *

Next morning, June 27, after a fitful night worrying about my troops and listening to the *thump-thump-thump* of nearby artillery fire, I set out with my driver, Corporal Curtis Ledet, to survey the roadway under the 291st's care. On June 17 the Germans had launched a massive counterattack to retake Carentan and their advance SS panzer elements had penetrated to within five hundred yards of the town. Evidence of the brutal fighting was everywhere in the form of burned out tanks, trucks, jeeps, half-tracks, and even dead German artillery horses. Battered rolls of barbed wire, shattered buildings, dead cows, cratered fields, and more stood in silent testimony to the horrors of war. As we inched forward along the narrow, crowded roadway, ambulances carrying wounded from the nearby frontline positions of the 30th Infantry Division passed us on their way to evacuation points along the beach.

German artillery was active everywhere within its reach, but especially around Tucker Bridge, a vital Bailey bridge just outside Carentan named for an engineer major who was killed there early in the invasion. The shelling there was so heavy and so sustained that engineers from our Company A had to build sandbag shelters for the MPs and reinforced dugouts for themselves so they could maintain the bridge for the heavy road traffic between Omaha and Utah beaches.

I approached Tucker Bridge through bumper-to-bumper traffic and was met by Lieutenant Arch Taylor and Staff Sergeant Melvin Champion. They told me that early that morning two German frogmen had come down the river underwater and had attempted to blow the bridge. Machine guns on the span and banks had prevented the demolition of the Bailey bridge by killing or at least driving off the two Germans. Next, Taylor and Champion showed me where jeeps that had sought shelter off the roadway had plowed into fields of German mines, and Champion pointed out how the German engineers had rigged elaborate booby traps within the minefield to slow the efforts of their American counterparts—us.

I sent Corporal Ledet to wait with the command car about a quarter mile west of the bridge while I stayed with Arch Taylor to study the local traffic pattern. The MPs were holding the slow-moving traffic about one hundred yards on either side of the bridge and sending individual vehicles across the resulting open stretch at top speed. The method increased congestion along the road, but it prevented a lot of sitting ducks from being caught by German artillery aimed at the bridge. As we watched from the east side of the bridge, Arch commented that the incoming artillery fire was so pinpoint accurate that he believed the Germans had an observer stationed somewhere nearby, within sight of the bridge.

Soon, the shelling started anew. As soon as the first rounds detonated, the MPs halted all approaching traffic well clear of the one hundred-foot-long Bailey bridge. Then everyone took cover in the bunkers. The drivers of a stalled ambulance on its way to the front tumbled out into the rubble of a destroyed building. The shelling lasted for about fifteen minutes. The shrieking of the incoming rounds was ear-piercing and the explosions were teeth-rattling. It was my first personal taste of war.

Shortly after the shelling stopped, Colonel Anderson, the engineer group commander, arrived and pulled over to discuss with me the importance of this connecting link between the two beaches. He also told me of the death of our friend, Colonel Danny Spangler, the commander of a sister engineer group. Dan had been killed by a German machine gun as he tried to bring a field telephone forward to a stalled infantry unit.

At around 1000 hours, I had Corporal Ledet drive me up toward Ste.-Mère-Eglise. Just north of Carentan, we encountered huge piles of dead bodies in a field—one pile of dead Germans, and one pile of dead Americans. Nearby, our graves registration troops were digging common graves. Here and there, French civilians were coming and going along the verge of the shell-cratered roadway, many with farm carts piled high with their treasured possessions. At one point, I was stunned to see civilian butchers cutting up dead livestock at a makeshift roadside stall.

About ten miles up the road from Tucker Bridge, I encountered Captain John Conlin, the Company B commander, and Lieutenant Frank Rhea, his 3rd Platoon commander. After John briefed me on Company B's first busy morning on the job, Frank explained that the many smashed gliders I had seen mired in roadside bogs were left over from the D-Day landings of the 82nd Airborne Division and that recovery of dead paratroopers and equipment had been severely hampered by heavily sown minefields within the wetlands. Then and there, we decided to send Company B mine-clearing parties into the swampy fields so that our dead countrymen could be recovered.

We were joined by Sergeant Charles Sweitzer, one of Rhea's squad leaders who was also Company B's demolitions and mine expert. Sweitzer explained that most of the numerous German vehicles abandoned along the edge of the roadway were booby-trapped and surrounded by antipersonnel mines. He went on to tell me that extreme care had to be exerted when moving through buildings beside the right of way, for they too had been elaborately mined and booby-trapped.

Like Jim Gamble's Company A, John Conlin's Company B would be working around the clock in three eight-hour platoon-strength shifts. The heavy work of the moment naturally revolved around restoring the cratered roadway and clearing mines and booby traps well out along the sides of the road. I particularly sympathized with the squads that pulled mine-clearing assignments at night. Later, after the sector had been decontaminated, the wrecked German and American vehicles would be removed and various buildings would be razed to the ground to widen the verges.

The front line was only two or three miles away, and the troops understood that any enemy counterattack could quickly drive through to the MSR. During my brief stay, I was gratified to see that the troops of Rhea's platoon looked battle-ready and secure as they went about their business or reacted appropriately to intermittent artillery barrages.

I left Conlin and Rhea to complete my inspection of the MSR north of Carentan with the Company C commander, Captain Larry Moyer. The traffic I encountered was a mixed bag of ambulances, bridging equipment, towed and self-propelled artillery, tanks, fuel and ammunition trucks, personnel carriers, troop-carrying trucks, command cars, and jeeps. It was particularly sobering to see so many ambulances filled with wounded making their way back to the beaches. The logistics of the traffic were beyond my comprehension. I could not imagine the amount of planning required to sustain fifteen divisions and their supporting units occupying an area sixty miles long by about ten miles deep completely dominated by enemy artillery and honeycombed with swamps, minefields, villages, hills, waterways, and hedgerow-enclosed fields. All this had to be done through several temporary ports and along just one deteriorating main supply roadway.

Ste.-Mère-Eglise, our MSR's northern terminus, had been the first town in occupied France to be liberated by the Allies on D-Day when three planeloads of 82nd Airborne Division troopers parachuted right into the streets. I picked up Company C's commander, Captain Larry Moyer, along the way and drove on to find Lieutenant Warren Rombaugh's platoon busily clearing debris and mines from the road net leading in and out of the ancient crossroads village.

After sharing a K-ration lunch with Moyer, I had Corporal Ledet drive us back toward Carentan. About five miles south of Ste.-Mère-Eglise, we found Lieutenant Don Davis's Company C platoon rebuilding the shoulders of the MSR following the completion of a thorough close-in mine-sweeping job. Along with Warren Rombaugh, Don Davis was one of Company C's two school-trained engineers, a fellow Penn State alumnus.

I left Larry Moyer with Davis's platoon and proceeded back into the Company B sector, where Lieutenant Wade Colbeck's 1st Platoon was also clearing mines and repairing the roadway. Wade, who had attended engineering school at Michigan State was, along with Frank Rhea, one of Company B's two school-trained engineers. I stopped to hear what Wade had learned about the huge twelve-foot gaps other engineer units had blown through nearby hedgerows during our infantry's advance through the area. Though only on the job one day, Wade had already given the matter considerable thought. He suggested that bull-dozers be equipped with makeshift armored cabs to protect their drivers and then be employed to breach the hedgerows alongside the infantry.

As Ledet and I made our way through heavy traffic back toward Carentan, I saw heavy black smoke ahead, near Tucker Bridge, and heard the unmistakable *boom* of detonating artillery shells. When the shelling stopped and we had worked our way to the bridge, I found Lieutenant Al Edelstein and Staff Sergeant Paul Hinkel, of Company A's 2nd Platoon, examining several nicked panels on one side of the bridge. As one of Edelstein's squads was filling holes in the roadway, medics were administering first aid to a pair of MPs who had been wounded by shrapnel. Al quickly commandeered an ambulance from the delayed column and had the MPs and a wounded officer passerby driven from the area.

I inspected the damaged bridge panels and agreed with Al's assessment that they did not need to be replaced. Al was Company A's only school-trained engineer, the recipient of postgraduate engineering training at Yale. I rarely disagreed with his informed recommendations.

Ledet and I next forged on down the road toward Périers so I could get my first real view of the front. As we approached the zone of the 29th Infantry Division, it became clear to me why

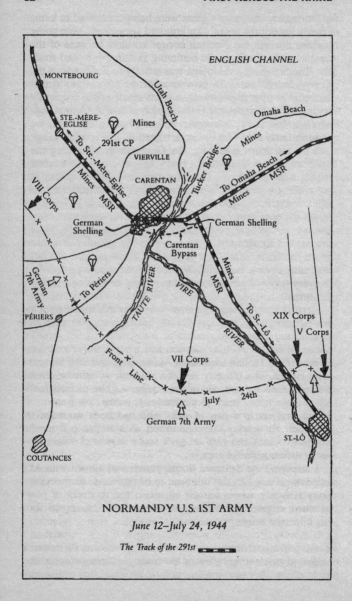

ENGLISH CHANNEL

MONTEBOURG

STE.-MÈRE-
EGLISE   Mines

Utah Beach

291st CP   Omaha Beach

VIERVILLE   Mines

To Ste.-Mère-Eglise   CARENTAN   Tucker Bridge

VIII Corps   Mines   To Omaha Beach   MSR

MSR   Mines

German
Shelling   German Shelling

Carentan
German   Bypass
7th Army

To Périers   Mines

PÉRIERS   TAUTE RIVER   VIRE   MSR

Front   To St.-Lô
Line
VII Corps   XIX Corps

RIVER   V Corps

July   24th

German 7th Army

COUTANCES   ST.-LÔ

NORMANDY U.S. 1ST ARMY

June 12–July 24, 1944

The Track of the 291st

the Normandy campaign's gains were being measured in terms of fields rather than miles. Our armored spearheads were going nowhere through the Norman *bocage* country because of the massive walls of hedgerows hemming in every field and roadway. The Normandy campaign was strictly in the hands of the infantry. Indeed, the entire invasion effort was almost at a virtual standstill. Everywhere we went, we saw small fields completely surrounded by massive hedgerows, each about twelve feet high and eight feet thick. Whenever we got close to the front, we encountered heavy incoming artillery fire and long-range machine-gun fire. Farther up, the Germans were blasting the American lines with mortars. Every time our troops smashed through a hedgerow, the Germans retreated, laying mines as they withdrew across the fields and along connecting roads. Both sides were dug in behind the hedgerows, but the Germans had the advantage in that they had dug-in tanks facing our unarmored infantrymen. Furthermore, the Germans were familiar with the terrain and they had the highly mobile 88mm dual-purpose antiaircraft/antitank gun, a direct-fire weapon of great range and uncanny accuracy. We, too, would be facing the vile 88s every time we moved forward to rebuild or replace a bridge the Germans had blown. In fact, it quickly became evident that the Germans were going to outpost every possible chokepoint with a covey of the dreaded 88s and supporting arms such as mortars and machine guns.

In addition to the hedgerows, the advancing armies faced numerous earthen banks, waterways, deep valleys, orchards, and wooded hills. The countryside for fifty or sixty miles around was broken up into a tank-defeating maze of squares and rectangles that had to be taken yard by yard mainly by infantry.

On the way back to Vierville, as I reflected on how our tanks could not penetrate the hedgerows, I gave more and more thought to Wade Colbeck's simple though high-risk solution involving our engineering equipment. In order to end the bloody stalemate in the hedgerows, I could see, bulldozers or tanks equipped with bulldozer blades would be needed to crash through the otherwise impenetrable growth.

Combat engineers were being used routinely to help the infantry advance through the mire of swamps and hedgerows. Each infantry division had a complete engineer combat battalion attached. Each of the organic divisional engineer battalions was charged with clearing mines and blowing pillboxes along its parent division's front. Indeed, individual squads of engineers could be attached to individual infantry companies, or doled out in whatever strength and configuration the infantry required.

Wade Colbeck's plan for defeating the hedgerows could have been undertaken exclusively by these organic division engineer battalions, but I knew they had their hands full clearing obstacles and directly supporting the infantry. Moreover, I knew we had the manpower and equipment to devote to the plan so, as soon as I got back to the battalion command post (CP), I phoned Captains John Conlin and Larry Moyer, my Company B and Company C commanders, and told them to find ways to protect bulldozer operators by means of makeshift armored driving compartments. Then I got on the phone to Colonel Anderson to outline my plan and ask him to find us an infantry unit willing to conduct an experiment.

Everything came together. By late the next afternoon, the first of our "armored" bulldozers were operating in direct support of infantry units mired in the hedgerows. Thereafter, while the bulk of the battalion maintained the MSR, detachments of B and C companies were crashing through the thick vegetation so the waiting infantry could instantly pour in against the startled German defenders. This quickly became an ongoing around-the-clock mission that eked out continual small gains across the broad, dangerously shallow beachhead. In time, an innovative American tank mechanic rigged a prototype hedgerow penetrator to the front of a tank. After this contraption proved out and was massively replicated, our bulldozers were allowed to stand down from this vital but extremely dangerous mission. Miraculously, none of the 291st bulldozer operators were killed in this exceptionally hazardous undertaking.

CHAPTER 5

On June 29, when I returned to the battalion CP following my daily tour of the battalion's zone of responsibility, the adjutant told me I was to return several calls from the 1111th Group commander. When I called, Colonel Anderson once again stressed the importance of Tucker Bridge, that it and our MSR were the sole link between the supply depots at Omaha and Utah beaches and the ten U.S. infantry and armored divisions then in the beachhead. He also told me that at least five more combat divisions would soon be ashore and that they would also need to be sustained by traffic moving along our MSR.

Word soon came down that General Omar Bradley, the 1st Army commander, also considered Tucker Bridge and the roadway between Carentan and Ste.-Mère-Eglise to be vital to the movement of supplies through the beachhead, and that he was extremely worried about them. If the Germans counterattacked again, as they had on June 17, and succeeded in securing the bridge and road, the beachhead would be sliced in two. Further, Cherbourg harbor was so badly demolished that when it fell on June 27 it was of no immediate use to us; the 1st Army would have to continue to be maintained entirely across the invasion beaches, and *everything* bound for the two corps manning the 1st Army's western front would continue to have to be moved through Carentan and across Tucker Bridge.

There's nothing like a little friendly pressure to keep people on their toes, but I was by then confident that the 291st would do its part without fail or misstep. There was little we could do to prevent the Germans from punching through the 1st Army divisions massed along the front, and there might be precious little we could do to stop a German breakthrough if it began, but I was by then certain that we could and would maintain the

MSR and Tucker Bridge against all the air strikes and artillery fire the Germans appeared capable of throwing at them.

Not all of the action was at the front of the dangerously shallow beachhead. In our bivouac areas, we had to dig foxholes to protect ourselves from air attack and frequent heavy artillery barrages. Everyone wore his helmet at all times. At night, "Bedcheck Charley"—a German medium bomber—and his pals flew over the beach and randomly dropped antipersonnel bombs. When our many antiaircraft guns tried to down the harassing intruders, we were further endangered by cascades of hot metal from hundreds of bursting "friendly" shells.

That night, as I lay in my cot listening to the rumble of the ongoing artillery exchange and the whine of Bedcheck Charley's engines overhead, I gave serious thought to how I felt about the battalion's performance thus far. The more I thought about all I had seen, heard, and discussed during our very few days of activity in the beachhead the more bolstered my sense of confidence became in the many independent decisions I had made in the long months since I joined the 291st at Camp Swift. I was unable to fault myself on a single officer assignment, or on a single enlisted leadership assignment. We had not faced all the problems and circumstances we could reasonably expect to face in the war—not by far—but I was sure that we were as well prepared for other new experiences as we had been for the new experiences of our baptism. Despite the rumble of the shelling and drone of aircraft, I finally fell into a deep, restful sleep. All seemed to be right with my world.

During our first few days ashore, my S-2, Captain Bill McKinsey, accompanied his recon team on regular visits to the front, where they collected samples of every type of mine and booby trap the Germans were using in Normandy. These were used to develop a training board, which Bill took out to the line platoons to demonstrate the characteristics of the explosives they would be encountering. It was a worthwhile effort because, in addition to maintaining the MSR, the 291st found itself responding to an increasing volume of calls to clear mines farther and farther out from the roadway.

Despite all our training and experience with mines, Private Francis Buffone, of Company C, suffered serious wounds on July 6 in a field along the MSR in which the fleeing Germans had booby-trapped the mines. He was our first casualty of the war. I conducted an immediate investigation, which offered important lessons we put to work right away. Despite the battalion's ongoing heavy work at clearing mines through the rest of the war, Private Buffone remained our only mine casualty.

On the plus side, despite the scheduling headaches we encountered in undertaking mine-clearing assignments, we were extremely well served by the independent organization of our engineer squads. Mine duty gave our junior troop leaders ample opportunity to hone their individual leadership skills far from potential interference by their superiors.

Except for manning local mine-clearing details, all of Captain Jim Gamble's Company A was committed to maintaining the bridge and adjacent roadway. Even though our armored bulldozers were vitally needed at the front, in the hedgerows, I withheld the Company A heavy equipment so it could be used to maintain the vital chokepoint. Miraculously, despite incessant German artillery barrages and air strikes and Company A's constant operation in the open, not one of our troopers was injured or killed at the bridge site during our first week ashore. However, several of the MPs assigned to regulate traffic at the bridge were wounded or killed, as were drivers and passengers in vehicles stalled or stopped by the incoming shells or followup repair work.

On the afternoon of June 30, I returned to the battalion CP from my daily inspection trip to find Captain Ed Lampp working over plans for a proposed two-mile bypass around Carentan to unblock the growing congestion within the battered town and at Tucker Bridge.

The main problem was that about half the accelerating volume of traffic was not headed to Ste.-Mère-Eglise and the VIII Corps front in the first place. It turned south toward Périers and the VII Corps front just outside of Carentan and west of—across— the bridge.

The main thrust of the plan, which had been proposed to me on June 29 by Staff Sergeant Elio Rosa, of Company A, was to cut a wide swath through the hedgerowed fields verging on the existing roadway east of the town. The new two-mile-long roadway would completely bypass Tucker Bridge and link back up to the VII Corps MSR south of the town. Traffic in each vital direction—south to VII Corps and west to VIII Corps—would be halved. For those critical two miles, the old MSR would support traffic heading toward the VII Corps front and the new bypass would support traffic returning from there. The plan was instantly approved by my boss, Colonel Anderson, and by his boss, Colonel Carter. My S-4, Captain Jim Walton, immediately began assembling the needed special equipment and materials while Ed Lampp oversaw the detailed planning.

On July 3, several of our Company A engineers spotted Generals Eisenhower and Bradley in person for the first time as their command car sped across Tucker Bridge. The quick passage of our two top commanders spurred our already frenetic efforts to begin the Carentan bypass as soon as possible.

On July 5, I moved B and C companies off the MSR, where they had completed the twin jobs of clearing and restoring the roadway. By then, Bill McKinsey and Ed Lampp had laid out the line of the new road, parallel to the old MSR through the hedgerowed field and across the east-west railroad line. As soon as B and C companies moved through Carentan, Captains John Conlin and Larry Moyer organized their companies so individual platoons and squads could simultaneously clear mines and booby traps, construct sections of the roadway, install culverts, drain swamps, build a grade crossing at the railroad tracks, dig drainage ditches, remove rocks, and demolish the many thick hedgerows along the right of way.

While Company A continued to maintain Tucker Bridge and patch the artillery-demolished streets of Carentan, B and C companies, supported by nine armored bulldozers, began work on the Carentan Bypass at dawn on July 6. A five-ton road grader had been obtained and Technician 5th Grade Charley Renson, our construction worker, stayed with it for eighteen unbroken hours as we rushed to complete the bypass in record time.

From July 4 on, the VII Corps, to our immediate front, advanced southward, in the direction of Périers, against incredibly stiff opposition. Despite the steady increases in the depth of the beachhead, the 291st's construction effort around Carentan was subjected to an average of a dozen artillery barrages per day. On July 7, shrapnel from one of the incoming rounds struck Private Robert Milositz, of Company C. On July 9, Staff Sergeant Paul Hinkel and Private First Class Walter Street were hurt by incoming artillery fire at Tucker Bridge. And Private First Class Patrick Libertelli, of Company C, was wounded on the bypass on July 11. Hinkel eventually made it back to the battalion, but Milositz, Libertelli, and Street did not.

The Carentan Bypass was completed on July 11—two miles of road built in five days—and the pressure at the Carentan chokepoint was relieved the moment the new roadway was opened to VII Corps traffic. Instantly—and miraculously—the familiar heavy German artillery barrages all but disappeared. For our clear-minded, practical solution and herculean efforts involved in planning and building the Carentan bypass, the 291st received a commendation—its first of the war—from Colonel Anderson, the 1111th Group commander.

Together with our early armored bulldozer innovation, the Carentan bypass helped speed the frustratingly slow progress of the 1st Army's consolidation and build up of the Normandy beachhead. At a strictly local level, the first arduous weeks in France afforded the 291st an opportunity the shake down and become accustomed to operating efficiently under fire. We proved we could take it and, more importantly, we proved we could, in our own manner, give it back.

CHAPTER 6

The 291st remained around Vierville and Carentan for a week after the completion of the Carentan bypass, improving the bypass and maintaining the road net in our zone of responsibility. Each day, the 1st Army front moved farther south, albeit at a grindingly slow pace. While we worked on the bypass, there occurred in the VII Corps sector a combined infantry-engineer river assault that was of tremendous interest to us in that it served as a model for much of the best, most important work we expected and hoped to accomplish in the war.

During the first week of July, the 30th Infantry Division's three infantry regiments had battled under their way through to St.-Jean-la-Raye, but the entire division became stalled on the east bank of the Vire River, a region of stiffly defended woods, swamps, and many small hedgerowed fields. The waterway at that point was about sixty feet wide and about nine to fourteen feet deep. While the 291st struggled to complete the Carentan bypass, directly behind the 30th Division, the three battalions of the 117th Infantry Regiment prepared to jump off on assault crossings of the river, and the 120th Infantry Regiment prepared to cross the Vire-et-Taute Canal, a shallow twenty-foot-wide waterway in its zone.

Rivers and other waterways are ideal obstacles behind which an army in retreat can at least momentarily rest and regroup while the army in pursuit usually must stop to prepare for tricky assault crossings in the absence of intact bridges. Though well trained and veterans of river-crossing exercises in the States, neither the 117th Infantry nor the 30th Division's 105th Combat Engineers had ever had to conduct an assault river crossing under fire, so preparations for the July 7 river and canal assaults were characterized by ample care and caution.

There were few methods available for crossing a defended waterway except a direct infantry assault closely supported by engineers. On July 7, the lead 117th Infantry assault elements would force their way to the far shore aboard engineer-manned assault boats. Once toeholds were established and laboriously built up by relatively small boat-borne infantry and engineer components, combat engineers in the forefront of the follow-on assault would drive footbridges across to the toeholds. Once the footbridges were in place, larger infantry units could move across rather quickly to aid in the expansion and consolidation of the assault toeholds. Meanwhile, as soon as the enemy had been pushed back somewhat, combat engineers would repair existing bridges that had been damaged and install wider, stronger vehicle-bearing bridges to the expanding bridgehead so tanks, tank destroyers, self-propelled and towed artillery and other combat-support vehicles could cross. As the bridgehead continued to expand, combat engineers would clear mines and debris from roads, fill in potholes and craters on the roadway, construct yet more bridges, and assist the assault elements at the point of contact with the enemy.

The Vire-et-Taute Canal offered different opportunities and solutions. Since the water was estimated to be no more than shoulder-deep, the 120th Infantry was ordered to wade across. Once the bridgehead had been secured, various engineer bridges would be emplaced routinely to extend the road net toward the front.

As soon as the river-crossing plan was promulgated, the 105th Combat Engineers prefabricated several footbridges and constructed scores of ladders with which the assault troops would scale the steep riverbanks. At the same time, various treadway and Bailey bridge companies brought up a large supply of components for each type of assault bridge and turned them over to the 1104th Engineer Combat Group's 246th and 247th Engineer Combat battalions, which would be supporting the 105th Combat Engineers, as would an independent engineer light pontoon company. The components of the various infantry and vehicle bridges were cached near the sites at which they would be installed and engineer assault boats were doled out among the 117th Infantry's assault companies.

Except for maintaining and expanding the heavily used VII Corps MSR through Carentan and on south, the 291st had no direct role in the assault. However, we were kept abreast of all the developments and preparations, both as a means of familiarizing us through a practical demonstration and to prepare us in the event any part of the battalion had to step in to assist our comrades in the 105th and other engineer battalions. Our S-2, Captain Bill McKinsey, spent most of his time with the 105th, writing detailed descriptions of their preparations that he would soon share with the rest of us. So did other observers from our S-2 and S-3 sections, who fanned out to join the various engineer units that would be taking part in the crossings.

The 117th Infantry's July 7 assault river crossings went off virtually without a flaw. Though the Germans defending the river line rallied with intense artillery fire, they were thrown back quickly and the assault battalions of the 117th Infantry made rapid significant gains despite heavy casualties. The hardest hit unit involved in the assault was a platoon of the 105th Combat Engineers that was struck heavily by the artillery fire as it attempted to build a footbridge across the Vire. A second 105th Engineers footbridge was torn loose from its moorings by the German artillery fire, but the span was resecured after several engineers swam into the river to recover the loose end.

As additional infantry units raced across the footbridges to reinforce the assault-boat elements, the 247th Combat Engineers got to work clearing and rebuilding a badly damaged seven-arch stone bridge so tracked and wheeled combat and support vehicles could wade into the fight. To complete the job, the 247th Engineers installed a 108-foot treadway bridge over the original cratered roadway. Despite vicious artillery fire, including barrages of deadly white-phosphorous shells, tanks and tank destroyers were crossing the rebuilt bridge by noon, just seven hours after H-Hour and only five hours after work on the bridge began. By then, other engineer units had built two additional vehicular bridges across the Vire: an eighty-four-foot pontoon bridge and a floating treadway. The pontoon bridge carried infantry toward the fight, the resurfaced stone bridge carried vehicular traffic toward the fight, and the floating treadway, installed just south of the stone bridge, carried ambulances and other traffic back from the front. All three of these bridges were fully operational before noon.

The 120th Infantry's assault at the Vire-et-Taute Canal stopped as soon as it began. Overnight, the canny Germans had opened the floodgates controlling the flow of water into the canal and the depth became too great for wading. The VII Corps chief engineer ordered the 1104th Engineer Combat Group to close the locks, but the job could not be completed in time to ease the assault crossing. Finding the canal deeper and wider than expected, the infantrymen clutched. There ensued a confusing fifteen-minute delay, following which the leading infantrymen finally plunged into the canal. Despite heavy artillery, mortar, and machine-gun fire that killed five and wounded twenty-six engineers, the company of the 105th Combat Engineers directly supporting the 120th Infantry erected a footbridge in only thirty-five minutes. This was a startling short-notice achievement. On the other hand, murderous German artillery fire at the site of a destroyed cross-canal bridge impeded efforts by the 1104th Group's 246th Engineer Combat Battalion to install a thirty-six-foot treadway bridge and thus delayed well into the afternoon the arrival of tanks in the 120th Infantry's hard-pressed bridgehead. Work on the bridge was finally begun beneath a smoke barrage laid by friendly artillery. Within twenty minutes, just as the smoke screen lifted, the bridge was fully installed and the waiting tanks surged into the bridgehead.

Problems ensued. A section of the pontoon bridge in the 117th Infantry's sector was weakened by incessant shelling; it collapsed that afternoon following a crash between two heavy vehicles. Also, the arrival that evening of a major component of the 3rd Armored Division caused a huge traffic jam on and around the 247th Combat Engineers' stone bridge.

Next day, July 8, the Germans counterattacked with the bulk of a parachute division and two crack SS panzer divisions. The initial German counterattack failed, but well-led, highly motivated makeshift German combat formations persisted. As the fighting raged nearby, the engineers repaired the pontoon bridge and added a second lane to the stone bridge, thereby immensely increasing the flow of traffic into the hotly contested bridgehead. On July 9, the engineers also added a ninety-foot Bailey bridge across the Vire to take yet more wheeled and tracked traffic. By then, nine six-hundred-man engineer combat battalions organic to or supporting VII and XIX corps units were involved in the vastly expanded and ongoing drive out of the Vire bridgehead.

The Germans put up fierce resistance. The American assault was not stopped, but it was slowed significantly. Over time, the offensive pretty much ran out of steam and had temporarily ground to a halt by July 20.

Despite the eventual outcome, the practical lessons available to the 291st by way of our observers' notes and subsequent briefings were to have a vital impact upon our own eventual involvement in literally countless stream and river crossings in France, Belgium, and Germany.

On July 17, the 1111th Group ordered the 291st to displace to St.-Jean-la-Raye to more closely support the VII Corps' continuing drive to a line running west from the fortified city of St.-Lô. The entire battalion quickly packed and displaced forward without incident on July 18. On that day, elements of the 1st Army's XIX Corps captured St.-Lô after twelve days of bitter, costly fighting.

St.-Jean-la-Raye was in the VII Corps zone, about eight miles west of St.-Lô and directly behind the by-then somewhat beleaguered 30th Infantry Division. Following our week-long respite around Carentan in the wake of the completion of the bypass, it was something of a shock to once again experience the incessant fall of artillery rounds and nightly visits by Bedcheck Charley. We immediately relieved the 30th Division's organic 105th Engineer Combat Battalion so it could prepare for the division's part in the next phase of the 1st Army assault out of Normandy. Thus, we faced the massive job of clearing as many as thirty-thousand mines and keeping VII Corps' north-south MSR open for the heavy traffic pouring in with supplies, equipment, and combat units needed to support the next assault, which was scheduled to jump off on July 24.

As the letter companies fanned out to relieve elements of the 105th Combat Engineers, Captain Bill McKinsey found a new and interesting way to reconnoiter the surrounding area. Somehow, our irrepressible S-2 hitched a ride aboard an artillery-spotting Piper Cub and thus viewed the area of operations from the air. His particular interest at that time was in locating German artillery positions that might endanger our efforts. Bill also located blown bridges and other obstacles that might impede the VII Corps' progress along its front. Bill's frequent aerial sojourns produced a series of useful photographs, but, most important, they guided Bill in the dispatch of stealthy night reconnaissance patrols for closer inspections of future engineering objectives.

Beginning July 18, the engineer missions of the 291st were many and varied. They included clearing minefields, building bypasses around blown bridges, operating quarries, filling craters in the roads, and patching road surfaces. We were tasked with removing American bodies from the battlefield as well. The fields were also strewn with German bodies, but we avoided

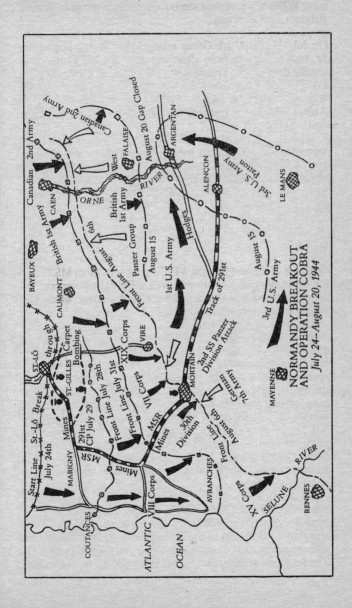

NORMANDY BREAKOUT
AND OPERATION COBRA
July 24–August 20, 1944

them out of reasonable concern over booby traps. The men of the 291st were now seeing war at its worst and were coming to realize how critical the combat-engineer mission was to our army's success in battle. We were experiencing most of the hazards of war, though most of us had not yet faced small-arms or machine-gun fire. Most sobering was the mute, horrible evidence indicating how easily the lives of the combat infantrymen were being snuffed out. Many of the men were eager to help extend the infantryman's life expectancy through a renewed commitment to hone their skills sharper than it was ever imagined they might be honed.

Taken together with our baptism centered on Carentan, the middle weeks of July provided the battalion with an unparalleled—and presumably final—opportunity to train under real-life conditions without actually having to stake our survival on the outcome.

CHAPTER 7

The equivalent of thirty-four Allied divisions suffered 122,000 casualties in the forty-eight days between June 6 and July 24 while taking only as much ground as the invasion planners had envisioned falling in just five days. The German defenders in Normandy admitted to casualties of 117,000 for the same period, but the German high command had yet to commit the armor-heavy 15th German Army Hitler had been withholding to repel the expected "main" invasion at Pas-de-Calais, about two hundred miles northeast of Normandy. Weeks behind their projected schedule and not unreasonably fearful that Hitler would soon release his strategic reserve for service in Normandy, the Allied commanders began casting around for some quick fixes to what they must have perceived as a grinding war of attrition they could not long afford. Thus, Operation COBRA was designed and billed as the decisive effort to break out of the Normandy box.

Beginning about two hours before H-Hour, nearly twenty-six hundred Allied bombers were to pave the way by saturating the German defensive sector across the river with a series of unbelievably dense "carpet-bombing" strikes in which forty-two hundred tons of bombs would be expended. The carpet-bombing technique had first been attempted on July 8, in front of Caen, whose defenders were stubbornly resisting attacks by the 2nd British Army. On that date, 470 heavy bombers dropped twenty-three hundred tons of light and medium antipersonnel bombs into an area only four thousand yards wide by fifteen hundred yards deep. The lighter bombs were selected in order to cause maximum German casualties without tearing up the terrain over which the British force would then have to advance.

The results had been mixed: many Germans had been killed,

wounded, or demoralized, but the infantry assault had been late getting started and it had encountered numerous unexpected obstacles created by the bombs. A somewhat modified second British effort on July 18 brought similarly mixed results in the 2nd British Army's renewed drive south from Caen.

The plot to assassinate Hitler erupted on July 20. It is arguable that some of the senior Wehrmacht conspirators became involved at least in part because of Hitler's stubborn refusal to release the strategic reserves held back at Pas-de-Calais. The German dictator survived, the plotters—including key generals responsible for the war in France—were quickly rounded up, and the 15th German Army remained in place.

The objectives of the carpet-bombing effort in front of the VII Corps were to mask the assault and saturate enemy defensive sectors as far back as their direct-support artillery positions. Following the bombing, the 1st, 9th, and 30th Infantry divisions were to deliver a coordinated assault across a relatively narrow front and punch a hole through which the waiting 2nd and 3rd Armored divisions would launch a pursuit of the presumably routed German forces.

The 1106th Engineer Combat Group was moved up to the VII Corps' left flank to support directly the 30th Infantry Division and the initially trailing 2nd Armored Division as they advanced along high ground on the west bank of the Vire River. On the VII Corps right flank, the 1120th Engineer Combat Group would support the 4th and 9th Infantry divisions in the assault and the follow-on 3rd Armored Division in the pursuit. Our own 1111th Engineer Combat Group would act as corps engineers in the VII Corps sector, devoting its efforts to opening and maintaining the supply routes and building and maintaining the longer, more permanent timber trestle bridges back along the MSR that would be opened by the advancing infantry and armor and initially cleared by the direct-support engineer combat battalions.

About a week before the scheduled assault, the 9th Infantry Division commanding general complained that his unit's front was too wide, so General Bradley added the 4th Infantry Division to the VII Corps. The completely motorized 1st Infantry Division was pulled off the line and added to the pursuit force of two armored divisions, and the 1106th and 1120th Engineer groups both were reassigned in their entireties—a total of six battalions—to the zone of the fresh 4th Infantry Division. The 1111th Group's support-engineering missions did not change.

* * *

The carpet-bombing plan for July 25—an Air Corps request for a one-day delay was granted at the last minute—outlined by far the largest such effort of its type. Initially, 350 fighter-bombers would hit the German front lines from west to east—parallel to the river line—to suppress defensive and antiaircraft fires. Then, as the American assault regiments withdrew twelve hundred yards behind their vulnerable lines of departure, fifteen hundred heavy bombers—also flying from west to east—would drop their payloads into a target area twenty-five hundred yards deep by six thousand yards wide. Next, another 350-plane west-to-east fighter-bomber sweep would catch surviving Germans as they dazedly lifted their heads to see what was left of their defenses. Finally, 390 medium bombers, also flying from west to east, would hit sectors immediately to the rear of the ravaged frontline target area to destroy longer-range artillery and reinforcements set in motion in the wake of the earlier strikes. By then, two and a half hours after the onset of the first fighter-bomber assault, the three assault divisions would be in motion across the river and canal, their leading elements already within the shattered German forward defenses.

The German Army Group B was obliging to the 1st U.S. Army's plans in that the bulk of its strength was deployed to the east, against the 2nd British Army in front of Caen, as was part of the 5th German Panzer Army. The 7th German Army, in front of our 1st Army, comprised about thirty thousand frontline and administrative troops, but only about five thousand of them, mainly from the SS Panzer Lehr Division, directly faced the VII Corps. Moreover, the German defenses in front of the 1st Army were extremely shallow and thus vulnerable to the piercing armored thrust General Bradley planned as a follow-on to the carpet bombing and infantry breakthrough.

The carpet bombing was nearly a disaster. American casualties from misplaced bomb strings amounted to 558, and much combat equipment was damaged or destroyed. On the other hand, the Panzer Lehr Division was shattered by the bombing because it had not been dug in deep enough. Thus, despite the shock and casualties sustained by our frontline battalions, our forces rolled over their forces. As our infantry advanced beyond the frontline sectors that sustained the brunt of the carpet bombing, German resistance stiffened and American casualties rose to a total of 1,060.

The 291st sustained no casualties in the carpet bombing, but we were close enough to the front to experience several near misses. The scariest moment was shared by a half-dozen men from Company B's 2nd Platoon who were patching shellholes in the MSR just behind the 30th Infantry Division. When the heavy bombers arrived, the engineers stopped work to watch the awesome spectacle and looked up just as a five-hundred-pound bomb landed in the field only ten yards away. The seven engineers at work there were sprayed with dirt from the impact of the bomb as they leaped for cover in a roadside ditch. A similar situation overtook a work party from Company C's 2nd Platoon.

On July 26, after the VII Corps achieved all its initial objectives against a dazed response, the corps commander, Major General J. Lawton Collins, exploited the breakthrough by committing two of his three mobile follow-on divisions. For the first time since the invasion seven weeks earlier, our forces waged a pursuit battle. For the next thirty-six hours, the battle became extremely fluid across the fronts of three adjacent corps (from west to east: VIII, VII, and XIX). The Germans evaded a trap designed to split their 7th Army and pin their left (western) wing against the Gulf of St.-Malo. Local counterattacks on our eastern flank by two panzer divisions detached from the adjacent 5th Panzer Army blunted the American armored breakthrough, but another of our armored columns overwhelmed a German corps as it withdrew across our center. The two British corps on the 1st U.S. Army's immediate left flank joined in the assault and also made significant gains in the direction of the city of Vire. The city of Coutances fell to the VIII Corps on July 28, and Granville and Avranches both fell—also to the VIII Corps armored divisions—on July 30. Next day, July 31, Lieutenant General George Patton's newly (and secretly) arrived 3rd U.S. Army assumed control of the VIII Corps and its sector. On August 1, the VIII Corps and its two freshly committed sister corps began a lightning armored drive toward St.-Malo and on into Brittany. As soon as Patton's 3rd Army became operational, General Omar Bradley turned the 1st Army over to Lieutenant General Courtney Hodges and moved up to command the newly created 12th U.S. Army Group.

The carpet bombing and subsequent breakout had an immediate and profound effect upon engineer operations all across the 1st

Army front. For the first time since the invasion, combat engineer units were being called upon to support the rapid motorized and armored drives originally envisioned at the time we were being organized, equipped, and trained. While not committed directly to supporting the frontline divisions, the 291st readied itself to undertake multiple tasks along potentially diverging axes of advance throughout the 1st Army sector.

As soon as the initial VII Corps assault began on July 25, Captain Bill McKinsey moved out with his reconnaissance team to develop information the operations section needed to plan the battalion's work in connection with clearing mines, repairing and replacing demolished bridges, removing vehicles and heavy equipment from the battlefield, and opening, widening, and expanding the road net for supporting tanks, all manner of logistics convoys, and, as always, returning ambulances.

Our letter companies followed directly behind the 30th Infantry Division as it advanced in the wake of the armored thrusts that had overrun its front. Beginning on July 25, within the frontline positions occupied by several of our infantry assault battalions, my engineers found huge craters in all the main roads, numerous German tanks and other vehicles knocked out by our air support, and extensive minefields strewn with the bodies of our infantrymen. We had been all through this on the Carentan—Ste.-Mére-Eglise and Carentan-Périers MSRs, but not at the frenetic pace required to support a full-blown breakthrough deep into enemy territory. When the enormity of the job we faced sank in, I thanked our lucky stars that we had been given an opportunity to become seasoned under the relatively mild conditions that had prevailed throughout the month prior to the breakout.

The first requirement—of which clearing lethal and nonlethal battle-connected obstacles was a necessary first step—was putting back in service the entire regional road net between the old VII Corps front and the rapidly receding new front line. Even in good times, the roads were in no way designed for modern traffic, much less for the demands of supporting armored and mechanized armies in the attack and defense, and the mass destruction of modern war made a shambles of what was already inadequate. Culverts had to be built, several miles of damaged, demolished, or merely abandoned German vehicles—including heavy tanks—had to be removed, and hundreds of dead German draft and artillery horses had to be disposed of along with hundreds of dead French cows and other livestock.

Our by-then battlewise troops began adding to the battalion's
authorized vehicle inventory by rehabilitating several choice former German vehicles. I quickly learned of these battlefield req-
uisitions, but I chose to turn a blind eye.

Every time we entered a newly liberated village or town, our
troops went right to work clearing mines and booby traps. Invariably, the French civilians responded to the dangerous efforts
by doing everything in their power and within their meager resources to return the necessary favor with profound acts of sharing. I noticed, also, that many of the younger men in the
battalion—youths of only eighteen or nineteen—were experiencing the first real dates of their lives in those war-torn French
villes. The work was brutal and never-ceasing, but the little time
the troops took out for play and frivolity seemed to lighten the
load.

The breakthrough along our front was so rapid and so deep
that we were not much bothered by incoming German artillery
or mortar fire, as we had been throughout our first weeks in
Normandy. In fact, most members of the 291st felt as if we were
undertaking difficult but nonlethal WPA or CCC projects in the
States. Nevertheless, Company C nearly came to grief when its
bulldozers were shelled as they raced to reopen the main road
through St.-Gilles. Fortunately, though the shells fell close to
our equipment and operators, we sustained no losses or damage.
It was, in the end, an exciting if rather benign reminder that we
still faced ample dangers along our road to victory.

From the outset, our platoons and squads were sent out on
their own, each with its own missions to complete. The many,
many hours I had devoted to selection of troop leaders paid off.
The various elements of the 291st rarely spent more than two
consecutive nights in the same place. Soon, our platoon and
company convoys looked like gypsy caravans, as indeed they
were, so adept had our youngsters become at purloining military
equipment, rations, and material from the battlefield—the spoils
of war that made their lives more bearable.

During this period, also, the 291st stabilized its method of
operation in support of a rapidly moving army. As the engineer
platoons worked around-the-clock shifts of *at least* twelve hours
each, my job was to visit the widespread work sites as frequently
as I could and to approve the plans and directives Captain Ed
Lampp wrote up for individual units. While Ed worked at the
center of the battalion, and I worked throughout, Captain Bill
McKinsey and his reconnaissance specialists worked at the pe-

riphery, collecting and assessing information the rest of us needed to plan details of the battalion's many engineering support missions. Among Bill's vital duties was locating suitable sites for our ever-shifting battalion command post—as close to the battalion's center of gravity as possible and as near the front as we could get without running the risk of drawing fire that could upset our fragile communications net and logistics effort.

While Bill and his troops worked between the front and the battalion's zone of responsibility, Captain Jim Walton's logistics section undertook the increasingly complex job of keeping us supplied with beans, bullets, fuel, and most important, bridging equipment. On one unforgettable day, Jim had to dispatch his section chief with a truck all the way back to the beach to collect enough fuel to keep us moving.

Lieutenant Don Gerrity, our personnel officer had an important job keeping morale up, mainly by handling the incoming mail for the troops. However, Don's major duty was to oversee the battalion's communications network; at times, this was the most important staff function any of us assumed. We simply could not get our many, many jobs done if our far-flung platoons and squads could not communicate their needs to the CP or if the CP could not instantly direct them to new job sites.

The mine clearing remained as tricky as ever. The Germans were masters at setting up minefields to restrict and canalize our opposing infantry and armor, and they employed all manner of mines and dirty tricks in the doing. We had no part in clearing lanes for our advancing infantry and armor—that extremely dangerous pastime was undertaken by the organic engineer battalions—but we had to clear bypassed sections of the road net and expand cleared areas well off the roads. It was dangerous, nerveshattering work, but we suffered no casualties.

One incident that amused me personally was my first ride in a German tank. Company A's Technician 4th Grade Jeff Elliott, Lieutenant Al Edelstein's personal driver, was an inveterate tinkerer who liberated a German Mk. V Panther tank near St.-Gilles and got it running. I came across Jeff and his tank while on one of my daily outings and Al Edelstein obligingly offered me a ride. Jeff cranked up the Panther and took me for a rather gingerly spin around a field that had been cleared of mines. After a few minutes, my apparent enthusiasm went to Jeff's head and he offered to show me all the tank's best traits. With that, he wound it up to full speed and attempted to drive it across a huge, looming bomb crater. As the Panther dipped into the crater and began rising as the treads bit into the opposite wall, its immensely long 88mm main gun dug itself in and stopped the tank dead in its tracks. Some embarrassed grunts filtered up from the driver's compartment as soon as the dust settled, but revving engine and grinding gears were not enough to budge us. Jeff finally admitted defeat and I climbed down to resume my inspection of the widespread battalion. Jeff did rescue the tank, but it was confiscated the next day by one of our army ordnance units. Soon Jeff rehabilitated a German half-track, but he spent so much time joyriding in it that he was fired as Al Edelstein's personal driver.

Talented souls like Jeff Elliott kept our vital rolling stock in running order and, indeed, added a huge number of rehabilitated and moonlight-requisitioned extra German and American vehicles to our inventory. I do not know what we would have done without our superb innovative mechanics or the extra vehicles.

Though the 2nd British and 1st Canadian armies remained bogged down or restricted to moderate gains on our left flank, Patton's 3rd U.S. Army, on our right, achieved spectacular breakthroughs mainly by going around the flank of the 7th German Army. The 3rd Army's VIII Corps virtually overran Brittany even as its two sister corps were turning south and southeast toward the distant Loire River and east toward Le Mans. Meanwhile our own 1st Army continued to advance in its sector, but gains were somewhat restricted because our frontline divisions directly faced the main strength of the 7th German Army.

While making a wide sweep which changed its facing from south to east, the VII Corps' 1st Infantry Division, on the 1st Army right flank, seized Mortain on August 2. The pivot into Mortain closed off the portion of the VII Corps frontage held by the 30th Infantry Division, which went into corps reserve to rest and reequip. We followed the Big Red One—as the 1st Division styled itself—doing what we did best: filling in craters you could lose a house in, clearing mines, picking up unexploded bombs and artillery shells, replacing bridges, removing debris, and generally improving the road net just to the rear of the fighting front.

While A and B companies cleared debris from the roads through and around Mortain, Lieutenant Warren Rombaugh's platoon of Company C quarried the vast amounts of crushed rock needed to fill huge holes in streets and roads throughout the net. Company C also constructed a bypass around St.-Fraimbeauet. My troops continued to work brutal twelve-hour shifts to keep the 1st Army's vital central MSR open to the front.

For several days prior to the fall of Mortain, we had been counting on being part of a projected lightning advance by three of the 1st Army's armored divisions, which were scheduled to drive another wedge through the German front. However, our expectations were shattered on August 6 when the just-recommitted 30th Infantry Division was struck at Mortain by the full force of a major German counterattack ordered by Hitler himself. The ultimate German objective was Avranches, on the coast, in the 3rd Army's sector, and the ultimate German aim was to sever the links between the 1st and 3rd armies and between the 3rd Army and the invasion beaches, over which we were all still being supplied.

As was so often the case by that phase of the war, the German strategy was grandiose beyond the means of their frontline field organizations, but the initial thrust at Mortain was nonetheless stunning. The 30th Division sustained exceptionally heavy casualties as it was sent reeling backward, but the Germans also sustained heavy losses and their advance slowed. Our two companies in and around Mortain were ordered to quickly abandon the town and the nearby quarry. Fortunately, they got out well before the German spearhead overran the quarry, and the entire battalion fell back on the small village five miles north of town at which my CP had been established the previous afternoon. We were not directly engaged nor even molested in the ensuing action.

Throughout August 6 and 7, in exceptionally bitter fighting, the two sides mauled one another repeatedly as key villages changed hands over and again. By the end of the day, August 7, the 30th Division was on the brink of collapse. However, help arrived in the nick of time.

As the fighting around Mortain raged on August 6 and 7, General Bradley ordered Patton to send two armored divisions to counterattack alongside two from Hodges's 1st Army. Meanwhile, Allied air power, particularly Normandy-based fighter-bombers, created havoc in the German tactical rear and a diversionary attack by the 1st Canadian Army drew off some German armor that might otherwise have been used to bolster the Mortain effort.

The tide decisively turned on August 8 when a renewed German armored thrust ran right into the vanguard of the arriving American armored divisions. The fighting was again exceptionally fierce, but the fresh American divisions fought the Germans to a standstill and, in some places, threw them back considerable distances. By the end of the day, the commander of the assaulting German corps conceded to his superiors that his divisions had suffered unsustainable losses. The Army Group B commander urged Hitler to allow him to pull back from in front of Mortain, but Hitler ordered him to continue the attack. Two more days of bitter, fruitless fighting ensued before Hitler gave in to the pleas of his frontline commanders.

Though the Germans backed off from the assault and, indeed, lost ground in several sectors, they did manage to hold onto some recaptured ground for several days. In the 30th Division sector, they held the remnants of an American infantry battalion surrounded until events far afield finally obliged them to withdraw on August 12.

Captain Jim Gamble's Company A drove through to Mortain once again on August 12, just as the Germans were withdrawing. As corps-level engineers, the 291st had not been directly involved in the action, though our ongoing efforts to refurbish and expand the local MSR had certainly helped support the 30th Division's stand and our multidivision armored counterattack. As my CP displaced forward to Mortain, I learned that the 30th Division alone had suffered approximately eighteen hundred battle casualties in six days, a virtually crippling percentage of its combat manpower. On the other hand, the 291st alone shoved over one hundred German tanks off the roads and streets in and around the town.

It took all of Company A's bulldozers and most of its manpower to gingerly sift the road-impeding wreckage of numerous buildings to recover scores of civilian, American, and German bodies. As difficult as it had been for Company A to clear and maintain the MSR through Carentan during our first week in the beachhead, that effort was in every way dwarfed by the frenetic pace of our second road-resurrection operation in and around Mortain. It appeared for a while that the 1st Army's most important job since Normandy hinged on this effort. Mortain stood every chance of becoming another bottleneck through which all of the 1st Army's vehicles might have to flow as the advancing infantry and armored divisions ground eastward in pursuit of the Germans. Fortunately for us, it was not to be; our efforts in the center were outrun by events on our flanks.

* * *

On August 8, even before the issue at Mortain was decided, General Bradley had ordered General Patton to pivot the 3rd Army's eastward-racing left corps—the XV Corps, which had just liberated Le Mans—to the north so that it could drive into the German 7th Army's left rear. At the same time, elements of the 1st U.S. Army's embattled VII Corps sideslipped eastward along the German left (southern) flank. These bold moves were made in concert with the 1st Canadian Army's simultaneous spoiling attack toward the right (northern) rear of Army Group B's three engaged armies. While the German center divisions pinned themselves down in fruitless combat around Mortain, the VII Corps and the 3rd U.S. and 1st Canadian armies made significant progress in what amounted to a massive pincers movement aimed at cutting off the main strength of Army Group B between Mortain and Falaise. Hitler's accession to his field commanders' pleas to stand down from the by-then pointless and extremely costly Mortain counterattack came just in time.

On August 13, the day after the 7th German Army began moving back from Mortain, the spearhead of Patton's XV Corps crossed the Orne River and drove into Argentan while the 1st Canadian Army's diversionary spearhead took on a life of its own and reached convincingly toward Falaise. However, in the perhaps mistaken notion that the Canadian drive from the north had been blunted, General Bradley redirected the XV Corps toward Dreux, far to the east. Bradley's new plan envisaged a wider pincers still aimed at encircling most of Army Group B's three active armies. The Falaise pincers were eventually closed on August 19, when 1st U.S. Army units met 1st Canadian Army units at Chambois. The entrapped Germans made one attempt to break out, but the effort failed and the remaining Germans surrendered. Over fifty thousand prisoners fell into our hands, and over ten thousand German corpses were buried within the pocket. However, by then Army Group B had saved most of its strategically vital panzer formations.

The wider pincers envisioned by General Bradley failed to bag Army Group B, but the 3rd Army's XV Corps reached Orléans and Dreux on August 16 and breached the Seine River at Mantes-la-Jolie on August 19.

Adding to German woes was the invasion of southern France by the 7th U.S. Army on August 15. This invasion was not seriously opposed and the 7th U.S. Army and the emergent

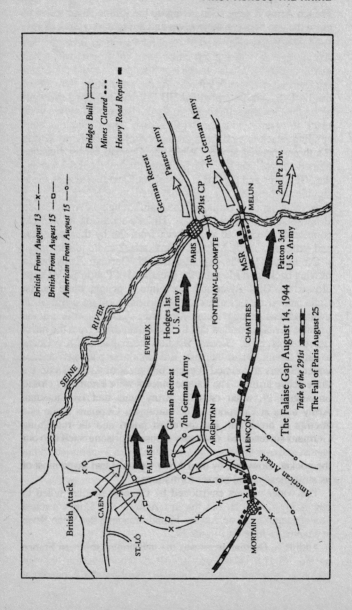

Bridges Built   ⋈
Mines Cleared   •••
Heavy Road Repair   ■■

British Front August 13 ——×——
British Front August 15 ——□——
American Front August 15 ——○——

SEINE RIVER

German Retreat
Panzer Army

291st CP

7th German Army

2nd Pz Div.

PARIS

FONTENAY-LE-COMPTE

MELUN

MSR

Hodges 1st
U.S. Army

EVREUX

CHARTRES

Patton 3rd
U.S. Army

German Retreat
7th German Army

ARGENTAN

ALENCON

The Falaise Gap August 14, 1944

Track of the 291st ■■■■■
The Fall of Paris August 25

FALAISE

American Attack

British Attack

CAEN

ST-LÔ

MORTAIN

French Army B were soon racing up the Rhone River valley to close the gap between themselves and the southern flank of Patton's 3rd Army.

CHAPTER 8

As elements of the 291st worked outward from the town of Mortain to refurbish the 1st Army road net, we found that the former German MSR through and behind the town—all the way to Falaise—was strewn with literally miles of wrecked and abandoned German trucks, half-tracks, and tanks, and hundreds upon hundreds of horse-drawn wagons and artillery pieces. Dead Germans and dead German horses lay everywhere. Apparently, though our ground forces were unable to close on the rapidly receding German main body, our tactical fighter and bomber groups were doing a fine job of breaking up their roadbound field units.

Lieutenant Wade Colbeck's platoon of Company B was dragooned briefly to build an enclosure for some of the many thousands of German prisoners who fell into the 1st Army's hands during the final phase of the retreat through Falaise. Word soon spread through the battalion from Colbeck's platoon that there were very few Germans among the prisoners; mostly they were Ukrainians and Cossacks who had rallied to the Nazi anti-Stalin cause.

As the Germans continued to run, our battalion zone of responsibility stretched out from Mortain all the way to Alençon, many miles to the east along the 1st Army's main axis of advance. The task was huge and demanded a great deal from the leaders of individual squads operating far from the battalion, company, or even platoon command posts. In general, the 291st had an enormous burden of responsibility and prestige riding on the outcome of our assignments. According to news filtering down through 1111th Group headquarters, we had come to be considered the 1st Army's premier road- and bridge-building battalion. This news certainly explained why we were always finding ourselves servicing the army's central MSR.

Despite the Allies' failure to trap Army Group B west of the Seine, the MSR and associated roads through and around Mortain were extremely busy and remained crucial to the 1st U.S. Army's immediate ongoing operations. The continued importance of the Mortain road net was at variance with the original logistics plan for Bradley's 12th Army Group following the Normandy breakout.

The VIII Corps' ongoing battles in Brittany to overcome the German defenders of Brest, Lorient, and St.-Nazaire were initially seen as being crucial to shifting a large part of the total Allied logistics burden from Normandy. However, the 3rd Army's lightning drive eastward out of Brittany toward the Seine—a drive attended by Army Group B's eventual retreat to the east bank of that river—caused General Eisenhower's staff at Supreme Headquarters, Allied Expeditionary Force (SHAEF) to lose interest in the Brittany ports. This was because it became reasonable to assume that the nearer Channel ports in northern France would soon be abandoned by or liberated from the Germans. Brittany was simply too many road miles from the Seine front to be of practical use to the Allied armies. Thus, until the various Channel ports fell, Mortain would serve as a road nexus between Normandy and the advancing front. In this regard—as in the matter of the hugely successful makeshift drive to the Seine—our herculean efforts at Mortain were not particularly fruitful in our own behalf. Events that were running very close together would soon conspire to render Mortain a backwater.

The main 12th Army Group objective following the action between Mortain and Falaise was naturally the Seine River. Given the VII Corps' central location in the 12th Army Group sector, it was reasonable for us to assume that we would be directly involved in rebuilding and replacing the many Seine bridges knocked out by the Allied air forces or by the retreating Germans. That is indeed what occurred.

The bulk of the 291st left the area around Mortain on August 24. As we leapfrogged our sister 1111th Group battalions all the way to the Seine, we temporarily dropped off individual squads here and there to undertake quick mine-clearing and road-repair assignments. In under thirty-six hours, the main body of the battalion motored nearly two hundred miles in company-size convoys through Domfront, Alençon, Mortagne, and Chartres to the vicinity of Melun, a river city about twenty-five miles south of Paris.

Along the way, we saw our sister battalions struggling to resurrect or replace the many bridges the coldly efficient German engineers had blown during the latter phase of their retreat. Of course, our enemies were not the only destroyers of vital bridges. Many spans had been demolished or damaged by our own air power, which for a time was our only combat arm capable of maintaining contact with the German main body. Every effort was made to slow the Germans so our ground forces could catch up, and that naturally meant bombing and rocketing bridges from the air before the Germans reached them or while they were in use.

To our immense relief, the Germans were too hard-pressed to put in many minefields. We witnessed some light bombing by German aircraft along the way, but we were not molested at all by German artillery.

On August 25, while we were racing up the road from Mortain, the Seine was crossed at three new bridgeheads south of Paris, which itself fell that day to the 2nd French Armored Division, part of the 1st U.S. Army's V Corps.

On August 26, the 291st's H&S Company arrived at Fontenayle-Compte, just south of Paris. There, we set up our tents on the beautiful estate's front lawn. The count graciously invited several of us into the château and fed us an exceptional, sumptuous, wine-accompanied seven-course meal from his linen-clothed table.

Leave was granted to the troops on a rotating basis and our battalion surgeon was immediately beset by an epidemic of Parisian venereal diseases. Strong measures were adopted instantly in the form of rigorous preventive education and the epidemic was quickly and almost completely controlled. Despite the liberal leave policy, our arrival at the Seine barrier set off an intense period of bridge construction and maintenance centered on Melun. Mainly, we had to replace existing Bailey assault bridges with heavier traffic—up to seventy tons—traveling at higher speeds—up to fifty miles per hour. Even as some of our platoons were constructing the heavier, more permanent timber spans, other platoons were throwing additional Bailey bridges across the Seine because the entire VII Corps would be jumping off again within a matter of hours after our arrival.

* * *

Immediately following the fall of Paris on August 25, all four Allied armies then operating in northern and central France wheeled eastward and northeastward on a line between the Loire River in the south and the English Channel in the north. While Paris was a strategically vital objective in its own right, the real objective—Germany—had to be approached by way of Belgium, through which the Allied armies could be directly resupplied from England by way of the Channel ports. In the shuffle of armies attending the Allied "left face," our own 1st U.S. Army shifted its zone of responsibility farther south and thus handed over Mortain to the adjacent 2nd British Army.

During the brief Allied reconsolidation on both sides of the Seine, divisional and corps engineer combat battalions in the 1st Army zone alone refurbished, replaced, or built from scratch twenty-nine bridges. Then the 1st Army resumed its attack to the northeast on August 27.

After crossing the Seine through and around Melun, the VII Corps sped across the American World War I battlefield at Château-Thierry on August 28. The 3rd Armored Division, on the VII Corps left flank, drove northeastward through Soissons and Laon and, on September 3, pocketed a large German force— a Wehrmacht panzer corps and an SS panzer corps—near the Belgian city of Mons. More than twenty-five thousand of the entrapped Germans surrendered. On the VII Corps right, the 1st and 9th Infantry divisions conducted a somewhat slower but equally breathless drive from Soissons and Laon before diverging eastward toward the Meuse. Following a brief respite in which the V Corps was pinched out of the 1st Army center by converging drives by the XIX and VII corps, all three corps of the 1st Army resumed somewhat converging drives toward the Meuse and beyond.

The V Corps sideslipped to the 1st Army right and crossed the Meuse at Mézières and Sedan before driving into Belgium through the Ardennes forest. The VII Corps, now in the 1st Army center, reconsolidated at Mons and drove across the Meuse at Namur before attacking toward Aachen by way of Liège. The left flank XIX Corps advanced across the Belgian frontier north of Mons and advanced eastward across the Dyle River in the direction of Maastricht, on the Meuse north of Liège. By September 14, the 1st Army's three corps were arrayed between Maastricht in the north to the city of Luxembourg in the south.

* * *

Patton's 3rd Army reached the Meuse River on August 30 but
was stopped there when its armored divisions literally ran out
of gas. (The last leg of Patton's drive to the Meuse was fueled
by means of aerial resupply and huge German fuel caches captured along the way.) That pretty much signaled the end of the
American juggernaut across France and Belgium. The 3rd Army
jumped off again on September 1, but as it advanced eastward
out of France beside the 1st Army it made extremely slow progress against the newly committed and grimly determined
German Army Group G. Patton was obliged to stop and
reconsolidate on a line along the Moselle.

The 2nd British Army jumped off on August 29 and captured
Brussels on September 3. Next day, as the 1st Canadian Army
ground up the Channel coast, liberating or investing one port
city after another, the 2nd British Army captured Antwerp's
strategically vital port facilities—intact! However, the Germans
rushed in crack troops to withhold the long Schelde estuary
linking Antwerp to the North Sea. It would thus be quite a while
before the Allies could exploit their immense good fortune in
seizing the port, the biggest in proximity to the Channel. The
Germans also continued to hold the bypassed ports of Boulogne,
Calais, and Dunkirk, but the flow of supplies shifted immediately to the Channel ports that *had* fallen to the Canadians—Le
Havre, Dieppe, and Ostend.

The U.S. 7th Army, driving up the Rhone valley from southern France, linked up with the 3rd Army's southern corps on
September 3 and it and French Army B wheeled eastward beside
the 3rd Army to occupy the southern end of the Allied line
across Belgium and France. Thus, the Allies held a solid line
between the English Channel and the Swiss frontier.

Between September 11 and 14, assaulting divisions in the 1st
and 3rd Army sectors actually crossed the frontier into Germany. The German town of Rotgen, southeast of the fortress
city of Aachen, fell to 1st Army units on September 13. At the
German frontier, the armies ground up against fiercely determined—fanatical—defenders manning hurriedly refurbished
sections of the vaunted Siegfried Line, or West Wall. The Allied
offensive immediately bogged down in the face of the deepening
German resistance. More than the German resistance, however,
the Allied pursuit ground to a halt because the Allied frontline
army groups were exhausted and disheveled and could no longer
be adequately maintained by means of their makeshift, fragile
logistics pipeline. Thus, for want of a reliable logistics infra-

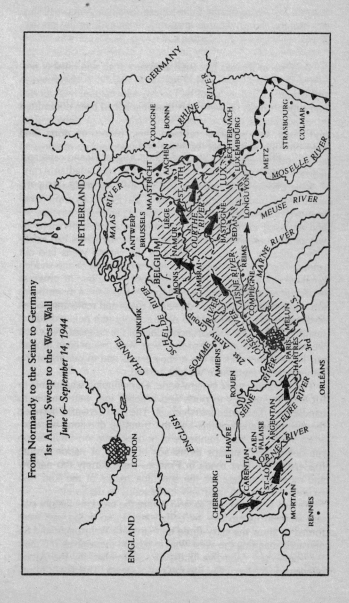

From Normandy to the Seine to Germany
1st Army Sweep to the West Wall
June 6–September 14, 1944

structure, the breathtakingly successful breakout from the Normandy beachhead, begun on July 25, ended on the approaches to the Netherlands and Germany on September 14.

It was time to rebuild liberated Europe's road and railway networks. Immense engineering resources had been stockpiled in the United Kingdom prior to D-Day, and engineering service and support units of every sort imaginable had been committed to supporting the combat units, building and maintaining bridges and roads, rehabilitating railroad lines, reopening ports (and even creating new ones), building and maintaining motor- and aviation-fuel pipelines, and rehabilitating and constructing airfields.

Nevertheless, the stunning victory we had achieved in the wake of our breakout from Normandy had caught us unprepared to move in an orderly manner the huge volumes of supplies we had amassed in England to the frontline combat divisions by way of the makeshift supply network our logisticians had established literally on the run. Most of the careful plans laid out prior to the invasion were obviated in the wake of the sudden breakout, which struck off in directions and a rate of progress no planners had foreseen. We engineers had done a magnificent job reopening blocked and damaged roads and replacing scores of blown bridges, but we had done so only in a field-expedient manner, to directly support operations of the moment. Now that we were stopped in front of the West Wall, we needed to plan our logistics network at the highest levels and to put aright the rather rickety nightmare we had created.

The problems were system-wide. Our shipping was unable to lift enough supplies to ports and beaches that were unable to handle even the inadequate tonnage. The road networks between the disembarkation points and the frontline divisions were inadequate for the task; hundreds of bridges were too small or too run-down, and perhaps thousands of miles of national-route roadways—the best roads in France—were simply too narrow and therefore unsafe for the speeding trucks of the Red Ball Express that wound their way inefficiently to the front.

We had no choice but to stop before the creaking supply system stopped us anyway by collapsing. In so doing, we were forced to allow the sixty-three half-strength Wehrmacht and SS divisions manning the West Wall to rebuild themselves and their long-neglected defensive lines. On September 14, the Allied offensive in Western Europe ran out of steam. This is not to say that the long front was quiescent. The 1st U.S. Army, in the center, mounted only limited corrective operations, as did the 1st Canadian Army, on the extreme left. The British 21st Army Group, with American support, launched its disastrous Arnhem airborne landings on September 17 while the 3rd and 7th U.S. armies unsuccessfully attempted to extend their drives into Lorraine and the Vosges mountains against immovable defenses.

The summer offensive was effectively over.

CHAPTER 9

Our brief respite around Paris provided a necessary break in what had become our endless toils under German guns. Mail call and passes were good therapy, and the men of the 291st got plenty of both. However, the rapidly receding front and the arrival of more heavily equipped engineering general service regiments obliged us to hit the road again. The battalion CP left Fontenay-le-Compte on September 3 so our S-2 and S-3 sections could once again reconnoiter our expanding zone of responsibility and plan jobs for the platoons and squads that were winding up their work along the Seine.

Beginning September 5, after restoring the Seine bridges in our sector south of Paris, the bulk of the 291st raced off in pursuit of the receding VII Corps. Our individual components typically motored many miles in a day, stopping only as long as it took to build timber trestle bridges to replace Bailey assault bridges thrown across rivers, streams, and defiles by the combat engineers in closer support of the speeding assault divisions.

Lieutenant Frank Rhea's platoon of Company B started things off on September 5 when it crossed the Seine to build a huge prisoner-of-war enclosure at Marolles-au-Hurepoix to accommodate the many thousands of German soldiers who had been bypassed by the 1st Army's racing armored and motorized spearheads. The bypassed Germans were surrendering in droves to our forces or makeshift units of the French Forces of the Interior (FFI), which is about all that passed for government throughout large regions of the countryside.

On September 6 the battalion CP convoy wound up its long journey from the Seine in Bastogne, a pleasant crossroads town in the Belgian Ardennes forest. There, we erected our pup tents in a field just outside of town and got to work reconnoitering our new zone of responsibility, which still stretched all the way back to Melun. As I stalked the CP area, I noticed that a huge percentage of our vehicles were of German origin. I had no problem with adding to our allotted inventory, but I was mildly concerned that, if the German trucks and *kübelwagens* ever outnumbered our American trucks and jeeps, we might be bombed or rocketed by our own aircraft.

On September 11, remarkably resourceful First Sergeant Bill Smith, of Company A, solved a temporary shortage of standard bridging materials by constructing a hay bridge at Marle, about thirty-five miles northeast of Paris. This structure was a superb payoff for all the trouble I had gone through in the selection of the battalion's senior noncommissioned officers. First Sergeant Smith had to fill in a collapsed bridge so our advance could continue and he knew that sufficient quantities of fresh-cut hay gathered from nearby fields would support the temporary roadway until one of our supporting bridge companies brought up Bailey components. This was one of the very few occasions when the bridging materials did not arrive ahead of or alongside one of our bridging details. Later, two platoons of Company A built a 110-foot timber trestle bridge near the site of First Sergeant Smith's hay bridge.

A much-appreciated nonstandard service provided by the 291st throughout this period was the ongoing collection and dissemination of road maps by Sergeant Charlie Sherman, a member of the S-2 section who spoke four languages. Sherman's map-collecting forays among the locals were vital to the continued flow of supplies to frontline units that had literally fought beyond the edge of tactical maps provided by the overburdened Army cartographers.

On September 18, the battalion CP displaced forward to the Hockai woods, a portion of the Ardennes between Malmédy and Eupen, about fifteen miles from the German frontier. Our arrival was not occasioned by the friendliness of civilians to which we had become accustomed through the drive across France. A little investigation by several of our nonplussed troops turned up the revelation that the original residents of many towns in the Belgian Ardennes had been evicted to make way for the resettlement of German nationals. Many of those Germans had not gotten back to Germany before our armies engulfed the area and, while they remained passive, they were by no means as demonstrably joyful at our arrival as truly liberated Frenchmen and Belgians had been and were being elsewhere. Many of the

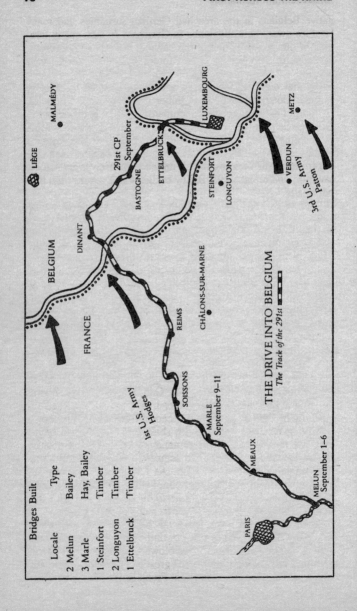

THE DRIVE INTO BELGIUM
The Track of the 291st ▪▬▪▬

Bridges Built	
Locale	Type
2 Melun	Bailey
3 Marle	Hay, Bailey
1 Steinfort	Timber
2 Longuyon	Timber
1 Ettelbruck	Timber

1st U.S. Army
Hodges

MELUN
September 1–6

MARLE
September 9–11

291st CP
September

3rd U.S. Army
Patton

PARIS

MEAUX

SOISSONS

REIMS

CHÂLONS-SUR-MARNE

DINANT

BASTOGNE

ETTELBRUCK

STEINFORT

LONGUYON

LUXEMBOURG

VERDUN

METZ

LIÉGE

MALMÉDY

BELGIUM

FRANCE

native Belgians in the area had German surnames and many families owed their allegiance to Germany. In fact, many families in our zone, including the sawmill owners at Sourbrodt, had sons in the German armed forces. All this made us very uneasy.

On that day also, following a madcap dash across eastern France, Company B built a timber trestle bridge at Jemelle, Belgium. On September 22, Company C leapfrogged 180 miles from the Seine to smooth out the road net on the 1st Army MSR by building a Bailey bridge and culvert bypass in one day near Willerzie, Belgium. Then the Company C troops cut fresh timber from the surrounding forest, milled it themselves at the local sawmill, and replaced the Bailey bridge with a seventy-ton timber trestle.

Finding and fixing sawmills throughout our zone of operations became a vital function for the battalion. It was as yet unclear if the drive that had started in Normandy and that had paused so briefly at the Seine was to be continued or if the Allied armies in France, Belgium, the Netherlands, Luxembourg, and Germany itself were to stand down for a protracted period. Whichever way it went, the scores of bridges that had to be rebuilt or maintained throughout the 1st Army tactical area needed massive quantities of fresh lumber, and the job of providing a great deal of it naturally fell to us. Before we knew it, we were operating sawmills at or near the Belgian towns of Malmédy, Stavelot, Born, Trois-Ponts, Montenau, Sourbrodt, and Vielsalm.

On September 23, Corporal Ledet drove me to Steinfort, Luxembourg where Captain Jim Gamble's Company A was building a 120-foot, 70-ton timber trestle bridge. I was struck instantly by the efficiency and speed of the building process, a gratifying result of our ongoing shakedown which had begun only two months earlier in Normandy. Here was proof positive of the reputation the 291st had acquired as the 1st Army's premier engineer combat battalion. As I watched Company A's awesome task unfold that afternoon, I was suffused with a depth of pride of leadership I had hitherto only hoped I might experience. These were now indeed crack engineering troops.

From Steinfort, Ledet drove me back into France, where Company B was building a pair or timber trestle bridges at Longuyon. There, the Germans had blown both ends of a 140-foot span on a curve. The job involved great technique on alignment, which was handled by Lieutenant Frank Rhea. The three Com-

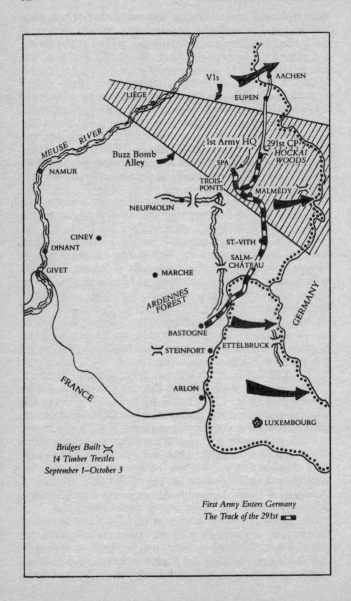

Bridges Built ⋈
14 Timber Trestles
September 1–October 3

First Army Enters Germany
The Track of the 291st ▭

pany B platoons were working around-the-clock eight-hour shifts to complete the massive job. Again, I was struck by the level of professionalism and economy of movement exhibited by the platoon that happened to be at work during my inspection. The result, completed in record time, was an engineering masterpiece.

Another task unearthed by Captain Bill McKinsey on one of his wide-ranging reconnaissance forays was a killer bridge-replacement job at Ettelbruck, Luxembourg, right on the German border. The retreating Germans had reduced the existing 180-foot span to rubble as they withdrew into their homeland. It took the combined efforts of A and C companies to furnish a new 130-foot structure virtually in the face of the enemy, who were entrenched right across the border. Adding considerably to my concerns over the safety of the troops was news from the locals that Germans in civilian clothing were watching us and could quite easily sabotage our efforts or call in artillery. Beginning September 28, after plans had been drawn up by Lieutenant Al Edelstein, of Company A, and Lieutenant Don Davis, of Company C, the timber for the Ettelbruck bridge was cut by Sergeant Joe Geary's squad of Company A from the woods near the sawmill town of Mersch, Luxembourg. Our group liaison officer, Captain Lloyd Sheetz, arranged with the steel mill at Esche-sur-Alzette, Luxembourg, to provide six-inch steel I-beams for the bridge's stringer system. As soon as the timber started to arrive from Mersch, most of Company A put in a full eight-hour shift constructing bents—the poured concrete piers upon which the bridge would rest. Then most of Company C took over for its eight-hour shift. This was by far the largest job the battalion had ever undertaken, the first involving more than the platoons of a single company trading shifts in one place. The job was completed without German intervention.

On September 29, Company B completed yet another timber trestle bridge at Berledang, Belgium. Company A completed one at Salm-Château, Belgium, on October 3, the same day Company C built another at Trois-Ponts. On October 5, Company B built a timber trestle across the Warche River at Malmédy.

Throughout the latter period, as the 12th Army Group appeared to be digging itself in for the winter, the Germans began sending their V-1 "buzz bombs" over our heads on the way to the vital logistics hub at Liège. Each V-1 carried a one-thousand-pound warhead and traveled at relatively slow speeds squirting burning ethyl alcohol propellant behind. Several of the buzz bombs fell into our area and blew huge craters where they landed, but these caused no damage and resulted in no injuries. Still, it was a startling experience to feel the ground rumble when one detonated nearby.

The 1st Army offensive had been stalled since mid September at the fortress of Aachen. Units of the VII and XIX corps finally broke into the besieged city on October 13, but the place was not secured by the 1st Infantry Division until October 21, by which time many hundreds of lives had been sacrificed in bitter house-to-house fighting. Aachen, the first large German city to fall permanently into Allied hands, was also the first place where the 1st Army breached the Siegfried Line. As soon as news of Aachen's fall reached the battalion CP, I had Corporal Ledet drive me there for a look around. As I walked through the streets, I saw no signs of life. The city was completely battered and deserted; the only sounds I heard were the occasional brick falling from a broken chimney or tile falling from a shattered roof. It was positively eerie, and very sad. The smell of cordite, dust, and burned wood was everywhere, as was the inescapable stench of death.

Despite the major moral victory at Aachen, all hopes of a renewed war-winning offensive came to nothing. Unyielding German resistance in front of the adjacent 3rd U.S. and 2nd British armies prevented the Aachen victory from being exploited. Patton's 3rd Army also breached the German barrier by capturing the fortress city of Metz on October 3, but the American force was obliged to give up the town on October 17 because adjacent units could not move up to exploit the breakthrough. Farther south, General Jacob Devers's 6th Army Group pushed the Germans back to the Vosges, but it too bogged down when it reached the Meurth River.

Following a period of consolidation and repositioning, the 1st Army found itself holding a front over a hundred miles in length encompassing the southeastern half of Belgium and nearly all of Luxembourg. Within that sector, the 291st had a massive zone of responsibility whose corner points were at St.-Vith, Monschau, Werbomont, and Houffalize. The pressure of maintaining so vast a front was somewhat alleviated in mid October when advance elements of the 9th U.S. Army arrived from Brittany to undertake limited patrol activities in Luxembourg. Word was that the entire Luxembourg half of the 1st Army front would eventually be turned over to the 9th Army.

While we were waiting for orders to resume the attack into Germany, life in the 291st's zone became routine. We knew where the front line was, but we never got there, nor were we shelled by German artillery nor harassed by German aircraft. It was a good life. Passes to Paris and Liège were frequent and of typically long duration. Closer to home was the 1st Army head-quarters town of Spa, where hot mineral baths beckoned. The routine nature of our work provided the troops with many eve-nings off, so they visited local cafés and dated local girls. It was considered by all to be a very fine way to fight the war.

In late October a cold spell with accompanying snow caught us unprepared and made living in tents utterly miserable. It was not until November 11, however, that the 291st CP group moved into buildings at Haute-Bodeux. At the same time, Company B moved to Malmédy and Company C took over a beautiful castle at La Gleize. Unlucky Company A was charged with manning numerous outlying sawmills and other installations, so its squads resorted to building elaborate dugouts with timbered roofs as proof against the deteriorating weather.

The long anticipated Allied offensive was set to jump off on November 16. Before that could happen, the 9th U.S. Army was shifted from between 1st and 3rd armies to the 12th Army Group's left (northern) flank because it was thought by General Bradley that he would be asked to attach one of his three armies to Field Marshal Bernard Montgomery's adjacent British 21st Army Group. Given the choice, Bradley wanted to retain the 1st Army. The 9th Army's move resulted in its assuming control of the XIX Corps while the 1st Army assumed control of the VIII Corps. When the 9th Army moved into a narrow zone right around Aachen, the 1st Army again had to spread itself south-ward into Luxembourg to a width of about eighty miles.

All the high-level machinations came to nothing. The November offensive went off straight into the face of the Siegfried Line, and the V and VII corps immediately bogged down in the densely wooden Hürtgen Forest. The leading assault divisions did push their way through to the Roer River by December 2, but the 1st Army attack then had to be redirected against the Roer dams to prevent the Germans from blowing them and literally drowning the offensive. Little additional progress was made in the new direction.

The attack in the adjacent 3rd Army sector went somewhat better. Patton's corps again ground up against the Metz fortress, which was besieged beginning November 18. The fortress city fell to Patton—for the second time—on November 22, but fighting in outlying areas would rage for another month. Sharply deteriorating weather severely hampered 3rd Army engineers trying to bridge the Saar River, and that all but stopped Patton. Farther south, the 6th Army Group's 7th U.S. Army attacked in a snowstorm but succeeded in taking Sarrebourg on November 20 and Strasbourg on November 23. The southernmost Allied army, the 1st French Army, closed on the Rhine River at the Swiss border but was unable to reduce a German salient around Colmar. The 6th Army Group made the greatest gains of the offensive, but it wound up well short of its objectives, as did the 12th Army Group to its north.

Following a needed breather, all three Allied army groups were to jump off again within the week on a final effort to end the war before the onset of deep winter shows. While frantic preparations were being made, the Germans launched their last best hope to stave off an Allied victory in the West.

PART THREE

THE BATTLE OF
THE BULGE

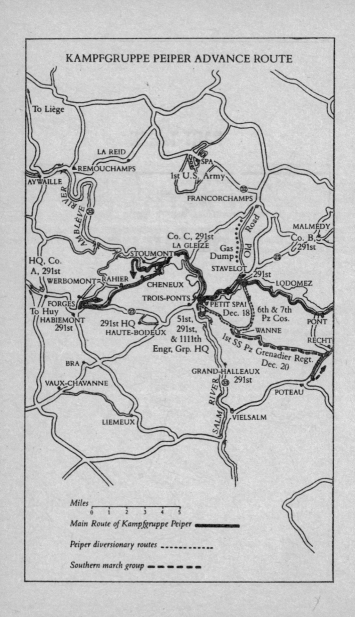

KAMPFGRUPPE PEIPER ADVANCE ROUTE

To Liège

LA REID

REMOUCHAMPS

AYWAILLE

SPA

1st U.S. Army

FRANCORCHAMPS

AMBLÈVE RIVER

MALMEDY
Co. B, 291st

Co. C, 291st

LA GLEIZE

Gas Dump

STOUMONT

HQ, Co. A, 291st

WERBOMONT — RAHIER

CHENEUX

STAVELOT

291st

LODOMEZ

TROIS-PONTS

FORGES

To Huy

HABIEMONT 291st

291st HQ
HAUTE-BODEUX

51st, 291st, & 111th Engr. Grp. HQ

PETIT SPAI Dec. 18

6th & 7th Pz Cos.

PONT

WANNE

RECHT

1st SS Pz Grenadier Regt. Dec. 20

BRA

VAUX-CHAVANNE

GRAND-HALLEAUX 291st

POTEAU

SALM RIVER

LIEMEUX

VIELSALM

Miles

0 1 2 3 4 5

Main Route of Kampfgruppe Peiper ——————

Peiper diversionary routes — — — — — —

Southern march group — — — —

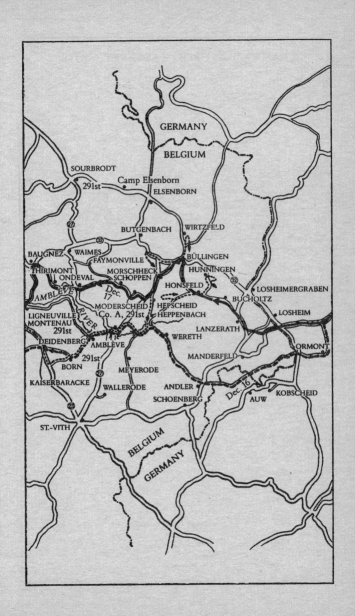

CHAPTER 10

Life was good. The 291st had its annual Thanksgiving football game—our second away from home—and the enlisted men trounced the officers. We were sure the next edition of the ongoing sports rivalry would be our coveted Homecoming game.

By Thanksgiving, we were all living in warm, comfortable, dry billets alongside our new-found civilian friends around Malmédy, Stavelot, Trois-Ponts, La Gleize, Vielsalm, Werbomont, Salm-Château, Sourbrodt, the Haute-Bodeux. Lieutenant Wade Colbeck was planning a major Christmas party for the kids living around the sawmill town of Stavelot, and other parties were being contemplated by other platoons and squads.

At our CP at Haute-Bodeux, Lieutenant Don Gerrity, Warrant Officer John Brenna, and I decided to send Christmas cards to the families of all the men in the battalion. We shanghied three helpers from H&S Company and got off 650 of the cards, all of which I had to sign in a marathon session. For our own Christmas, we planned to decorate a huge tree and pass out some Spam and other food to our Belgian friends in the area.

John Brenna, our assistant personnel officer, pointed out that 1944 would be our second Christmas away from home even though we had all spent the summer thinking we would be sharing it with our families. The war was bogged down, but not our spirits.

On December 15, 1944, I made a quick trip from my CP at Haute-Bodeux to visit with Captain Jim Gamble, the Company A commander. I had received orders from Colonel H. Wallis Anderson, the 1111th Group commander, to establish one of the 291st's companies in the vicinity of Born, Belgium, to support the 9th Armored Division's imminent assault on the Roer River dams. Company A's job would be to quickly remove explosives and mines from the dams to prevent their being blown by the Germans.

I met with Jim in the afternoon and gave him instructions to move immediately and set up his CP near Born. The news startled Jim somewhat because it marked the first time that Company A—or any 291st component—would be directly involved in an assault operation.

The remainder of the afternoon and evening was spent at Château Froidcoeur, a castle in La Gleize, with Captain Larry Moyer and the Company C command group. I planned to get an early start on the morning of December 16 so I could visit Captain John Conlin's Company B in Malmédy and then head to Born, where Lieutenant Arch Taylor's Company A platoon was already maintaining the road net and running the local sawmill.

I received a call from John Conlin at 0715, December 16, that advised me that at 0530 four mammoth shells had fallen near the site of the 44th Field Evacuation Hospital, in Malmédy. John reported, "Three medics have been killed and several civilians were wounded. There are four damaged buildings along the street and we have repaired a large crater in the road."

The event was unprecedented in our experience. Our zone of operations had not been molested for months. I told John that I was ready to drive out to Malmédy anyway and that I would inspect the damage and attempt to divine the cause as soon as I arrived. I was mildly concerned for the safety of Jim Gamble's Company A, which already should have been on the road between Werbomont and Born. I decided to proceed to Malmédy to view the damage and then go on to Born, as planned, to get a firsthand look at conditions along the front.

After poking around for a while, Conlin and I agreed that the shells that had struck Malmédy were probably 310mm rounds that could very well have been fired by a railroad gun far inside Germany. We had no idea what had triggered the shelling, why it was of such short duration, nor why Malmédy of all places had been molested. I spoke briefly with Lieutenant Frank Rhea, who had recently patrolled the Siegfried Line along the so-called Losheim Gap, the region of the 1st Army's penetration. Frank told me that the front was covered by the 2nd Infantry Division, the rather new 99th Infantry Division, and the 14th Cavalry Group. Coverage along the heavily wooded main line was light but it appeared adequate to Frank. John Conlin mentioned that

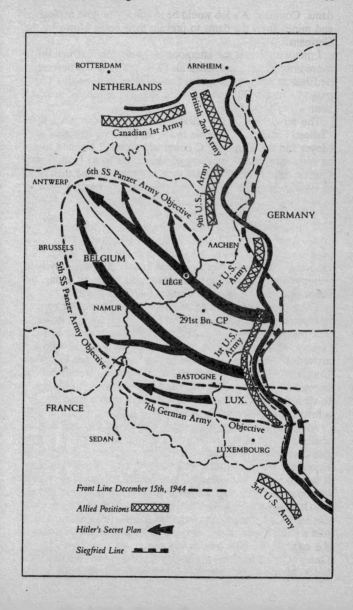

Front Line December 15th, 1944 — — —

Allied Positions ⚔⚔⚔⚔⚔

Hitler's Secret Plan ◄◄◄

Siegfried Line ▬▬▬

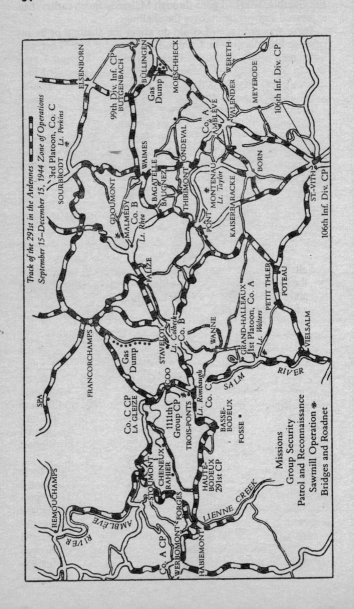

Track of the 291st in the Ardennes
September 15–December 15, 1944 Zone of Operations
3rd Platoon, Co. C
Lt. Perkins

Missions
Group Security
Patrol and Reconnaissance
Sawmill Operation
Bridges and Roadnet

Jim Gamble, who had gone through Malmédy much earlier, had expressed some concern over the shelling.

There was not much I could do about the shelling or its results, so I had lunch with Conlin, First Sergeant Earl Short, and Lieutenant Wade Colbeck. Then Corporal Ledet and I proceeded down route N-23 toward a road junction we called Five Points, in the village of Baugnez. As we reached Five Points, Ledet swung the command car to the right and headed toward Born by way of Ligneuville. We arrived at Born to find the village swarming with troops from the fresh, green, utterly untested 106th Infantry Division. Our troops manning the sawmill near town told me that Jim Gamble and the main body of Company A had moved to Amblève, Belgium, where Jim planned to set up a temporary CP.

Ledet and I went on to Amblève and found that Jim had already bedded down his command group and Lieutenant Al Edelstein's platoon in the local schoolhouse. I thought the troops around the CP looked tense, and I found out why when First Sergeant Bill Smith told me that the local German-speaking civilians were discussing openly a German build up and imminent assault. Lieutenant Frank Hayes, the Company A exec, added that the 106th Division troopers billeted locally had been hearing unusual sounds of activity emanating from the nearby German side of the lines.

I finally tracked down the industrious Jim Gamble and discussed with him the shelling at Malmédy. I did not mention to Jim that I was becoming increasingly concerned about all the little incidents indicating heightened activity in this long-quiescent sector. Jim told me that Arch Taylor's platoon was still running the sawmill in Born and that he had sent Lieutenant Bucky Walters's platoon to Vielsalm to run the sawmill there until the 9th Armored Division's attack jumped off. All of Company A's components were tied into the battalion tactical radio net and all were as well prepared as they could be to support the renewed drive to the Roer River dams.

I thought of spending the night with Company A, but there was too much going on. At 2200, December 16, Ledet and I started back to the battalion CP, at Haute-Bodeux. As we proceeded through the Ardennes forest that dark, dreary night, I noticed that the 106th Division troops we encountered were unsettled and jumpy. As we reached Five Points (Baugnez) and turned onto the N-23, we saw civilians heading west through the thick, eerie fog that had settled over the region. The realiza-

tion that the locals were spooked alarmed me more than any of
the many little incidents I had seen throughout the long day.

Stavelot was quiet. The mist from the adjacent Amblève River
was unusually thick all the way into Trois-Ponts. From there,
the going got slow because of the dense fog obscuring the N-23
roadway. We did not reach the battalion CP until after midnight.
When I checked in, the duty officer—Lieutenant Leroy Joehnck,
the assistant intelligence officer—told me that the battalion tactical net was dead quiet. I went over the messages on my field
desk and noted that Colonel Anderson and the 1st Army engineer, at Spa, had been given details of the shelling at Malmédy.

I was getting ready to turn in when Sergeant John Scanlan,
our communications chief, stuck his head in to tell me that a
telephone wire to 1111th Group headquarters, at Trois-Ponts, had
been severed. A little later, Scanlan reported back that the break
had been traced and repaired, and that we were once again in
firm communication with Group.

Shortly after 0300, December 17, Major Dick Carville, the
1111th Group liaison officer at VII Corps headquarters, called to
relay a report that German paratroopers had been dropped
somewhere north of Malmédy.

That did it! All the little incidents crystallized in my mind as
being parts of one big event. However, I still had little upon
which to base a plan of action. I directed the duty officer to pass
the news along the entire battalion and order a heightened state
of vigilance. Then I fitfully settled back into my cot and tried
to rest up for what I assumed would be a busy day.

First thing in the morning, Captain John Conlin called in from
the Company B CP, in Malmédy. He insisted upon speaking
directly with me. "Colonel, Lieutenant Rhea has sighted a German armored column heading our way, running free and clear.
Shall we prepare to defend?''

German armor? In our rear? I told John that Company B should
definitely prepare to defend and that I would be along as quickly
as possible to check the situation. John immediately dispatched
patrols and went to work consolidating and hardening the Company B positions around Malmédy.

Before I could get away from the CP, Colonel Anderson called
from Group to verify that German armored units had indeed
broken through the 99th Infantry Division's front along the
Losheim Gap, in the V Corps sector. While I was speaking with
the colonel, Major Dick Carville also weighed in from VII Corps

headquarters with similar news. Colonel Anderson directed me to go to Malmédy and take command of all 1111th Group units there and do whatever I thought was necessary. In addition to the bulk of my own Company B, the engineering units at or bound for Malmédy were the 629th Engineer Light Equipment Company and the 962nd Engineer Maintenance Company, neither of which could be remotely classed as a combat unit.

My job had suddenly become much larger than I had earlier thought it might. I asked newly promoted Major Ed Lampp to go with me, and Captain Lloyd Sheetz, our liaison officer with Group. We also took Lieutenant Tom Stack, Lampp's assistant S-3, and Lieutenant Leroy Joehnck, the assistant S-2. Together with several enlisted assistants and command-post technicians, we drove quickly through Trois-Ponts and Stavelot and made the S-turn down into Malmédy. We encountered many civilians as we drove beneath the railroad viaduct just outside of town, and numerous U.S. Army vehicles from a wide variety of units were streaming past us, heading west, away from the front. Brief shouted exchanges with drivers and passengers in the departing vehicles indicated that the German breakthrough was spreading.

The battalion forward command group met with Captain Conlin and Lieutenants Rhea and Colbeck, whose platoons had already begun setting up roadblocks. Conlin had several small patrols cautiously probing forward in search of the reported German armor. As soon as I knew what was going on in and around Malmédy, I radioed Captain Jim Gamble, at Amblève, to move all of Company A back to his former position at Werbomont, where his troops could serve as the battalion reserve. Jim reported that some action was taking place in the local area and that elements of Company A could hear sounds of firing in the near distance.

After Ed Lampp and I identified a dozen sites at which Company B was to establish roadblocks—including the four or five already outposted—Ed left Malmédy bound for Haute-Bodeux to resume control of the battalion rear command post. I hated losing Ed at that crucial juncture, but the battalion had been without an executive officer for some weeks, and Ed was covering that and his S-3 job. My parting words to Ed were that I felt we could hold the vital road net until he convinced higher headquarters to send infantry and, above all, some antitank weapons. Ed detoured to deliver a map overlay, showing the roadblock positions, to Colonel Anderson, at Trois-Ponts, and proceeded to Haute-Bodeux without incident. As soon as Ed

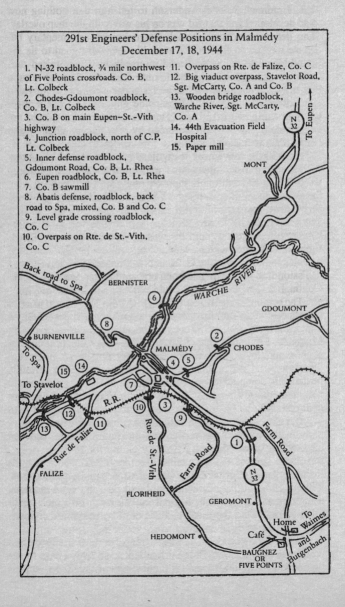

291st Engineers' Defense Positions in Malmédy
December 17, 18, 1944

1. N-32 roadblock, ¾ mile northwest of Five Points crossroads. Co. B, Lt. Colbeck
2. Chodes-Gdoumont roadblock, Co. B, Lt. Colbeck
3. Co. B on main Eupen–St.-Vith highway
4. Junction roadblock, north of C.P. Lt. Colbeck
5. Inner defense roadblock, Gdoumont Road, Co. B, Lt. Rhea
6. Eupen roadblock, Co. B, Lt. Rhea
7. Co. B sawmill
8. Abatis defense, roadblock, back road to Spa, mixed, Co. B and Co. C
9. Level grade crossing roadblock, Co. C
10. Overpass on Rte. de St.-Vith, Co. C

11. Overpass on Rte. de Falize, Co. C
12. Big viaduct overpass, Stavelot Road, Sgt. McCarty, Co. A and Co. B
13. Wooden bridge roadblock, Warche River, Sgt. McCarty, Co. A
14. 44th Evacuation Field Hospital
15. Paper mill

left, I radioed Colonel Anderson to tell him that nothing new had developed and that Ed was on his way with the map overlay. Our defensive posture—which was extremely rudimentary because we had so few troops available—was designed to tie the roadblocks at bridges and road intersections to the raised railroad embankment that curved south from east to west around Malmédy. The embankment was a godsend in that it provided superb fields of fire for our machine guns and adequate cover for our thinly spread troops. However, the position would not be viable until we were reinforced by professional infantry and their organic heavy weapons.

By 1130 the movement of civilians and retreating U.S. Army units through Malmédy was extremely heavy. It naturally dawned on me that the manpower and weapons I needed were slipping westward through our lines, so I tried to convince passing units to throw in with us. I failed miserably. I was not able to convince officers of routinely transiting elements of the 7th Armored Division to commit even modest combat resources to the defense of Malmédy. I could not believe the 7th Armored Division was actually still transiting Malmédy to undertake a mission that so clearly had been obviated by the German breakthrough farther east. That I could elicit no aid was stupefying.

The last organic element of the 7th Armored Division to enter Malmédy was a mobile antitank gun battalion commanded by a Major Boyer. I advised Boyer of the situation to the east of us and he asked about the best route to St.-Vith. I told him his best bet would be to move west to Trois-Ponts, south to Vielsalm, and then east to St.-Vith, but I also emphasized that I certainly would like to add the weight of his antitank guns and troops to my defenses. Boyer thanked me for the information I had provided, said that he felt obligated to carry out his original mission, and left. As Boyer's column proceeded west out of Malmédy, many American troops and townspeople panicked and followed it.

I went through the town to try to locate intact American units that could be integrated into our defenses. I quickly discovered that a 150-man replacement depot and the personnel manning an entire Army field hospital had vanished, as had a tank-repair unit. There was no one left in Malmédy except diehard civilians and my own valiant engineers.

With reports of German paratroopers north of Malmédy and German armor to the east, I conceded that I would have to depend solely upon my men for manning our roadblocks—unless someone up the chain in 1st Army headquarters dispatched some spare infantry and armor to assist us. For me, there was no turning back. I had made my decision. I trusted my men and I believed they trusted me. We were going to hold Malmédy, or die trying.

At about noon, there appeared at one of our roadblocks an *east*-bound convoy carrying Battery B, 285th Field Artillery Observation Battalion. I went out to meet with the senior officers in the convoy—a Captain Mills and Lieutenant Virgil Lary—who told me they were bound for St.-Vith. I advised the two of the situation and suggested that they either change their route or remain in Malmédy to help us defend the town. Captain Mills, a battalion staff officer, told me that he was under firm orders to get through to St.-Vith to support the 7th Armored Division. Lieutenant Lary, the battery commander, concurred. With great reluctance, I let them proceed, though I was especially uneasy with my decision.

Next, news arrived from one of our two-man jeep patrols that sixty-eight Mk.IV medium tanks and Mk.V Panther medium tanks, halftracks, and armored cars had been spotted on a secondary roadway south of Route N-32, in the direction of Thirimont. The news, which made me feel extremely naked, was duly passed to Group headquarters. Moments later, Colonel Anderson called to say that, for security reasons, he was severing direct radio links with us and that I was to communicate with him only by messenger or by telephone via the battalion rear CP at Haute-Bodeux. That was definitely not reassuring.

I called a meeting of my available officers and senior NCOs: Captains John Conlin and Lloyd Sheetz, Lieutenants John Kirkpatrick, Wade Colbeck, Frank Rhea, Tom Stack, and Leroy Joehnck, and 1st Sergeant Earl Short, Master Sergeant Ralph McCarty, and Staff Sergeant Walt Smith. I knew all of them well, except for John Kirkpatrick, who had just joined the battalion. I told them that we were going to stay to defend Malmédy and that I was hoping that help would be arriving soon. I told them to get back to the troops to tell them of my intention and to prepare them for any eventuality.

Shortly after most of the officers and senior NCOs left, John Conlin and I were alone in the command post, except for my communicator, Sergeant Bill Crickenberger, and a pair of Company B medics. We heard firing way off to the east that sounded like mortars or tank guns and machine guns. Until that moment, we had only heard *about* the battle; now we were hearing it firsthand. We all reacted to the new stimulus. I said aloud what we all must have been thinking: "That little field artillery observation battery must have run into that column of German tanks."

John Conlin had to stay back in the CP, from which he was in touch with all his roadblocks by radio, and the company medics could not be sent out on a patrol, so Bill Crickenberger and I each grabbed a Thompson submachine gun and jumped into my command car to investigate. We rushed east out of Malmédy toward Five Points.

We reached Sergeant Charles Dishaw's roadblock within minutes and had to stop while the troops pulled in a daisy chain of mines so we could pass. While I waited, Dishaw explained that we had reached the front line and that it was extremely hazardous to venture farther along the N-32. While he was talking—I had no intention of turning back—I quickly glanced around to inspect his squad's defensive posture. I was gratified but not particularly surprised to see that they had fashioned a by-the-book engineer block. Manning the block were ten engineers armed with rifles, a .30-caliber light machine gun, and a .50-caliber heavy machine gun mounted on the squad truck. I knew that mines had been laid and I could see where trees along the roadway had been fitted with blocks of TNT so they could be blown across the road to form an obstacle known as an abatis.

Suddenly, matter-of-factly, Sergeant Dishaw mentioned that he had personally fired the squad's .50-caliber machine gun at a lone German armored car that had dashed up the road, clearly oblivious of the roadblock. The German vehicle had swerved off the roadway, turned around, and run from sight. Then, with an aplomb I could not have matched, Dishaw completed his account with news that all the distant heavy firing had stopped about five minutes later. I hoped that was a good sign as Crickenberger pulled ahead toward Five Points.

We stopped and parked the jeep about a half mile beyond Dishaw's block and set off on foot to the top of a nearby hill so I could look over Five Points in relative safety. By all appearances, the heavy firing had occurred at or near the road junction.

The field in front of us appeared to be a pasture. It was set off below a barn and surrounded by what happened in the mist to be a line of Lombardy poplars. Crickenberger and I were both concerned that we might be spotted by unseen enemy troops hidden in the tree line, so we both crouched to reduce our sil-

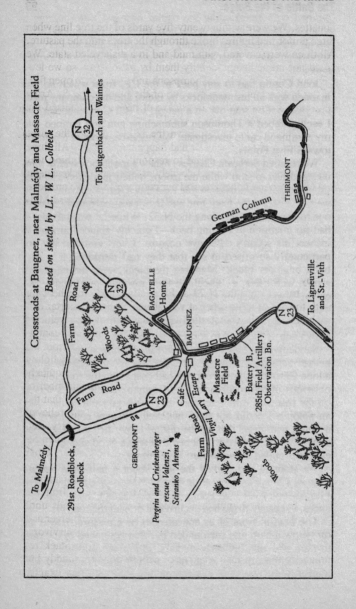

Crossroads at Baugnez, near Malmédy and Massacre Field
Based on sketch by Lt. W. L. Colbeck

To Butgenbach and Waimes

To Malmédy

291st Roadblock, Colbeck

N 23

GEROMONT

Pergrin and Crickenberger rescue Valenzi, Sciranko, Ahrens

Farm Road

Café

Virgil Lary Escape

N 23

Farm Road

Farm Road

N 32

Woods

BAGATELLE Home

N 32

BAUGNEZ

Massacre Field

Battery B, 285th Field Artillery Observation Bn.

Woods

German Column

THIRIMONT

To Ligneuville and St.-Vith

N 23

houettes. We were within twenty-five yards of the tree line when three uniformed figures broke through the trees into the pasture. All three were covered with mud and in a disheveled state. We could not immediately identify them by nationality, so we leveled our lethal .45-caliber Thompsons and prepared to open fire. At the last instant, I saw that one of the men had U.S. Army sergeant's stripes sewn to the sleeve of his jacket. I raised my weapon and yelled, "They're ours!"

Crickenberger and I ran down the hill to waylay the three Americans and find out what had happened to them. All three were wounded and too dazed to respond. Their clothing was wet and torn. They followed docilely as Sergeant Crickenberger and I gently herded them toward our command car. We crowded them aboard and turned back down the main road toward Malmédy at top speed, stopping only to fill in Sergeant Dishaw. The Company B medics went to work on the three as soon as we pulled up in front of the battalion CP, but it was another hour before any of them could coherently relate their story.

After leaving Malmédy, Captain Mills's and Lieutenant Lary's convoy of Battery B, 285th Field Artillery Observation Battalion, turned onto the N-23 at Five Points and were heading south toward St.-Vith when it was struck by heavy mortar and machine-gun fire. The startled GIs leaped from their vehicles and took what little cover they could find. The Germans continued to spray the roadway and verges, adding direct fire from the main guns of their tanks. The Americans, who were very lightly armed, were unable to withstand the terrible fire and quickly surrendered with their hands in the air. The senior member of the trio I picked up, Sergeant Kenneth Ahrens, told me that the Germans herded the survivors into a nearby field and relieved them of their weapons, sheath knives, watches, jewelry, and other valuables. The Germans, who appeared to be Waffen SS troops, then left the field. As soon as they were clear, other Germans manning machine guns opened fire on the dazed captives. Though wounded, Sergeant Ahrens led his companions, Corporal Mike Sciranko and Corporal Albert Valenzi, from the killing field and stumbled off through the nearby woods until they broke into the clear in front of Sergeant Crickenberger and myself. As far as the three knew, they were the only survivors. Shortly after our return, however, Lieutenant Tom Stack returned from a two-man jeep patrol with three more muddy but uninjured survivors of the massacre. Their stories exactly matched Sergeant Ahrens's.

Absolutely firm in my determination to hold Malmédy, I phoned in the incredible news of the massacre to Ed Lampp and told him to inform higher headquarters both of the incident and of the last known position of the German panzer column. I then radioed Captain Larry Moyer, two thirds of whose Company C had consolidated at Froidcoeur, and told him to leave a squad to man a roadblock and bring every other man he could muster straight to Malmédy. It appeared that the German armor could continue on toward Malmédy or take a secondary road from Ligneuville. If the Germans took the secondary road, they would have to go through Stavelot. I then asked Ed Lampp to send forward every bazooka and machine gun he could find and to hold Company A in reserve as soon as it arrived from Amblève.

By 1630 hours, December 17, the main body of the 291st was concentrated in and around Malmédy, but we had squads spread out all the way through the Ardennes. We were in radio contact with every element of the battalion, but that did little to alleviate my concern, particularly for two thirds of Lieutenant John Perkins's platoon of Company C, which was isolated at Sourbrodt. As far as we knew, German paratroops were between Perkins and the rest of the battalion. I was also deeply concerned lest Jim Gamble's Company A run into German armor while it was on the road back from Amblève.

Until Larry Moyer could get forward with most of Company C, I was holding Malmédy with only 128 lightly armed engineers from the 291st. I knew that there was a strong, ruthless German SS panzer column in the area and I had reason to believe that German paratroops were also threatening our sector. I wondered momentarily if I had put myself and my troopers in an impossible situation, but I throttled the doubt. I was absolutely certain that Colonel Anderson and his 1111th Group staff would not let us down, would not leave us unsupported. I hoped that help would arrive quickly, for all the other units that had been occupying Malmédy were gone, had run out on us.

At about 1700 hours, Sergeant Joe Connors, one of Wade Colbeck's Company B squad leaders, brought in a terribly wounded GI, Private John Cobbler, another member of the massacred Battery B, 285th Field Artillery Observation Battalion. Cobbler, who had nine major wounds, died while our medics were working on him. By then, we had eight survivors in the Company B aid station. As soon as they were all treated, I sent them to the rear with Lieutenant Tom Stack.

Late in the afternoon, Bill Crickenberger and I made another

reconnaissance down toward Five Points. I had not seen everything I had wanted to see during the first trip, and I had to get
it done before dusk. We parked where we had earlier and walked
clear down to the tree line we had only approached earlier. A
building at the crossroads was burning and I could clearly see
wrecked jeeps and trucks just south of the N-23 cutoff. Bill and
I were just turning back toward our jeep when two more injured
and dazed survivors staggered out of the woods. We loaded the
two men aboard the command car jeep and headed back to Malmédy. Among the many things I knew I had to do was somehow
beef up the little Company B medical detachment by getting a
doctor and more medics forward.

As the evening wore on, Malmédy was shelled sporadically
by German artillery, and light ground probes began to test our
roadblocks. I was unable to respond. After one light shelling,
Larry Moyer arrived with forty-eight troopers and Lieutenant
Don Davis. I had hoped that more men could be spared from
important duties farther in the rear, but I knew that Larry had
done his very best. The bulk of the new arrivals were from Don
Davis's platoon and the company headquarters, but a few were
from Lieutenant Warren Rombaugh's platoon. One of Rombaugh's squads, under Sergeant Chuck Hensel, had been left at
Stavelot, per my orders, to build and man a roadblock there.

Larry reported that the road between La Gleize and Stavelot
was jammed with retreating troops and vehicles but that the road
between Stavelot and Malmédy was deserted and eerily quiet.
A major manning a 7th Armored Division roadblock had stopped
Company C outside of Stavelot and had told Larry that Malmédy
was in enemy hands. Larry, who was in direct radio communication with us, scoffed at the news and doggedly proceeded
after dropping off Sergeant Hensel's squad. As soon as Larry
reported, I had him dispatch a squad and a makeshift headquarters group to develop two of the several contemplated roadblocks we had thus far been unable to man.

Shortly after Company C arrived, Colonel Bill Carter, the 1st
Army chief engineer, sent word for me to send the 629th Engineer Light Equipment Company and the 962nd Engineer
Maintenance Company to Trois-Ponts to join the 1111th Group
headquarters. I was sorry to lose the manpower, but I knew in
my heart that neither unit was equipped or trained to participate
in the defense of Malmédy. The only outsiders left in town were
a few military policemen who would not leave us in the lurch,

as had everyone else we had encountered that long, miserable day.

Survivors of the Battery B massacre continued to trickle into our roadblocks and on into the forward aid station, at which the Company B medics had been beefed up by the newly arrived Company C medics. All of the survivors had been wounded and several had been grievously wounded, but we lost only Private Cobbler, who had died earlier. Though I hated to lose the men and vehicles even temporarily, I felt obliged to send the worst cases back to Spa, where the 47th Evacuation Hospital was in full operation. I spoke with every survivor who was able to cogently relate the story and thus slowly filled in details of the outrage. Painstakingly, we were able to piece together a picture of the German force, its composition, and the direction it might be taking.

We did not know it at the time, but Malmédy had become, in effect, the northern shoulder of the 1st Army's efforts to contain the main German assault toward the distant Meuse River and the strategically vital cities of Liège and Antwerp.

Another key fact we did not know yet was that the German panzer spearhead in our sector—the elusive German armored column that had massacred Battery B—had been stymied by thirteen 291st combat engineers manning the roadblock on a hill south of Stavelot.

CHAPTER 11

The Germans we had been facing for most of December 17 comprised a special battle force—*kampfgruppe*—commanded by Lieutenant Colonel Joachim Peiper. An ad hoc task-oriented component of the 1st SS Panzer Division, Kampfgruppe Peiper consisted of about four thousand Waffen SS troops manning seventy-two Mk.IV medium and Mk.V Panther medium tanks; five medium flak tanks; about twenty-five self-propelled tank destroyers and assault guns; a battalion of SS panzer grenadiers mounted in about eighty half-tracks; a reconnaissance battalion equipped with light armored cars; a mechanized light flak battalion; and two assault engineer companies (which were equipped with bridges and bridge-construction equipment). Early in the action, Peiper's force was bolstered informally by a battalion of the 3rd Parachute Division.

Kampfgruppe Peiper was literally the armored spearhead of the main German thrust into the Ardennes, the last best hope Germany had of putting off the inevitable outcome of the war in Western Europe. Together with other elite panzer and parachute units, Kampfgruppe Peiper was to open the route from the Losheim Gap to Antwerp and Liège, the strategically vital logistics centers in northern Belgium.

Also facing us, though less directly than Kampfgruppe Peiper, was a three-thousand-man commando force commanded by Lieutenant Colonel Otto Skorzeny. Many of Skorzeny's elite Waffen SS troops had infiltrated behind the 1st Army's lines where, dressed in American uniforms and driving American jeeps, they had sown confusion and dismay among the many roadbound columns of retreating or relieving American troops and armored vehicles. However, the main body of Skorzeny's battle group was deployed in three roadbound tank-heavy de-

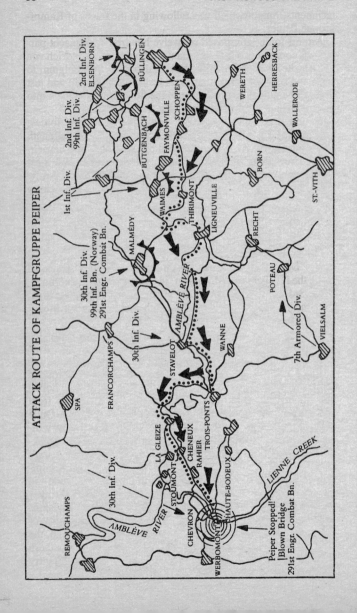

tachments, one of which was following in the traces of Kampfgruppe Peiper.

A third force, composed of twelve hundred Wehrmacht paratroops commanded by Lieutenant Colonel Baron Friedrich von
der Heydte, was assigned the task of dropping into Belgium to
seize and secure the road junctions just south of Eupen and just
north of Malmédy in order to stop the flow reinforcements into
the area which Kampfgruppe Peiper was traversing.

Behind the Peiper, Skorzeny, and von der Heydte forces,
holding the German northern attack sector, was the main strength
of the 6th Panzer Army commanded by General Sepp Dietrich,
an SS street thug who had become Hitler's favorite and most
trusted field commander. In the center was the 5th Panzer Army,
which was to drive straight through to the Meuse in the vicinity
of Dinant. Farthest south, attempting to break through in Luxembourg, was the 7th German Army, the reinforced remnant of
the force the 1st U.S. Army had battled in Normandy and across
most of France.

Generally speaking, the main German assault opened at 0530
hours, December 16, when all three attack armies struck all
along the line between Monschau, in the north, and Echternach,
in the 3rd U.S. Army zone. The attack in our immediate area,
near the northern shoulder of the 6th Panzer Army's break-
in, occurred in the northern sector of the 1st U.S. Army's V
Corps, which the 291st happened to be supporting following the
9th U.S. Army's northward shift. It had been launched by the
12th SS Panzer Division. The 99th Infantry Division was
knocked aside by the sheer force of the assault, but it regrouped
somewhat around Butgenbach while the adjacent (to the north)
2nd Infantry Division attempted to deploy to defend its front
and deliver a counterattack into the 99th Division's zone. Quite
early in the action, the efforts of the 99th and 2nd Infantry divisions succeeded in defining the northern shoulder of the break-
in. Immediately to the south of the 12th SS Panzer Division's
zone was that of the 1st SS Panzer Division, of which Kampfgruppe Peiper was part. Farther south in the V Corps zone—in
the center of the breakthrough, facing the 5th Panzer Army—
the 14th Cavalry Group and the 28th and 106th Infantry divisions
were overwhelmed and overrun. At the southern extremity of
the attack zone, in the 3rd U.S. Army's northernmost zone, the
7th German Army was held to minimal gains and the southern
shoulder of the break-in was defined by the 4th and 5th Infantry
divisions just south of Echternach.

Although there were three complete and heavily reinforced German armies in the assault, the northernmost—Dietrich's 6th Panzer Army—was assigned the main effort. Unfortunately for the Germans—and most fortunately for me, personally—Dietrich was a Nazi sycophant who, though a proven brave battle leader, was utterly out of his depth when it came to controlling as complex an organism as a modern panzer army. The December 16 break-in centered on Losheim went like a dream, but the German follow-on divisions immediately bogged down because of inadequate administrative planning in such vital areas as road assignments and spacing between units. In effect, the 6th Panzer Army's attempt to rush headlong through the Losheim Gap created one of the Western world's truly magnificent traffic jams. Farther south, the three panzer corps of General Hasso von Manteuffel's extremely well-handled 5th Panzer Army plunged to the west bank of the Ourthe River along a broad front.

By far the greatest threat to our security behind the northern shoulder of the break-in was the utter confusion sown by von der Heydte's paratroopers and Skorzeny's American-uniformed commandos. Along with Kampfgruppe Peiper's initial thrusts in back of Butgenbach, the efforts of these forces so completely confused our corps and army commanders as to render moot any effective means of sealing the breach. Our leaders were so beset by conflicting information that they could not accurately gauge the magnitude of the break-in, nor the direction of the main German efforts. Failing to pinpoint the enemy, they could not mount effective countermoves. Worse, from my standpoint, they were so beset with brushfires that they failed to get any word out to support units such as the 291st. We figured out on our own that ''something'' was going on, but we did not know what or where or how we were to respond. That condition prevailed through all of December 16 and most of December 17.

Fortunately for us, the German spearhead in our area—Kampfgruppe Peiper—also spent most of December 17 groping through the fog of war. Peiper's slow advance allowed us to maintain and strengthen our blocking position at Malmédy, and the retention of Malmédy's important road net allowed the 7th Armored Division to traverse our sector southward toward St.-Vith, where its sudden appearance blocked the main effort of the 5th Panzer Army's otherwise successful northern corps.

The essence of armored blitzkrieg warfare is for the attacking force to seek, find, and exploit weak spots along the defender's front. If the defenders stand solidly along a projected route of advance, they are to be contained and held in place (if they cannot be swiftly overrun) while a highly mobile armored spearhead searches for a weak spot at which a new breakthrough can be achieved. This goes on and on until the defending army collapses or the attacking army achieves and exploits a breakthrough of such magnitude as to render moot any defensive posture the defending army might contrive. Above all, the attacking force must not lose its forward momentum or allow the situation to become anything but highly fluid. The essence of constant movement is to keep the defenders ignorant of the attacker's true strength and intentions and guessing where the next blow might fall. The immediate goal, beyond advancing to seize the ultimate objective, is to paralyze the thought processes of the defensive leadership and prevent those leaders from making decisions. The blitzkrieg technique is mainly psychological in nature.

The Germans had employed the technique with unbelievable results in Eastern Europe and France in 1939-41 and with ultimately somewhat less successful results in North Africa in 1941-42. The decline of the German technique had many reasons, but the key to Allied successes was the coolheaded development of their own versions of blitzkrieg warfare and, above all, the development of a series of standard countermoves aimed at sealing German armored breakthroughs and following up with armored counterattacks. Taken together, the stand of the bulk of the 99th Infantry Division at Butgenbach and the timely counterattack by the 7th Armored Division through Malmédy toward St.-Vith were the beginning of the end of the German Ardennes offensive in the V Corps zone. The stand by the 99th Division was very much a matter of will, and not grand design. However, the exploitation of the 99th Division's stand by means of the 7th Armored Division's counterattack toward the German center was very much the result of coolheaded, on-the-spot planning by General Bradley and the V Corps commander, Major General Leonard Gerow.

However, locally around vital Malmédy, there was no thoughtful overarching response for as many as forty-six hours after the German Ardennes offensive jumped off. The 291st happened to be centered on Malmédy when the shooting started and I happened to decide to concentrate my companies in that town. Mine was entirely a visceral response to an unbelievably opaque situation, but it happened to be about the best thing any

American officer could have done with respect to denying the German armored spearhead access to our soft rear.

It happened this way:

Kampfgruppe Peiper had been organized as the unit responsible for breaking through into the 99th Infantry Division's rear. This it had done near Butgenbach, and it had gone on to surprise and capture the American force holding Honsfeld. In a grim precursor to events at Five Points, several of the 250 American prisoners taken during the initial breakthrough were ruthlessly murdered by their SS captors.

From Honsfeld, Kampfgruppe Peiper left the 1st SS Panzer Division's zone and encroached on territory that was in the zone of the 12th SS Panzer Division. Finding the route clear and believing it to be quicker than the route that had been assigned, Peiper advanced toward Büllingen, overrunning several American units and detachments along the way. Büllingen fell without a fight, but Peiper's immensely long column—it stretched fifteen miles back to Honsfeld—was attacked by American fighter-bombers and many German vehicles left the road to find cover. The Germans refueled from American gasoline stocks in Büllingen, which was attended by the cold-blooded murder of a wounded American prisoner.

Unknown to Peiper, the capture of Büllingen effectively trapped the main bodies of the 2nd and 99th Infantry divisions, which had their backs to an impenetrable, virtually trackless wilderness and which had suddenly lost their road connection through Büllingen to the outside world. Had Peiper continued north to Butgenbach, the two American divisions inevitably would have been obliged to retreat or capitulate for lack of supplies and munitions. However, Peiper chose that moment to return to his own division's zone of operations.

During a brief halt outside Büllingen, Peiper was advised by one of his reconnaissance teams that a dirt road led more directly to his next objective, Moderscheid, than the paved road he had intended to follow. The road looked good and there was the need to make up for some lost time, so Peiper plunged ahead with his column in train. Along the way to Moderscheid, Peiper again turned into a side road in the hope he would be able to avoid a possible bottleneck at the crossroads town of Waimes. The dirt side road carried Peiper's vanguard to Ondeval, which Peiper reached at about noon on December 17. From there, the column wound across country lanes in the direction of Thirimont, a little way station within the secondary road net south of Five Points.

Peiper's vanguard left Thirimont on its way to the north-south N-23 between Five Points and Ligneuville, the Germans' next main objective. Halfway to the N-23, the lead German tank became bogged down in a ford across a tiny forest stream. Kampfgruppe Peiper had to turn back to Thirimont and proceed around to Five Points before turning south on the N-23 toward Ligneuville. Retracing its steps to Thirimont was a lengthy, time-consuming process.

As Peiper's vanguard was closing on the N-32 east of Five Points, our two-man jeep patrol was turning left onto the N-32 in the direction of Waimes. Sensing movement off the main highway, our men drove a little way down the secondary road to Thirimont and spotted the Germans before they themselves were spotted. Despite understandable fear and their extreme vulnerability, the two engineers managed to count the oncoming German tanks and halftracks with amazing accuracy. They fled to deliver their report as Peiper's oblivious vanguard ground ahead to the N-32 and turned left toward Five Points.

As all this was happening, Battery B, 285th Field Artillery Observation Battalion was passing through Five Points before turning right—south—along the N-23 toward Ligneuville. The last vehicle passed an MP checkpoint at Five Points just as Peiper's vanguard arrived at the road junction from the east. The two MPs on duty at the checkpoint were swept up and the German vanguard turned left onto the N-23 and quickly overtook the Battery B column from the rear. The Americans were swiftly overrun, rounded up, herded into a roadside field, and mown down on orders from the vanguard panzer battalion commander, Major Werner Poetschke. While the massacre was taking place, a single armored scout car was sent to probe up the road from Five Points to Malmédy, but it was turned back by Sergeant Dishaw's .50-caliber machine gun.

After completing their grisly outrage south of Five Points, the SS troopers remounted their vehicles and continued down the N-23 toward Ligneuville, which had just been cleared by the bulk of the 49th Antiaircraft Artillery Brigade, a battery of which eventually wound up at Malmédy. Ligneuville fell to Kampfgruppe Peiper virtually without a fight.

Peiper's next objective was Stavelot, from which he planned to proceed to Trois-Ponts and then on to Werbomont. As Peiper contemplated his route over a hasty dinner in the local hotel,

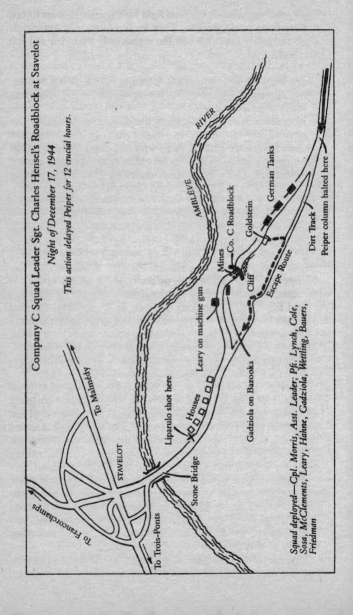

Company C Squad Leader Sgt. Charles Hensel's Roadblock at Stavelot
Night of December 17, 1944
This action delayed Peiper for 12 crucial hours.

RIVER

AMBLÈVE

To Malmédy

STAVELOT

To Francorchamps

To Trois-Ponts

Stone Bridge

Liparulo shot here

Houses

Leary on machine gun

Gadziola on Bazooka

Mines

Co. C Roadblock

Cliff

Goldstein

Escape Route

German Tanks

Dirt Track

Peiper column halted here

Squad deployed—Cpl. Morris, Asst. Leader; Pfc. Lynch, Cole, Sosa, McClements, Leary, Hahne, Gadziola, Wettling, Bauers, Friedman eight prisoners taken in the brief fight for Ligneuville were forced to bury three dead Germans. Then seven of the eight Americans were ruthlessly executed and the eighth was wounded and left for dead.

There were thirteen Americans manning the roadblock at Stavelot: Sergeant Chuck Hensel's twelve-man squad of Company C and a truck driver.

Hensel had reached Stavelot in the dark, at about 1830, December 17. He was met in town by our assistant motor-transport officer, Lieutenant Cliff Wilson, who had just arrived from the 291st rear CP at Haute-Bodeux on orders from Major Ed Lampp to direct Hensel to the proper roadblock site. After passing through town, which was awash in fleeing U.S. Army vehicles, the squad's truck descended to the Amblève River viaduct and on up to the top of the facing ridgeline, where Lieutenant Wilson set Hensel's men to work installing mines.

As Hensel's squad got to work, Lieutenant Wilson told Chuck that Colonel Anderson was at work getting a company from the 202nd Engineer Combat Battalion forward to Stavelot but that no one had any idea when—or really if—it would arrive. In addition, a company of the 51st Engineer Combat Battalion was bound for a similar blocking position at Trois-Ponts, the next big town back down the road and the site of the 1111th Group's headquarters. Wilson told Hensel that *any* traffic coming up the road would definitely be German and that it was to be engaged. After escorting Hensel to the roadblock and telling him everything he knew, Cliff Wilson returned to Haute-Bodeux.

As soon as Lieutenant Wilson left, Chuck selected three of his troops to man two tiny outposts. Two of the men were given a bazooka and some ammunition and placed beside the road just beyond the mined belt. Private Bernard Goldstein, who was armed only with his M1 rifle, walked down the road beyond the first curve and took up residence in a small stone shed. If anything came his way, Goldstein was to warn the rest of the squad.

Private Goldstein had only just settled into his lookout when he heard the unmistakable sound of a tracked vehicle approaching from dead ahead. In fact, as Goldstein listened in numbed surprise, he distinctly heard several tracked vehicles—and perhaps *many* tracked vehicles. Then he heard men muttering phrases in what he knew must be German.

Unbelievably, with the lead tank only a few yards away, Private Bernard Goldstein stepped to the middle of the roadway, held his 8-round, .30-caliber M1 rifle at the ready, and yelled "Halt!"

At this incredible juncture, Sergeant Hensel was rounding the bend with another engineer he planned to place alongside Goldstein in the tiny outpost. Before the scene quite registered on Hensel, German paratroopers riding the lead tanks leaped to the roadway and opened fire with many automatic weapons. Hensel and his companion dropped to their knees and briefly returned the fire, but they withdrew seconds later, prodded by a stream of machine-gun bullets from the lead tank. As Private Goldstein retreated up the slope hemming in the west side of the roadway, the two-man bazooka team charged into the fray and got off a single round that luckily hit the lead German tank. Then Hensel, his companion, and the bazooka team ran back to the roadblock position.

Hensel's squad waited for twenty long minutes at the roadblock, but nothing happened. No Germans appeared. Several volunteers tried to advance back around the curve to find Goldstein, who already had fled up the hill, but Germans waiting out of sight fired on them and they pulled in their horns. Suddenly, tank engines which had been idling for the twenty minutes roared to life. It sounded to Hensel like the engine noises were receding, but he could not be sure. He herded everyone aboard the squad truck and ordered the driver to coast silently back down the hill to the viaduct. As the truck braked at the bottom of the hill, Hensel and his remaining men jumped out and deployed. If the Germans advanced, they would have a fight—however brief—on their hands.

But the Germans did not advance. Exhausted, behind schedule, and understandably concerned about what he might run into in the dark—clearly Stavelot was defended—Peiper decided to call it a day. The entire German armored vanguard backtracked and went into a night defensive posture on a high hill overlooking Stavelot.

Peiper's hesitation and withdrawal turned out to be decisive.

CHAPTER 12

Unknown to me, my messages through 1111th Group to 1st Army headquarters throughout December 17 were having a chilling effect upon the top Allied military leaders in Europe, including General Eisenhower himself. Based largely on news from the 291st, it was dawning on the 1st Army, 12th Army Group, and SHAEF commanders that a German armored force of undetermined but adequate size was rampaging well in the rear of breached front line. Apparently, we were the only Allied unit in the vicinity of Kampfgruppe Peiper with sufficient composure to report what we were experiencing with any degree of accuracy. As the pattern emerged on our leaders' maps, General Omar Bradley, the 12th Army Group commander, ordered Major General Leland Hobbs's 30th Infantry Division (now part of the 9th U.S. Army) to counterattack from Aachen toward the point in the Losheim Gap at which the Germans had broken in. General Eisenhower himself freed up Major General James Gavin's 82nd Airborne Division, then resting in Reims, France, for a counterattack toward Losheim through Werbomont. Closer to home, Lieutenant General Courtney Hodges, our own 1st Army commander, was scouring the rear for any intact infantry and antitank units he could send to stiffen our truly meager defenses at and around Malmédy. As I was to learn much later, my personal resolve to stand at Malmédy had somehow been communicated up the chain of command and had become the core of SHAEF policy. However, for the moment, it remained to be seen if the convergence of thought could outrace the convergence of events.

It might very well have seemed to the generals that I knew what was going on at the potential point of contact with the elusive

German armored spearhead, but information was slow in arriving at Malmédy, and it came in spurts by devious means.

Often faced with communicating information literally too hot to commit to the airwaves, Major Ed Lampp repeatedly dispatched his personal driver, Technician 5th Grade Mike Popp, with verbal messages. On one run between from Trois-Ponts to Malmédy, Popp brought news that part of Jim Gamble's Company A had arrived safely at Trois-Ponts, thus allowing me to infer that Jim's route from Amblève through the forest and across the Salm River was free of Germans. At about 2100 hours, December 17, I sent Popp back to Haute-Bodeux with orders for Ed Lampp to collect several machine guns from Company A and send them up to Malmédy. Ed dispatched eight Company A engineers under Corporal Isaac "Black Mac" McDonald to man the guns. Popp's repeated and utterly heroic trips offered ongoing inferential confirmation that our road net to the rear remained unsevered, an important bit of tactical news and a relief of major magnitude.

Mike Popp was by no means the only hero testing the road net or the limits of our luck that evening. Warrant Officer Coye Self, our assistant supply officer, ran an incredible risk in behalf of Malmédy's defense. He drove a six-by-six truck loaded with volatile ammunition, mines, and TNT along the lonely, threatened road from Haute-Bodeux so we could complete the awesome task of wiring all the bridges and setting out minefields on all the major approaches.

Captain Paul Kamen, the battalion dentist, arrived with seven medics at 2115 hours. Neither Paul nor any of the medics had ever been over the road to Malmédy—not even in daylight—and their truck was outfitted, as were all our vehicles, only with cat-eye headlights. They were as pleased to arrive in Malmédy as we were to have them. Paul consolidated the medical services and set up in the area precipitously abandoned that forenoon by the 44th Evacuation Hospital.

While reporting in, Paul Kamen mentioned that, on the way through Trois-Ponts, he had seen four American-uniformed men in a jeep who did not look quite right. I could not imagine why that might be the case or what I could do about it, so I let the matter drop.

At about 2200 hours, Lieutenant Frank Rhea, who was in charge of patrols scouring our rear, reported that a long column showing cat-eye headlights was slowly approaching from the direction of Spa. This sent an immediate chill through the battalion CP, for we had received no warning from higher headquarters that a relief column actually was on the way.

Despite the uncertainty, Company B's Sergeant Joe Chetnicki, bravely stood in the middle of the roadway and flagged down the lead vehicle of the approaching column. I cannot begin to imagine Chetnicki's relief when he was greeted cheerfully by Lieutenant Colonel Harold Hansen, commander of the 99th Separate Infantry Battalion, the first available unit 1st Army headquarters had been able to dispatch to our aid. Hansen's battalion, about nine hundred strong, was composed mainly of Norwegian-Americans, like himself, and native Norwegians who had fled from Hitler's occupation of their country and who somehow wound up in the United States. By all appearances, the 99th Norwegian Battalion, as Hansen's unit proudly styled itself, was a crack outfit.

Lieutenant Colonel Hansen led his column into town and reported to me at 2215 hours. I was almost moved to tears as this big blond man greeted me with his outstretched hand. Hansen showed an expression of amazement when, in briefing him, I noted that we had been holding all day with no more than 180 lightly armed engineers. He had been told along the way that Malmédy was in German hands, and he had expected to enter town by means of an infantry assault. When Hansen learned that we had not one antitank gun to our name, he just shook his head.

I told my newly arrived colleague that Malmédy appeared to be hemmed in by Germans to the east, south, and southwest, and we had been shelled intermittently throughout the afternoon and evening, and that for some reason the Germans were withholding their expected assault on the town. I gave Lieutenant Colonel Hansen all available details of the massacre at Five Points—gleaned from accounts of the twenty-eight known survivors we had treated—and everything I knew about the wraithlike, murderous SS panzer column. I next quickly reviewed our defensive plans and showed him on my map where thirteen roadblocks had been set in and minefields had been laid. In response, he agreed with my judgment that his infantry companies be emplaced along the railroad embankment, by far the best defensive feature in the immediate area. My roadblocks would remain in place, anchoring and extending the infantry main line of resistance by covering all the bridges, overpasses, and defiles that would inevitably tend to canalize any possible German approach on the town.

After hearing me out, Hansen agreed to share command of Malmédy with me, a truly magnanimous gesture in view of my tyro status as a combat leader. Then his first act was to send a message to 1st Army headquarters in which he requested the urgent dispatch of at least a company of armored infantry and at least a platoon of tank destroyers to defend Stavelot. I was gratified to see that this calm, professional infantryman had confirmed my belief that an adequate defense force in Stavelot could very well prove to be a key to preventing the Germans from achieving their goals in our sector.

Shortly after the 99th Norwegian Battalion pulled into town, we heard that the remainder of the 1st Army's hastily contrived Task Force was on the way. The main elements were the 526th Armored Infantry Battalion and Company A, 825th Tank Destroyer Battalion, both of which were 1st Army units that had been dispatched directly and independently from Spa. The safe arrival of the additional infantry, armored fighting vehicles, towed 57mm antitank guns, and, above all, a dozen towed 75mm tank destroyers, would mean that Malmédy could reasonably be defended against a fairly significant armored assault. It remained to be seen if the reinforcements could get through.

While Hansen went off to establish his own command post, which would be linked to mine by telephone lines and messengers, I went back to the business of strengthening and consolidating my network of roadblocks.

The arrival of sorely needed combat reinforcements at Malmédy was only a small part of local efforts to build up a defense in the 1st Army's rear that could stand up to and perhaps deflect the progress of the 1st SS Panzer Division's Kampfgruppe Peiper and the slower-moving spearhead of the 12th SS Panzer Division. At about 1630 hours, December 17, on receipt of my first message outlining the massacre at Five Points, Colonel H. Wallis Anderson, the 1111th Group commander, had ordered the 51st Engineer Combat Battalion to send a full company to begin fashioning defenses at Trois-Ponts, where the group headquarters was located. Also, Anderson ordered the 202nd Engineer Combat Battalion, which had been attached to 1111th Group on December 11, to scrape together a company-size force and dispatch it to Stavelot. As soon as those messages had been sent, Colonel Anderson assumed authority over the 1st Army Map

Depot and ordered it to withdraw from Stavelot. The 202nd was also advised of the apparent German parachute drop north of Malmédy and ordered to dispatch a force to investigate the situation and contain the Germans, if any were found.

Nothing much actually happened before Peiper's vanguard ran into Chuck Hensel's squad at Stavelot. News of the encounter was somehow delayed until my liaison officer, Captain Lloyd Sheetz, happened to stop off to talk with Sergeant Hensel while en route from Malmédy to Trois-Ponts with a written message I was sending Colonel Anderson. That was at about 2245 hours. After that, the appearance and disappearance of the German armored force was reported through various links to higher headquarters, including my forward CP and the 1111th Group CP.

I became greatly concerned about the vulnerability of the Stavelot bridge across the Amblève River. If the Germans renewed their drive into the village, we would have to blow the span to deny them access to our rear. Stavelot was only ten miles from 1st Army headquarters at Spa and less than two miles from a huge fuel dump at Francorchamps. Thus, at 2315 hours, December 17, I called Colonel Anderson and asked him to blow the bridge. I further advised him that Captain Sheetz believed that the German armored column was consolidating on a hill overlooking Stavelot and that, since Sergeant Hensel's well-advised withdrawal, there was no one actually defending the key span.

After I added news of our situation at Malmédy (Hansen's battalion was digging in), Colonel Anderson said he would report my situation to the V Corps and 1st Army headquarters. Next, he filled me in on the measures he was taking to cover the various bridges with elements of the 1111th Group engineer battalions. According to the colonel, Major Lampp had sent Lieutenant Cliff Wilson back to Stavelot to oversee Sergeant Hansel's squad and a full company of the 202nd was also en route and expected any time. After some discussion it was also decided to have a squad of Lieutenant Bucky Walters's platoon of Company A, 291st, put out roadblocks on the approaches to Trois-Ponts.

As soon as Lieutenant Wilson returned to Stavelot, at around midnight, he dispatched Private First Class Lorenzo Liparulo and Private Bernard Goldstein in a jeep back to the tiny hut Goldstein had been manning when he had turned back Kampfgruppe Peiper's vanguard at sunset. The two engineers were ambushed by a handful of German Scouts when they stopped in front of a gaggle of houses on the far side of the bridge—out of sight and sound of the rest of the squad. Liparulo, who was driving, was wounded several times in the head and shoulder and Goldstein was wounded in the left side. The Germans left them for dead and Goldstein, whose left hip was shattered, began crawling back toward the bridge to get help for his wounded companion. Since nothing was heard from the two, it was assumed that everything out ahead was quiet.

By midnight, the 1111th Group's 291st, 51st, and 202nd Engineer Combat battalions were moving to form the framework of a defensive barrier about seventy-five miles long from east of Malmédy, through Stavelot and Trois-Ponts, and westward toward the Meuse. While infantry units with which we had no contact were holding the shoulder at Butgenbach or attempting to seal the breach in the 1st Army front, we were arrayed along precisely the line of rivers and streams Kampfgruppe Peiper needed to breach if it was to lead the 6th Panzer Army toward the Meuse and the strategic objectives of Liège and Antwerp.

While Peiper idled away the night waiting for his fifteen-mile-long column to close up on Ligneuville, we engineers did everything we could think of to prevent his renewed efforts to break through the river line. The key to our defense was readying various bridges for demolition, an ancient and trusted method for stopping attacking armies at river barriers. Once it arrived, the company of the 202nd assigned to Stavelot was to prepare the Stavelot viaduct for demolition, and the company of the 51st assigned to Trois-Ponts was to do the same for two of the three river bridges there. Wiring the third Trois-Ponts river bridge fell to Sergeant Jean Miller's squad of Lieutenant Bucky Walters's platoon of Company A, 291st. Farther back, two companies of the 51st were preparing to demolish bridges between Trois-Ponts and the Meuse.

However, for all the good intentions and might have beens, there still remained an enormous gap at Stavelot. After Lieutenant Cliff Wilson reported at 0005, December 18, that no reinforcements had yet arrived in Stavelot, I called Colonel Anderson again to plead outright that he get a unit of some strength to the bridge as quickly as he could. I was sure the Germans were going to attack there and that, if they did, they would get through into our rear and cut Malmédy off from the rest of the world.

Company C, 202nd Engineer Combat Battalion, commanded by Lieutenant Joe Chinlund, finally arrived in Stavelot at about

0100 hours, December 18. Guided by Lieutenant Cliff Wilson, Chinlund's company went straight to work preparing the Stavelot viaduct across the Amblève for command detonation. I would have blown the bridge outright, but higher headquarters thought it was more prudent to see how the situation developed. Eventually, Colonel Anderson ordered the bridge demolished, but the charge failed to detonate. We did not know it then, but it appears that two American-uniformed Skorzeny commandos had infiltrated Lieutenant Chinlund's working party and had somehow sabotaged the charge.

Shortly after midnight, a Belgian farmer named Martin was passed through one of our roadblocks to Dr. Paul Kamen's aid station in Malmédy. Martin told Kamen that a wounded American officer was at his home, a farmhouse just south of town. Paul sent sulfa and bandages home with the farmer, and Martin returned at about 0100 hours, December 18, with Lieutenant Virgil Lary, commander of the massacred Battery B. As it turned out, Lary was the last of twenty-nine survivors we had taken in since 1530 hours, December 17. Though wounded, he was in good mental condition and quite able to relate a perfectly coherent story with many new details, including a complete description of the SS armored vehicles and a fairly accurate accounting of the German column's strength.

I was speaking with Lieutenant Lary when I learned that Corporal Black Mac McDonald had arrived with his detail of eight Company A machine gunners and an assortment of .30-caliber and .50-caliber machine guns. We sent the guns to beef up Master Sergeant Ralph McCarty's two roadblocks at the railroad viaduct west of town and McCarty used the bonus in manpower to help establish a new block at the Warche River timber trestle bridge, which was immediately wired for demolition.

The last 291st engineers to get through to Malmédy that night were Technician 4th Grade Jeff Elliott and Private First Class Red Richardson, hands down the battalions' ablest scavengers. I wished that Jeff had brought us one of the German tanks he had been refurbishing from time to time since Carentan, but I gladly settled for the extra bazookas and ammunition he brought forward from Company A in response to my urgent plea for both.

That plea for Company A's bazookas and bazooka ammunition, transmitted around midnight by radio via the battalion rear CP, was the last radio message we succeeded in getting through to Haute-Bodeux. Subsequently, our radio communications with the battalion rear became intermittent.

By the time Elliott and Richardson arrived, we were being probed regularly at various roadblocks. For some reason, the Germans mounted no direct, overwhelming assaults but contented themselves with quick hit-and-run confrontations apparently aimed at getting our troops to give away their positions. Artillery and mortar fire continued to strike the town sporadically, robbing us of any sleep we might have contemplated.

Between 0300 and 0400, December 18, the headquarters and two companies of the 526th Armored Infantry Battalion and two platoons of Company A, 825th Tank Destroyer Battalion arrived intact. I learned from the 526th's commander that, in response to my many pleas, the rest of the force—an armored infantry company and a tank destroyer platoon—had been diverted toward Stavelot. Shortly after the 526th arrived with the tank destroyers, we were unexpectedly bolstered at Malmédy by a battery of 90mm antiaircraft guns from the 49th Antiaircraft Artillery Brigade. These were placed on a hill overlooking the town and dug in in such a way as to act as antitank weapons covering several vital roads.

Other than the failure of the Stavelot bridge detonation, the news continued to be good for most of the rest of the dark hours. Sometime after 0430 hours, Lieutenant Colonel Hansen received a radio message from Major Paul Solis, the executive officer of the 526th Armored Infantry Battalion. Solis had been diverted before reaching Malmédy with a company of the 526th and a platoon of Company A, 825th Tank Destroyer Battalion to defend Stavelot. He told Hansen that he had reached Stavelot and was linking up with Lieutenant Chinlund's company of the 202nd Combat Engineers and Sergeant Hensel's squad of the 291st. As that news made its way around the regional command net, Major Ed Lampp decided to send Captain Jim Gamble and the rest of Lieutenant Arch Taylor's platoon of Company A to help at Stavelot by establishing new roadblocks south and west of the bridge. Somewhere along the line, Sergeant Hensel decided to leave Stavelot and rejoin Lieutenant Warren Rombaugh's Company C platoon, which he heard was at Trois-Ponts.

At 0500 hours, I contacted Colonel Anderson on our restored telephone line to advise him that we were being harassed by light artillery barrages and minor probes and that the rear elements of the 526th Armored Infantry Battalion and the tank-destroyer company were arriving and being committed by Lieutenant Colonel Hansen.

Things were getting better and better at Malmédy, where Harold Hansen's hard work was paying off in the establishment of an integrated defense in depth. I also had the impression that Stavelot was becoming stronger, though I felt there were not yet enough infantry or antitank weapons in town to defend the unblown bridge against a renewed and determined thrust by the armored unit that had contacted Sergeant Hensel's squad the evening before.

At 0600 hours, Lieutenant Chinlund, of the 202nd Combat Engineers, called to advise me that Captain Jim Gamble and Lieutenant Arch Taylor, both of Company A, 291st, had arrived in Stavelot. He also confirmed that Major Solis's armored infantry and tank destroyers were moving into defensive positions in the town and that Major Solis had formally assumed control of all the engineers in town.

At 0650 hours, Ed Lampp was contacted by Colonel Anderson, who told him that Captain Gamble had reported to Group with news that the Stavelot viaduct was prepared for demolition. Ed also learned that Jim and Arch Taylor had personally gone forward to locate Private First Class Lorenzo Liparulo following the return of Private Bernard Goldstein, who had been wounded around midnight. Jim and Arch found Liparulo in the jeep he had been driving and brought him back to Stavelot, where they picked up Goldstein. The word was that both men were alive but that Liparulo was in critical condition with wounds in the head. After reporting to Ed Lampp by radio, Jim Gamble personally drove Goldstein and Liparulo to the battalion aid station in Trois-Ponts. For the time being, we had no idea how the two engineers had been attacked, for the German bushwackers were either gone or had laid low in the presence of Gamble and Taylor. (Lorenzo Liparulo succumbed to his wounds on December 19, but Bernard Goldstein survived and reached the States in April 1945.)

I conferred at length with Lieutenant Colonel Hansen at 0700 hours. He outlined the deployment of his reinforced battalion and then we got to work trying to match up reports of sightings of enemy units. According to reports brought in by patrols sent from Malmédy by Hansen's headquarters and mine, it appeared that a German armored force was on a big hill south of Stavelot, apparently poised to attack the town, and that German paratroopers were north of us, around Hockai, on the road to Eupen.

Hansen had somehow inferred that the German armored force
was part of the 1st SS Panzer Division, which was accurate. So
far, no one had turned up any signs of the German paratroopers
reported as being on our road net north of Malmédy, Stavelot,
and Trois-Ponts.

As best Hansen and I could determine, our defensive positions from Malmédy through Stavelot and Trois-Ponts to Werbomont were as complete as they were going to be before the
Germans mounted their expected armored assault. The bulk of
our force was at Malmédy, but a strong blocking force had been
established under Major Solis at Stavelot. Company C, 51st
Combat Engineers, and Sergeant Jean Miller's squad of Lieutenant Bucky Walters's platoon of Company A, 291st, had all
three bridges at Trois-Ponts covered and nearly ready to blow.
Captain Jim Gamble, of Company A, still had his headquarters
platoon, Lieutenant Arch Taylor's platoon, and part of Lieutenant Al Edelstein's platoon at Werbomont, in reserve. At the
moment, our radio and telephone networks—not to mention the
messenger-supporting road net—were all functional.

Hansen and I agreed that the main blow would probably fall
at Malmédy, which had the best road net and thus would provide
the German spearhead commander with virtually endless options.

We were wrong.

CHAPTER 13

Major Paul Solis's defensive deployment in and around Stavelot was a makeshift effort brought about by his unfamiliarity with the terrain—he had never seen it in daylight—and his uncertainty over the location and intentions of the German armored force that had tangled with Sergeant Chuck Hensel's squad. Solis did not even begin deploying his armored infantry company and tank destroyer platoon until the last elements of both closed on Stavelot at around 0400 hours.

Major Solis's mission at Stavelot was largely undefined and extremely complex. In addition to the bridge, Solis felt obliged to look after the southern approaches to the vast, vulnerable gasoline dump that extended four or five miles alongside the road to Francorchamps. There was a troop of Belgian armored cavalry in the vicinity, but it is uncertain if Solis even knew it was there. Certainly, he did not put the Belgian force to use. In any case, the fuel dump appeared to be Kampfgruppe Peiper's immediate objective, so Solis was completely justified in guarding its approaches. Thus, the major sent two squads of his armored infantry company and a 57mm antitank gun up the road to establish a block where the railroad spur from Malmédy cut the road to Francorchamps. A 75mm antitank gun from the tank destroyer platoon was dispatched with some infantry to a blocking position on the main road to Malmédy and another 75mm tank destroyer was set up where the Malmédy-Trois-Ponts road intersected the Stavelot-Francorchamps road. That left Solis with two infantry platoons and several 57mm antitank guns from his 526th Armored Infantry Battalion and two more 75mm tank destroyers from the 825th Tank Destroyer Battalion.

After seeing to his rear, Solis placed the remaining two platoons of the armored infantry company in the Stavelot town

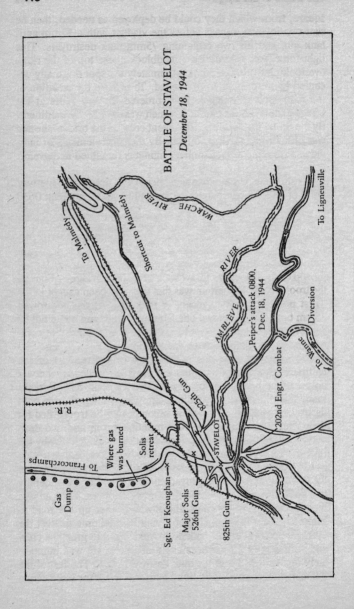

BATTLE OF STAVELOT
December 18, 1944

square, from which they could be deployed as needed, then he sent two infantry squads across the viaduct with a 57mm anti-tank gun and his two remaining 75mm tank destroyers. This light force was to establish a roadblock at the top of the ridge overlooking the bridge, at approximately the spot originally occupied by Sergeant Hensel's squad. To obviate the isolation of the roadblock contingent, Solis ordered the engineers at the bridge to delay the demolition, which was apparently imminent. By the time the roadblock contingent crossed the bridge, the sun was on its way over the horizon. By then, no elements or individuals from the 291st Combat Engineers remained in Stavelot.

It was still dark and the roadblock detail was nearing the halfway point of its long climb up the Stavelot hill when, at about 0630 hours, the artillery accompanying Kampfgruppe Peiper opened with a fearsome barrage aimed at scattering the opposition around the bridge. Caught in the open beneath a sky suddenly filled with brilliant light and sound, the roadblock detail instantly became paralyzed with indecision. Should it advance to the top of the hill or withdraw back across the bridge? About all the troops knew for certain was that they had been caught in the worst possible place to receive a tank assault; the two towed 75mm tank destroyers and one 57mm antitank gun could not be deployed on so steep an incline. At last, the detachment commander decided to turn back to the bridge.

The laborious process of reversing the direction of the halftrack-towed tank destroyers was progressing slowly, and was only half completed when one or two German Mk.IV tanks topped the hill and opened direct fire. Both halftracks and both destroyers were disabled within seconds and the troops fled for their lives, abandoning the 57mm antitank gun and two dead comrades. Six more troopers could not be accounted for by the time the survivors thundered back across the bridge.

As soon as the shooting started, Major Solis ordered one of the two tank destroyers deployed north of the bridge to redeploy to a spot from which it could fire across the river. The gun was reconnected to its halftrack and towed farther up the road to Malmédy. The Belgian civilian living in the home nearest the eventual position of this tank destroyer ran out to greet the crew and volunteered his services as an observer. He was immediately incorporated into the tank destroyer crew. The last of the 825th Tank Destroyer Battalion's guns was left at the intersection

in the middle of town and aimed straight down the road leading
north from the bridge.

While Major Solis frantically worked to defend the bridge
with his diminished antitank resources, the German tanks that
had destroyed the two tank destroyers pulled back out of sight
and the intense artillery barrage continued. At length, December 18, 1944, dawned rainy and overcast with little or no ceiling.
The Ardennes forest was murky and miserable in all directions.

The German artillery barrage intensified between 0745 and
0800. Then Peiper's tanks charged down the hill toward the
bridge. It took a long time before the lead tanks drove into the
killing zone of the tank destroyer deployed up the road to Malmédy, and it took several rounds before the tank destroyer crew
settled in. One or two German tanks were hit and disabled,
obliging the German armored spearhead to grind to an impatient
halt as efforts were directed to clearing the roadway of the two
Mk.IV obstructions. The tank destroyer continued to fire, but
about all the damage it caused was to several roadside houses
and outbuildings, which started burning.

The roadway was eventually cleared and the lead tank rapidly
advanced to the bottom of the hill, pulling behind it a tank
column that stretched impressively all the way to the top of the
hill. It was by then 0830 hours.

Incredibly, no one blew the bridge.

The lead tank slowed and then raced at full speed across the
span. Several other tanks followed, and then the bridge was
completely overrun.

The leading tanks were passing the first intersection in the
main part of town when they were engaged by heavy machine-gun fire from the right. A battery of halftrack-mounted quadruple .50-caliber antiaircraft guns from the 7th Armored
Division happened to be transiting Stavelot when the armored
thrust overtook the bridge. The withering .50-caliber fire briefly
stopped the German tanks where they stood, but, inexplicably,
the American antiaircraft battery commander immediately withdrew all his halftracks through town and up the Francorchamps
road.

As the German vanguard tanks approached the main intersection in the center of town, the 75mm tank destroyer posted there
opened fire and immediately scored several hits. Fearing an
even larger, more extensive trap that would mire the single column on Stavelot's narrow main street, the vanguard commander

reflexively turned left at the first available intersection. The narrow street he chose carried him to an intersection with the Malmédy-Trois-Ponts highway. If he turned right, he would outflank the tank destroyer while tanks to his rear took it on from dead ahead. The pincers attack on the main intersection would easily overcome the tank destroyer and open the road to the fuel dump.

Far beyond belief in this unbelievable action—it never should have happened; the bridge should have been blown—was the fact that Peiper had not a clue that all the fuel he would ever need was stored in an open roadside dump less than two miles from the bridge his vanguard had just seized. Certainly, Skorzeny's American-uniformed commandos knew the fuel was there, and the huge dump could not have been overlooked by even the sparse Luftwaffe aerial reconnaissance flights that had preceded the Ardennes Offensive. But it is plain to see that no one had ever told Peiper or his vanguard commander, the sanguinary Major Werner Poetschke. As several squads of Lieutenant Joe Chinlund's company of the 202nd Combat Engineers spread out to defend various intersections leading toward the fuel dump, the lead German tanks turned left down the road to Trois-Ponts.

Just before the German vanguard turned left, away from the main intersection, the tank destroyer crew blew up the barrel of their gun to prevent its capture by the flanking German force that appeared certain to overrun the position. For all practical purposes, the main intersection fell without a fight, but the German vanguard had committed the entire trailing column to a run on Trois-Ponts via the road along the north bank of the Amblève.

As the Germans appeared about to overrun the main intersection, Major Solis retired to the block he had set up earlier on the road to Francorchamps—one 57mm antitank gun and two armored infantry squads. He also sent word for every other American who could be located to withdraw up the main road toward Malmédy. As these troops passed, the crew of the last tank destroyer hitched up their gun and followed. Except for Solis's tiny blocking force north of town and a few isolated groups of Chinlund's company of the 202nd Combat Engineers in the town, Stavelot had been abandoned.

Minutes after Major Solis cleared the town and hunkered down at the roadblock in front of the fuel dump, Staff Sergeant Ed

Keoughan approached from the north with about half of the Company C, 291st platoon that had been at Sourbrodt until I had ordered it to Trois-Ponts in the middle of the night. The entire platoon had left Sourbrodt in four trucks, but two of the trucks and Lieutenant John Perkins had gone one way while Keoughan, the platoon sergeant, had gone the other. Thinking he was going to get through Stavelot and on the road to Trois-Ponts, Keoughan was mightily disappointed when his trucks had to pull up beside some farm buildings because of the sound of heavy firing ahead. As the engineers jumped down to listen and discuss alternatives, Major Solis pulled up in his jeep and asked if they had any antitank weapons. Staff Sergeant Keoughan replied that he had one antitank rifle grenade, to which Solis replied, "Okay. Deploy your men in these farm buildings. . . . Guard this road. German tanks are coming." Then, as the Company C engineers gaped, Solis pulled back onto the road, followed by the 57mm antitank gun and the two squads of jogging armored infantrymen. Keoughan's engineers complied with Major Solis's order, prepared to battle German tanks with their M1 rifles and their single antitank rifle grenade.

The sounds of short, sharp fire fights reached Keoughan's roadblock for sometime—indicating that elements of Chinlund's company were harassing the Germans—but no Germans appeared on the road to the fuel dump. In time, well before the tail of the German column cleared Stavelot, the Belgian cavalry troop guarding the fuel set fire to the southernmost section of the roadside dump, but even the huge, billowing spires of black smoke failed to attract the Germans' attention.

At around noon, Major Solis reappeared at Keoughan's roadblock and ordered the engineers back to the dump to help the Belgians set more fires. Almost as soon as Keoughan's two troop-filled trucks set out for the dump, they were confronted and stopped by the inflow of many vehicles carrying the 30th Infantry Division's 1st Battalion, 117th Infantry Regiment, to Stavelot.

It was not until nearly noon that Lieutenant Colonel Hansen and I learned that the Stavelot bridge had been captured. The first news arrived with the leading elements of the troops Major Solis had sent in our direction following the seizure of the bridge. I was shocked, certain that the Germans would soon be on us from the direction of our best link with our rear. However, nothing happened; no Germans appeared as Lieutenant Colonel

Hansen worked to shift part of his infantry force to cover the Stavelot road. Hansen was still working when the vanguard of the main body of the 30th Infantry Division's 117th Infantry Regiment and 118th Field Artillery Battalion appeared from the north. Eventually, we learned that the 1st Battalion, 117th Infantry, had been diverted toward Stavelot and that the whole rest of this superb, battle-tested regimental combat team was bound for Malmédy. For the first time since the nightmare began, I experienced a real hope that we would actually hold Malmédy. In time, over the 117th Infantry's communications net, I learned both that the Francorchamps dump had been set afire and that all available troops were trying to extinguish the flames and save the precious fuel.

We were by no means out of the woods. We held Malmédy in considerable and increasing strength, but Kampfgruppe Peiper had crossed the Amblève at Stavelot and was on its way toward Trois-Ponts, which was still only lightly defended. We needed to retake Stavelot and, if possible, deny Peiper any of the three bridges across the Salm and Amblève rivers at Trois-Ponts. If what had happened at Stavelot—the capture of an intact bridge—happened again at Trois-Ponts, our defense of Malmédy and throughout the region would be moot, for the road to Liège and Antwerp would be open.

CHAPTER 14

Two squads of Lieutenant Bucky Walters's Company A platoon had left the sawmill at Grand-Halleaux on my order at about 1600 hours, December 17. Upon learning of the German breakthrough toward St.-Vith from a passing column of the 7th Armored Division, Bucky left the main road and began moving over the logging trails, fire breaks, and farm roads his platoon had been traversing for some time while operating the Grand-Halleaux sawmill. The going was extremely slow, particularly when trails debouched onto main roads, which were jammed with slow-moving or unmoving traffic retreating from the front. However, well before sunup, December 18, Bucky found the Salm River bridge, less than two miles south of Trois-Ponts, in the hands of Sergeant Jean Miller's squad of his own platoon.

Under orders to report to the Company A CP, at Werbomont, Bucky reluctantly left about half of Sergeant Miller's squad alone at the bridge and eventually made his way to the battalion rear CP, at Haute-Bodeux. There, he gave Major Ed Lampp a complete report of all he had seen along the way from Grand-Halleaux and bedded down with his troops; none of them had slept in nearly forty-eight hours.

Bucky Walters's return to Haute-Bodeux brought Captain Jim Gamble's Company A to full strength, except for Sergeant Miller's half squad, a detachment of machine gunners in Malmédy, and a Company A squad under Staff Sergeant Paul Hinkel, which was guarding the 1111th Group CP in Trois-Ponts.

There was no lack of engineers in Trois-Ponts by sunup, December 18. In addition to Sergeant Angelo Magliocca's resident Company C squad, which had been running the local sawmill for some weeks, Colonel Anderson had pulled in all of Company C, 51st Engineer Combat Battalion. When the 51st Company C arrived at around midnight, it immediately relieved the two squads of Lieutenant Warren Rombaugh's platoon of Company C, 291st, which were by then wiring one of the two bridges inside town for demolition. Rombaugh rejoined the main body of Company C, 291st, at Château Froidcoeur, in La Gleize, and Company C, 51st, completed the job of preparing both Amblève bridges for demolition by about 0800 hours, December 18.

During the night, also, the tiny defense force at Trois-Ponts was bolstered unexpectedly when the halftrack towing one of the 526th Armored Infantry Battalion's 57mm antitank guns toward Malmédy threw a track in town. Before the antitank gun crew quite knew what was happening, they and their gun had been dragooned by 1111th Group headquarters and set out about a half mile in front of twin railroad underpasses just east of the railroad viaduct running alongside the N-23 road bridge across the Amblève. Alongside the gunners was a half squad of Company C, 51st Engineers, including a bazooka team. The engineers built up a roadblock of daisy chains of mines.

After the main body of Lieutenant Bucky Walters's Company A platoon had had a few hours' sleep at Haute-Bodeux, Ed Lampp sent it back to Trois-Ponts to help Sergeant Jean Miller's half squad set out the explosives with which the Salm bridge would be blown. The charges were set and Sergeant Miller was again left at the bridge with about half his squad while the rest of the platoon went up to the 1111th Group CP to act as an infantry reaction force.

At about 1000 hours, shortly after Walters's platoon left Haute-Bodeux, Lieutenant Arch Taylor's Company A platoon was dispatched from Werbomont in response to a report that German paratroopers had landed south of Haute-Bodeux. A little after that, Captain Jim Gamble received orders to send engineers to prepare to blow a wooden trestle bridge across Lienne Creek, at Habiemont, on the N-23 just east of Werbomont. Aside from the Company A headquarters, the only troops at Werbomont were members of two understrength squads of Lieutenant Al Edelstein's platoon. Staff Sergeant Paul Hinkel's squad of Edelstein's platoon was guarding the 1111th Group CP at Trois-Ponts and Al himself was with the battalion rear CP, at Haute-Bodeux, so Jim Gamble phoned the platoon sergeant, Staff Sergeant Edwin Pigg, and told him to send a squad-size force to undertake the demolition job. Thus, before 1100 hours, the 291st's reserve company had been broken up and sent off on three separate

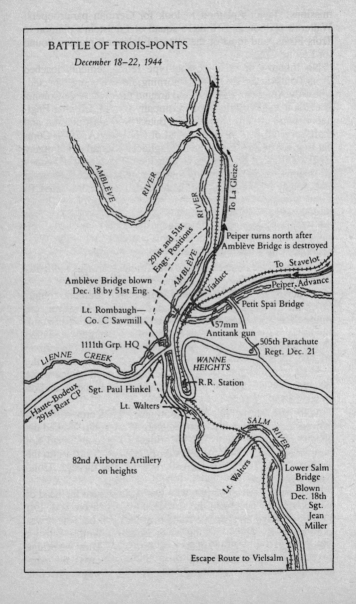

BATTLE OF TROIS-PONTS
December 18–22, 1944

AMBLÈVE RIVER

AMBLÈVE RIVER

To La Gleize

291st and 51st
Engr. Positions

Peiper turns north after
Amblève Bridge is destroyed

To Stavelot

Viaduct

Peiper Advance

Amblève Bridge blown
Dec. 18 by 51st Eng.

Petit Spai Bridge

Lt. Rombaugh—
Co. C Sawmill

57mm
Antitank gun

505th Parachute
Regt. Dec. 21

1111th Grp. HQ

LIENNE CREEK

WANNE
HEIGHTS

Haute-Bodeux
291st Rear CP

R.R. Station

Sgt. Paul Hinkel

Lt. Walters

SALM RIVER

82nd Airborne Artillery
on heights

Lt. Walters

Lower Salm
Bridge
Blown
Dec. 18th
Sgt.
Jean
Miller

Escape Route to Vielsalm

missions: Taylor's platoon to look for German paratroopers,
Walters's platoon and Hinkel's squad of Edelstein's platoon to
Trois-Ponts, and most of the rest of Edelstein's platoon bound
for Lienne Creek.

No infantry or other combat-type reinforcements reached
Trois-Ponts during the night or morning, nor were any expected.
The only American troops in and around the town were Colonel
Anderson and his group staff; Company C, 51st Combat Engineers; two squads of Lieutenant Bucky Walters's platoon and
Staff Sergeant Paul Hinkel's squad of Company A, 291st Combat Engineers; Sergeant Angelo Magliocca's squad of Company
C, 291st Combat Engineers; and the lone 57mm antitank gun—
all under Colonel Anderson, a large part of whose CP group
was already in motion toward Haute-Bodeux to set up a safe CP.
These sparse defenders heard firing from the vicinity of Stavelot
during the early morning, but the scene in front of Trois-Ponts
remained peaceful up until about 1100 hours.

The lead Mk.V Panther medium tank of Kampfgruppe Peiper
nosed around the bend leading to the Amblève bridges moments
after 1100. Instantly, as the engineers pulled their daisy chain
mines across the road, the 57mm antitank gun fired one round,
which hit the Panther in a track and disabled it. However, the
Panther's unimpaired turret motors brought the long 75mm tank
gun to bear and one shot destroyed the American gun and killed
all four crewmen. Shrapnel or a bullet from the hail of German
machine-gun fire wounded one of six engineers supporting the
antitank gun, but he slipped back across the road bridge while
the other five headed through the other railroad viaduct and on
up the La Gleize road.

At the precise moment the 57mm gun and its crew were destroyed, a great detonation immediately to the south marked the
demise of one of the Amblève bridges. The sound had not
stopped echoing before the second bridge was dropped into the
Amblève. The N-23 and railroad right of way through Trois-
Ponts were blocked.

Lieutenant Colonel Peiper, who was waiting near the head of
the column for news that the Amblève had been crossed, lost
no time locating an alternate route over the river barrier. It was
to be along the N-33, leading north along the Amblève to La
Gleize, and then by a secondary road across the Amblève bridge
at Cheneux. If Peiper could force his way across the Amblève at Cheneux, he would regain the N-23 highway connecting

Trois-Ponts with Werbomont. If he got there, he was certain he could reach the Meuse by dusk.

During the earlier approach on Stavelot, before the Stavelot bridge had been captured intact, Peiper had taken out a small insurance policy by detaching an infantry-supported company of Mk.IV tanks along a narrow dirt track toward the village of Wanne. The company had arrived at Wanne without difficulty and had proceeded toward Trois-Ponts to deliver what amounted to a secondary flanking attack on the third Trois-Ponts bridge, the one across the Salm that Bucky Walters's platoon had wired and prepared for demolition. The Mk.IV company was approaching the Salm bridge at about the time the vanguard of Kampfgruppe Peiper's main body was approaching the railroad underpass several hundred yards to the north.

If the Salm bridge could be taken intact, Peiper would gain possession of a route considerably shorter than the La Gleize alternate for which he had opted. The entire German column could be rerouted through Wanne and then across the Salm. Peiper turned his main body north along the Amblève, but he kept one eye on the proceedings undertaken by the detached Mk.IV company.

The German medium tanks cautiously approached the bridge, but tank commanders standing tall in their turret hatches saw no hint of any defenders. At length, the tanks stopped in front of a hastily installed minefield and paratroopers scrambled off them to begin clearing a path. Not a peep was heard from any defenders, convincing the Germans that they had found a safe back door into Trois-Ponts.

As the main body of paratroopers worked gingerly to clear the mines, several of them—no doubt including several officers—ventured out onto the span to see what they could see. When the small knot of Germans reached the halfway point, Sergeant Jean Miller activated the detonator in his sweaty hand, blowing them and the Salm bridge to smithereens.

The Salm and Amblève rivers at Trois-Ponts were firmly blocked, leaving Kampfgruppe Peiper with no alternative but to proceed to the Amblève bridge at Cheneux.

Lieutenant Colonel Peiper's turn north onto the N-33 toward La Gleize caused deep consternation among the engineers watching from in and around Trois-Ponts. They sent word to Colonel Anderson, who had just reached Haute-Bodeux to rejoin his displaced CP. The 1111th Group Commander sent word over to Major Ed Lampp, at the adjacent 291st rear CP, and Lampp ordered the 291st's communications chief, Technical Sergeant John Scanlan, to radio the Company C CP in the clear and order it to *run* from La Gleize to Modave before the Germans arrived.

There being absolutely no force on hand or in the offing that was strong enough to defend La Gleize, Company C moved with alacrity. The entire unit was out of Château Froidcoeur before noon. Lieutenant Warren Rombaugh and twenty men headed back toward Trois-Ponts by a circuitous route while the rest of the company fell back on Modave.

Soon after Company C was ordered to Modave, Colonel Bill Carter, the 1st Army chief engineer, ordered the 1111th Group CP and the 291st's rear CP to go there as well to help in the establishment of a barrier line directly in front of the Meuse River.

At 1210 hours, Ed Lampp reached me by radio to tell me of the withdrawals from La Gleize and Haute-Bodeux, of the plan to build up a barrier centered on Modave, and to fill me in on plans to more fully develop the defenses at Trois-Ponts in the event the Germans were forced to fall back on the town. Toward that end, Ed told me, Lieutenant Warren Rombaugh and twenty Company C engineers were driving from La Gleize to Trois-Ponts by a circuitous route. Other 291st units already in Trois-Ponts were Lieutenant Bucky Walters's platoon and Staff Sergeant Paul Hinkel's squad, both from Company A. According to Ed, Company C, 51st Combat Engineers, was to remain in Trois-Ponts. Major Robert "Bull" Yates, the 51st Engineer Combat Battalion's executive officer, had assumed command there, so there was thus no need for me to divert any attention to Trois-Ponts. I told Ed that the reinforced 117th Infantry Regiment of the 30th Infantry Division was in Malmédy and Stavelot and that it appeared that we had amply fortified the northern shoulder of the German break-in from Butgenbach as far west as Stavelot.

The destruction of the Trois-Ponts bridge forced Kampfgruppe Peiper far to the north of its route, well into the zone of the sluggish 12th SS Panzer Division vanguard, far from the objectives of the 1st SS Panzer Division it was spearheading. The Germans had lost precious time—first at Stavelot, for the entire night, and now in their detour toward La Gleize. More important, their presence and probable route were well known to the blocking forces with which they had collided. When knowledgeable engineers looked at their maps of the region and factored in Peiper's actions and probable aims, it was clear that he had two options upon clearing La Gleize. Since there was no way of knowing that Peiper was out of his divisional zone and needed to run back in a southerly direction, it was easy to assume that he would leave La Gleize in the direction of Spa, at which the 1st Army headquarters was still located. Considerable efforts were thus made to defend Spa. On the other hand, it was possible that Peiper was on his way to Werbomont, in which case he needed to cross the Amblève at the first available bridge, the span at Cheneux. If so, he would also need to cross Lienne Creek at the Neufmolin bridge, outside Habiemont.

Spa was beyond 1111th Group's reach; other engineers and part of the 82nd Airborne Division would have to muddle through without us. And there was nothing we could do to blow the Cheneux bridge—no time and no engineers left. But we already had a scratch squad from Company A, 291st, in motion toward the wooden trestle bridge across Lienne Creek. It remained to be seen, however, who would get there first—the Germans or Staff Sergeant Pigg's Company A engineers.

We got lucky because a pair of brave pilots pinpointed the Germans after Peiper turned southwest out of La Gleize—toward Werbomont, away from Spa. Acting on reports from ground units at Stavelot and Trois-Ponts, Major General Elwood "Pete" Quesada, commander of the IX Tactical Air Command, found two pilots willing to volunteer to fly reconnaissance planes below the low cloud ceiling overhanging the Amblève valley. Often flying at less than one hundred feet, the two pilots eventually located Kampfgruppe Peiper's vanguard southwest of La Gleize and followed the roadbound German column almost as far back as Stavelot. The thoroughly nonplussed Germans eventually opened fire from 37mm flak tanks and 20mm antiaircraft gun carriers spotted along the column, but the pilots brought back a remarkably accurate count of German vehicles and types and, more important, the column's exact route and location.

As soon as the reconnaissance pilots reported, General Quesada scrambled sixteen P-47 Thunderbolt fighter-bombers, which also groped beneath the low cloud ceiling. At about 1300 hours, the P-47s found the tail of the German column at Stavelot and delivered furious bombing and strafing attacks. Only several light vehicles were destroyed and only a handful of Germans

were wounded or killed, but the Germans were thoroughly un-
nerved. A second strike of sixteen Thunderbolts caught the German vanguard at 1330 hours, just as it was crossing the Amblève
via the stone bridge at Cheneux. Quite a bit more damage resulted. A Mk.V Panther was seriously disabled and blocked the
roadway, and two halftracks and most of the panzer grenadiers
riding in them were destroyed, as was a command car and the
officers in it. The German light flak damaged several of
the P-47s and sent one crashing in flames at Francorchamps.

The head of the German column was forced to stop at the
Cheneux bridge in order to clear the disabled Panther from the
roadway. The delay was of strategic importance.

That Kampfgruppe Peiper was heading toward Werbomont was
both good news and bad news for the tiny group of Company A
engineers still there. It was bad news in that there were very few
engineers and absolutely no infantry at or near the town, but it
was good news in that there were plenty of explosives on hand
at the Company A CP—more than enough to blow the Neufmolin timber trestle bridge across Lienne Creek.

The job of planting and wiring the explosives at Lienne Creek
fell to Staff Sergeant Edwin Pigg, Lieutenant Al Edelstein's platoon sergeant. (Edelstein was with the battalion rear CP.) The
core of Pigg's team was most of Sergeant Robert Billington's
squad, which boasted several of the battalion's best explosives
handlers—experienced engineers who had served from Carentan onward.

Getting to the Neufmolin bridge took major effort and pa-
tience. The N-23 east of Werbomont was overrun by civilians
fleeing the return of the hated Germans, and nothing could make
them give way. It took until 1500 hours to negotiate the relatively
short distance to the bridge, and Pigg would easily have lost his
race against Kampfgruppe Peiper had not the Germans been
delayed by the P-47 strikes at Cheneux.

Staff Sergeant Pigg was in possession of firm orders: After
wiring the bridge, he was to blow it up upon direct orders from
his platoon commander, Lieutenant Al Edelstein, or upon a
direct approach of the German armored spearhead. The demolition order was withheld for the time being because the bridge
was still of use to our side. In fact, 1111th Group headquarters
and our own 291st rear CP expected to cross the Neufmolin
Bridge on their way directly up the N-23 from Haute-Bodeux to
Modave via Werbomont. On no account, however, was Kampf-

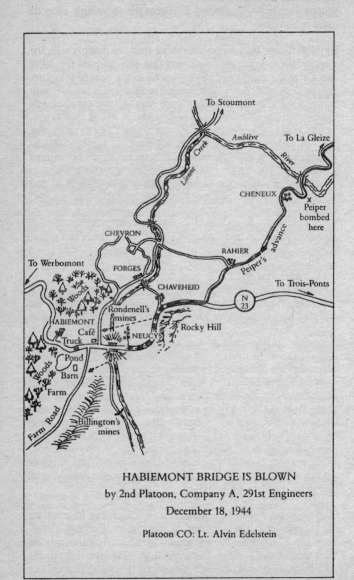

HABIEMONT BRIDGE IS BLOWN

by 2nd Platoon, Company A, 291st Engineers

December 18, 1944

Platoon CO: Lt. Alvin Edelstein

gruppe Peiper to be allowed to repeat the morning's coup de main at Stavelot.

By 1400 hours, Ed Lampp was about ready to comply with the directive from higher headquarters that he withdraw the 291st rear CP to the vicinity of Modave, well to the west of Werbomont. By then, the rear CP had lost all radio communication with my forward CP and had long since sent all the weapons and troops at its disposal forward to Malmédy. At about 1530 hours, by which time the rear CP group was about ready to move, the flow of civilians moving westward on foot through Haute-Bodeux had noticeably increased, and talk among them centered on Kampfgruppe Peiper's vanguard being dangerously close to the town. Located a few hundred yards south of the N-23 and only a half mile west of Trois-Ponts, the rear CP was thus well within range of Peiper's mobile artillery. Indeed, as Ed was about to give the order to move out, a pair of headquarters men manning an observation post he had sent out east of town reported that they could see movement by Peiper's troops along the highway south of Trois-Ponts. Ed told the men to return to the CP immediately.

As the last of the headquarters troops cleared out of the CP buildings, Ed contacted Captain Jim Gamble, of Company A, and told him to withdraw all the men he had with him behind Lienne Creek and to give clearance to Staff Sergeant Pigg to blow the Lienne Creek bridge as soon as Peiper's lead tanks came into his view. Ed's last act before climbing into his own command car was to ask Technical Sergeant John Scanlan if he had heard anything from me on the radio. When Scanlan said that he had not, Ed asked him to stay behind alone for as long as he could and keep trying to reach me by radio to tell me that the rear CP had moved. When Scanlan agreed, Ed cautioned him to stay only as long as he thought it was safe, then to destroy his radio equipment and attempt to make his way to Malmédy. When Scanlan agreed to the plan, Ed left with the main body of the rear CP group, hopeful that he would reach the Lienne Creek bridge before Peiper's vanguard.

Staff Sergeant Pigg's mixed squad was completing its work on the Lienne Creek bridge when, at 1600 hours, Colonel Anderson's and Major Lampp's CP groups arrived simultaneously on their way up the N-23 to Werbomont and Modave. Lieutenant Al Edelstein, who was Pigg's platoon commander, jumped out of one of the vehicles and thus assumed responsibility for blowing the bridge. The column moved into the gloom of the early winter dusk, leaving Edelstein, Pigg, and ten other Company A engineers with the responsibility for stopping and turning Kampfgruppe Peiper.

Minutes after a pair of 1111th Group jeeps crossed the bridge from west to east and disappeared up the N-23 in the direction of Haute-Bodeux and Trois-Ponts, the tiny demolitions team was visited by Major General James Gavin, commanding general of the 82nd Airborne Division and acting commander of the XVIII Airborne Corps. In a characteristic display of sangfroid and his take-charge attitude, Gavin was in fact *the* leading element of his division and his corps (the 82nd and 101st Airborne divisions), which were slated to transit our area in the direction of Bastogne that evening. Gavin asked Al Edelstein why he was there and what he expected to happen and then toured the bridge site with Al. When Gavin noticed a smaller bridge just north of the Neufmolin span, at nearby Forges, he asked Al if it too was set for demolition. Al replied that the Forges bridge was a rickety span barely strong enough to carry jeep traffic and certainly not up to carrying German medium tanks. Besides, Al declared, he had only enough TNT on hand to set off a decisive explosion on the Neufmolin span. Edelstein added that several engineers had been sent up to Forges to lay mines that would stop or delay the approach of light vehicles. With that, General Gavin wished Lieutenant Edelstein well and headed south along the Lienne Creek road.

When the sun set at 1635 hours, the mine-laying details were still at work north and south of the Neufmolin bridge, but the demolitions on the timber trestle span were set, wired, and ready to blow. In fact, the engineers had set a fail-safe back-up charge and wired it to a second detonator. As a precaution, Corporal Fred Chapin, the group's best demolitions man, stood in an old German sentry box, which had the best all-around view of the eastern approaches to the Neufmolin bridge.

After seeing to his wounded following the air attack at the Cheneux bridge, Lieutenant Colonel Peiper reorganized the point of his column and set off down the road toward Rahier, a tiny crossroads village about two thirds the way from Cheneux to the N-23 intersection he was seeking. A halt was called at Rahier so the column could close up on the vanguard.

While the Germans waited, two Belgians, René Simonet, a

resident of Trois-Ponts, and his brother-in-law, a local farmer, decided to do something to stop the return of the hated Germans. The pair ran across country all the way to the Neufmolin bridge where, in perfect English, Simonet reported the exact whereabouts and estimated strength of Peiper's vanguard. Lieutenant Edelstein set out the squad's .30-caliber machine gun and deployed seven engineers with rifles and hand grenades on either side of the west end of the bridge.

Following a brief halt, Peiper's vanguard, including Peiper himself, forged ahead to the N-23 and turned toward the Neufmolin bridge by way of Chauveheid and Neucy. Somewhere between the two tiny roadside villages, the German vanguard ran into a pair of American jeeps manned by two 1111th Group staff officers and their drivers, all on their way from Spa to Trois-Ponts. The Germans spotted and fired on the lead jeep, killing the 1111th Group's motor transport officer and his driver, but the second jeep, carrying the group operations officer, pulled off the road and evaded the German tanks. Unknown to the Germans, who did not stop to take booty, the dead American officer was carrying documents outlining the proposed Modave defensive line. Peiper's on-again, off-again haste cost his side a vital intelligence coup.

At 1645 hours, about midway through the evening's period of dusk, Corporal Chapin spotted the first German tank as it nosed out of the gloom not two hundred yards east of the Neufmolin bridge. It was, of all possible types, a Mk. VI Tiger Royal, a battlefield monster bearing a long deadly 88mm tank-destroying gun and more armor than most antitank guns could penetrate. It was one of several of its type that had joined Kampfgruppe Peiper during the overnight stay in front of Stavelot. During the enforced delay at the Cheneux bridge, following the P-47 strike, Peiper had moved it and several more of its type to the head of the column.

The engineers were ready and so were the Germans. The gunner of the lead Tiger Royal saw activity on the bridge and opened fire with his main gun. The engineers ducked in every direction. The detonator, which had been left in the open, presumably for Sergeant Billington, was grabbed up by Corporal Chapin, who paused to look around until he spotted Lieutenant Edelstein. When Chapin spotted Al, the platoon commander was waving his arms frantically. Chapin took the nonverbal signal to mean he was to blow the bridge, so he twisted the key on the detonator in his hand and thus set off the twenty-five hundred pounds of TNT he and the rest of Staff Sergeant Pigg's team had set out.

The Neufmolin bridge, rebuilt by Captain Larry Moyer's Company C, 291st, in September, was reduced to kindling. Legend has it that Lieutenant Colonel Joachim Peiper waited until the niose died down before uttering what would become a fitting epitaph for the dreams of Kampfgruppe Peiper, the 1st SS Panzer Division, the 6th Panzer Army, and the German high command in the West: "The damned engineers," Peiper exclaimed, "The damned engineers."

The leading Tiger Royals advanced to the bridge and opened fire with their machine guns at the handful of engineers who were fleeing in the direction of the squad truck, which was parked just out of sight at the nearest intersection. Corporal Chapin, who had started out closest to the Germans, was nearly cut down, but he made it to the truck, as did all the others who had been at the Neufmolin bridge.

As the truck, which had damaged valves, slowly coughed its way back in the direction of Werbomont, it was waylaid by an American officer leading a pair of self-propelled 75mm tank destroyers from the town toward the bridge. These were part of a mixed defense force built around the 30th Infantry Division's 2nd Battalion, 119th Infantry Regiment. The reinforcements were just arriving in Werbomont—only minutes after their mission had been obviated by the destruction of the Neufmolin bridge.

The squad truck struggled all the way back to Werbomont, where the troops found that the company A CP had pulled out with the 1111th Group CP and the 291st rear CP. The only American troops the "damned engineers" found in Werbomont were members of an advance party of the 92nd Airborne Division. After some discussion, Staff Sergeant Pigg and the men with him drove west and eventually found the 1111th Group's 629th Light Bridge Company setting up in Huy. They settled in with the 629th, ate, and bedded down for the night.

Most of the tiny mine-laying detail at the Forges bridge took off in the direction of the squad truck when the Neufmolin bridge was blown, but Private Johnny Rondenell did not. Alone and a little lost, Rondenell burrowed into the woods about halfway back to the Neufmolin bridge and decided to wait and see what

happened next. Four other engineers, including Sergeant Billington, also missed the truck, but they were picked up by the
jeep carrying General Gavin back to Werbomont from his tour
of the 82nd Airborne Division's proposed route of advance. On
advice from the general, who dropped them in Werbomont, the
four eventually attached themselves to one of the 82nd Airborne
Division's antiaircraft units. Lieutenant Edelstein also missed
the truck, so he began the long trek to Modave, to which he
alone knew that the battalion rear CP was bound.

Lieutenant Colonel Peiper did not leave the site of the blown
Neufmolin bridge for some time. He desperately needed to get
across Lienne Creek, so he dispatched light reconnaissance
teams upstream and downstream to find an intact bridge capable
of bearing the weight of the Tiger Royal monster tanks. In the
meantime, Major Hal McCown, the commander of the 2nd Battalion, 119th Infantry, accompanied a mixed force of infantrymen and tank destroyers from Werbomont to Lienne Creek to
see if the Neufmolin bridge had indeed been blown and to learn
the disposition of the German force last seen approaching the
creek. The Germans arrayed along the creek near the former
bridge spotted the approaching Americans and some shots were
traded before McCown pulled back a little and set in his tank
destroyers around the village of Habiemont, just to the west of
the bridge site.

Sometime before approaching the Neufmolin bridge, Peiper
had ordered two SS panzer grenadier companies mounted in
halftracks to test a pair of bridges upstream from the Neufmolin
span. One company crossed Lienne Creek on a rickety wooden
bridge west of the Rahier cutoff and the other proceeded northwest from Chauveheid to the Forges bridge. All the halftracks
eventually joined forces in Forges and headed south toward the
N-23.

Tucked into a roadside hidey-hole halfway between Forges
and the N-23, Private Johnny Rondenell heard the sound of the
approaching halftracks and quickly strung his daisy chain of
mines across the narrow roadway. The mine-laying was no
sooner completed than the leading halftrack rolled across the
daisy chain and set off one or more mines. Private Rondenell
raced deep into the forest as the panzer grenadiers instinctively
fired their machine guns and personal weapons in all directions.

The lead halftrack had been permanently disabled, but the
others probed hither and yon along the local road net until they

ran smack into the two self-propelled tank destroyers Major McCown had posted around Habiemont. Several halftracks were destroyed and the remainder of the German reconnaissance column ran straight back to the Forges bridge and crossed to the east bank to report that no local bridges could bear the weight of Kampfgruppe Peiper's tanks.

Lieutenant Colonel Peiper decided to call it a night. He had left a strong force to hold the Cheneux bridge, so he turned his column around and headed back up the road toward La Gleize.

Peiper was right: "The damned engineers" had stopped him, had removed all his options, had boxed him in, had delayed him while regiment upon reinforcing regiment moved down to strengthen and claim the many road towns along a line that would, next day, seal the Bulge's northern shoulder.

December 18, 1944, was the critical day in the northern Bulge. Peiper captured the Stavelot bridge, but we blew the three vital bridges at Trois-Ponts in his face, forcing him onto narrow, unimproved secondary roads not entirely suited for the passage of a heavy armored force. Our fighter-bombers had seriously disrupted Peiper's schedule and, though Peiper captured the Cheneux bridge intact, our engineers blew up the by-then strategically vital Lienne Creek bridge in his face. Also, as important as the contribution of the engineers in deflecting and frustrating Peiper were the delays we caused. During December 18 small groups of engineers purchased immeasurably valuable time so that whole divisions of American tanks and infantrymen could move in to begin sealing the battlefield and prepare to evict the German intruders.

As much as my engineers were doing to deflect and delay Peiper, it must be noted that the real seeds of Peiper's frustration lay within the framework of his own prior combat experiences—and in the mind-set of German blitzkrieg commanders in general. From the earliest days of the war in Europe, German armored and mechanized spearheads had achieved their stunning breakthroughs largely as a result of lightning-swift seizures of intact bridges from their Polish, French, British, and Russian adversaries. Over time, though they possessed superbly trained engineers and good prefabricated combat bridges, German commanders came to *rely* upon the seizure of bridges from their adversaries; they planned for it. Peiper had had enormous personal success in Russia in precisely the sort of blitzkrieg attacks he was leading in Belgium, but he had never before faced American combat engineers, whose training made them particularly adept at blowing bridges in the face of enemy threats. (I had made a personal fetish of bridge destruction during my earliest days as a training officer at Fort Belvoir, and I carried my proclivity into the 291st.) The point is that we were not *afraid* to blow bridges because we were confident of our ability to replace them in the attack, in a matter of a few hours, with Bailey or floating treadway structures.

Peiper had engineers and bridges, but they were back in his column and could not be brought forward speedily along the narrow tank-congested roadways onto which his spearhead was being diverted. It was Peiper's overly sanguine dependence on capturing bridges and the inaccessibility of his engineer bridges—coupled with our willingness to blow our bridges—that doomed his effort to reach the Meuse on December 18.

CHAPTER 15

The definition of the northern shoulder of the German break-in by tiny elements of the 1st Army was important, but it was not the decisive element in what would soon be called the Battle of the Bulge. Immense efforts and battles were shaping up to the south, particularly around St.-Vith and Bastogne, in the zone of the infinitely better-run 5th Panzer Army, and efforts similar to our own were defining the southern shoulder of the break-in. Through it all, our most senior commanders—Eisenhower, Bradley, Hodges, Patton, and the 9th U.S. Army's Lieutenant General William Simpson—were creating advantages by throwing division after division toward the shoulders and, indeed, across the advancing German front toward the center, around St.-Vith and Bastogne. Their answer to fluid blitzkrieg break-in techniques was a fluid response aimed at keeping the Germans off balance, to make them pause to respond to unexpected counterattacks and pockets of resistance. We won some, and the Germans won some. The point of it all for us on December 16, 17, and 18 was to buy time so our leaders could shift *decisive* weight onto the battlefield.

Throughout December 18, as Kampfgruppe Peiper probed westward along the Amblève, three trusted American combat divisions moved into the northern shoulder: While the 2nd Infantry Division continued to hold at or near the old front around Elsenborn, the Big Red One strengthened the 99th Infantry Division line between Butgenbach and Waimes, our old comrades in the 30th Infantry Division reinforced us in strength from Malmédy as far west as Werbomont, and the leading elements of the freshly rested 82nd Airborne Division began arriving in Werbomont. Facing the 99th, 2nd, and 1st Infantry divisions was the bulk of the 6th Panzer Army, which was represented

from Waimes on back to Butgenbach and around to the north by
the 12th SS Panzer Division. The main strength of the 1st SS
Panzer Division had followed in the traces of Kampfgruppe Peiper and had established its forward headquarters at Ligneuville,
which Peiper had captured late on December 17.

Our divisions holding the northern shoulder from Butgenbach
to Werbomont were as yet far from capable of mounting any
sort of general counteroffensive—it was all we could do to establish viable defenses—but help was on the way. Before it would
arrive, however, our side had to develop a solid line from Werbomont to the Meuse in order to stave off expected (and planned)
German follow-on attacks aimed at broadening the salient in
that direction. The 1st Army headquarters evacuated Spa during
the evening of December 18 and reestablished itself in Chaud-
fontaine, near Liège. Most of Major General J. Lawton Collins's
crack VII Corps—the 75th and 84th Infantry and 2nd Armored
divisions—was pulled out of the line north of the break-in and
rushed to cover the plain from Marche, Belgium, to the Meuse
River at Huy. The 9th U.S. Army's 3rd Armored Division was
also on its way to bolster the new line or conduct counterattacks
in the direction of Werbomont or La Gleize.

Of particular interest to the 291st was the 1111th Group's reat-
tachment to the VII Corps and the rather symbolic attachment
of the 291st itself to the 84th Infantry Division. All there was of
the 291st at Modave, in the center of the VII Corps zone, was
Major Ed Lampp's rear CP, the Company A command group,
two skeletal Company C platoons, and a few other odds and
sods who had been pulled along by the displacement during the
afternoon of December 18. The 1111th Group was rather more
complete, though a company of 51st Engineer Combat Battalion
remained in Trois-Ponts. It fell to Colonel Anderson and the
available 1111th Group assets to develop the engineer combat
barrier for the VII Corps in what was then seen as the ultimate
stand before the Meuse.

Those few of us holding the northern shoulder during the afternoon of December 18 were powerless to defeat the Germans,
but we were not powerless to hurt and hinder them. Most of the
pain we inflicted—aside from destroying key bridges at Trois-
Ponts and Habiemont—was at Stavelot. The first shot of pain
was rendered by a platoon of towed 75mm tank destroyers that
had accompanied Lieutenant Colonel Robert Frankland's 1st
Battalion, 117th Infantry, to Stavelot late in the afternoon. De-

ployed on a hill overlooking the road to which the German column was restricted, the tank destroyers were suddenly engaged by a charge of ten Mk.V Panther tanks from Kampfgruppe Peiper's rear echelon at around 1300 hours. However, just as the tanks attacked, they were attacked by the IX Tactical Air Command's first P-47 strike of the day. Neither the tank destroyers nor the P-47s caused much damage, but all the German vehicles in the area scattered for cover and the tank attack was quite forgotten. The tank destroyers fired intermittently at the passing German convoys but apparently caused little damage and drew no blood.

At around 1600 hours, the afternoon fog rising from the Amblève forced patrolling P-47s to return to their bases and prevented the tank destroyer crews from observing more targets. At that moment, when the Germans appeared to be off the hook, Lieutenant Colonel Frankland delivered an assault on the German-held center of town with two of his battalion's three infantry companies. There was momentary confusion when the American riflemen ran into a group of American-uniformed Skorzeny commandos, but the Germans settled the matter when they opened fire. Frankland's troops were veterans who instantly fired back without giving the matter any more thought. The German impostors were swept aside and, by nightfall, the American companies had retaken roughly half of Stavelot. By then, thanks to the arrival of fresh 30th Infantry Division units at Malmédy, we were able to send the entire 118th Field Artillery Battalion—eighteen 105mm howitzers—to Stavelot, where they and three M-4 medium tanks arrived as the infantry companies stopped to consolidate their gains.

The arrival of the 118th Field Artillery Battalion was virtually decisive. The unblown, German-held Stavelot bridge was easily within range of the 105mm battery positions, and it was no time at all before our shells were falling on the bridge and its approaches. The Germans bravely defied the artillery fire, but the flow of troops, tanks, equipment, and supplies across the Amblève was reduced to a trickle. That was terrible news for Peiper's spearhead.

Throughout December 18, and long into the night, Lieutenant Colonel Peiper remained ignorant of events beyond the range of his personal senses or the senses of the men reporting to him. The deep, high-walled river valleys he had been traversing prevented him from maintaining direct radio links with higher headquarters, notably the headquarters of his own 1st SS Panzer Division. It was not until hours after Peiper settled in at La Gleize on December 18 that a division staff officer arrived at Peiper's headquarters with a radio capable of reaching the division headquarters. Peiper then reviewed his day's adventures and frustrations with Colonel Wilhelm Mohnke, the division commander, and heard about all the problems and delays that had been and were being faced by the 1st and 12th SS Panzer divisions.

To Peiper, the most disturbing news pertained to the artillery interdiction of the Stavelot bridge. Kampfgruppe Peiper had not suffered many vehicle casualties during the day—indeed, it had been reinforced—but it had used a great deal of its fuel reserves running hither and yon along the valley of the Amblève. Peiper had no idea that a major fuel dump had been within his grasp as he passed through Stavelot, and he had no idea that an even larger and relatively undefended fuel dump lay within only a few miles of La Gleize. Thus, he fretted the night away worrying about how he was going to reach the Meuse even if the Allied defenses gave way before him.

For the moment, because of the arrival of fresh regiments and the shifting of divisional boundaries, the actions of Kampfgruppe Peiper diverged from the actions of the 291st Engineer Combat Battalion. For the bulk of the 291st, the immediate concerns that night were centered on Stavelot and Trois-Ponts, where our enemy was the main body of Colonel Wilhelm Mohnke's 1st SS Panzer Division.

The 1st SS Panzer Division was the oldest unit of Hitler's praetorian guard, the primary guardians of the Nazi flame. Only the most dedicated, the most rabid Nazis were admitted to the "old" SS, and, as keepers of the flame, the 1st SS Panzer (*Liebstandarte Adolf Hitler*—Adolf Hitler's Household) Division fielded more than its share of bloody-minded Nazi scum. This is no place to decry the excesses of the SS, but it must be noted that, contrary to some new and inexplicable notions, the Waffen SS, of which the 1st SS Panzer Division was a part, was not merely an organization of elite stormtroopers. It was an organization of men perfectly in agreement with Hitler's most rabid racial theories. While the standards of other Waffen SS divisions had slipped in the course of five years of war, the racial standard of the Liebstandarte Division had not slipped one iota. We faced an organization of absolutely dedicated, absolutely ruthless Nazi

fanatics whose only purpose in life was to save Hitler's war from
an untoward end. The massacre of Battery B, 285th Field Artillery Observation Battalion, and other groups of uniformed
and civilian captives taken along the way, merely points up the
ruthlessness and utter derangement of our immediate adversaries. The indisputable fact that the 1st SS Panzer Division had
been amply tested on the Eastern Front and was an extremely
good *military* organization only added to our potential woes.

Fortunately for the troops in Malmédy, Stavelot, and Trois-
Ponts, the main body of the 1st SS Panzer Division was inter-
ested initially in St.-Vith and Vielsalm, to the south, and not in
following Kampfgruppe Peiper toward La Gleize. Nevertheless,
the 6th Panzer Army's road net in the northern Bulge was too
restricted and too congested and needed to be expanded and
shortened in any direction possible—southward via St.-Vith or
northward around Peiper's MSR. The St.-Vith route, via Vielsalm, to the Meuse was the preferred route, but there was also
a noticeable tug toward the northern side of the corridor because
of the advances and ultimate plight of Kampfgruppe Peiper. The
American units in Malmédy, Stavelot, and Trois-Ponts escaped
direct confrontations with the main body of the 1st SS Panzer
Division throughout December 18 because the issue around St.-
Vith and Vielsalm remained in open debate. When this southern
door was slammed shut by the 7th Armored Division and other
newly arrived units late on December 18, Colonel Mohnke's
attention became riveted to the north.

By the evening of December 18, Kampfgruppe Peiper's meandering course was the only one of five routes assigned to the
1st and 12th SS Panzer divisions that was in German hands. The
U.S. 2nd and 99th Infantry divisions had blocked the 12th SS
Panzer Division along the three northern routes, and the 1st
SS Panzer Division had been blocked through Vielsalm and St.-
Vith in the south. The 12th SS Panzer Division was totally
bogged down, but the 1st SS Panzer Division zone remained
fluid. If the Germans adhered strictly to their own blitzkrieg
doctrine, heavy follow-on commitments would be made in the
1st SS Panzer Division zone in order to strengthen and exploit
Peiper's gains.

In order for the 6th Panzer Army to achieve *any* of its strategic
goals, the 1st SS Panzer Division first had to clear Stavelot of
its American defenders and push the Americans back beyond
the range of the 118th Field Artillery Battalion's 105mm howitzers.

* * *

The first German attempt to clear Stavelot was inexplicably weak in view of the powerful armored forces that were advancing nearby by means of the Stavelot bridge. Three Mk. VI Tiger Royals advanced on the town square without infantry support and were destroyed or disabled by bazookas in the hands of Lieutenant Colonel Frankland's infantrymen. Far from then allowing his plans to be put off by the attack, Frankland sent his troops deeper into the lightly defended German half of town. By noon, December 19, all of Stavelot except a few western outbuildings was back in American hands. Even buildings directly overlooking the bridge fell to Frankland's infantrymen, and without much resistance.

The Germans pushed in a force of Panther-supported panzer grenadiers from the south bank of the Amblève, but this attack also was remarkably inept and desultory. The panzer grenadiers were easily pinned by the guns of the 118th Field Artillery Battalion and three of the four Panthers were disabled quickly by a single towed 75mm tank destroyer. With that, the attack force withdrew, having inflicted no casualties upon the defending force.

As the German survivors withdrew south of the Amblève, Frankland's troops defending the west side of town were threatened by the 1st SS Panzer Division's reconnaissance battalion. This unit had been attached to Kampfgruppe Peiper after passing through Stavelot the night before. In the morning, as soon as Peiper had heard that virtually all of Stavelot was back in American hands, he had ordered the reconnaissance battalion to secure Stavelot once and for all.

The attack was launched from two directions, but it immediately ran afoul of the 118th Field Artillery Battalion. Except for three attached Mk. IV medium tanks, the reconnaissance battalion was equipped solely with light tanks, scout cars, and halftracks, all of which were particularly vulnerable to 105mm artillery fire. The persistence of the attackers was noteworthy, but the artillery battalion fired over three thousand rounds and eventually drove them back with heavy losses.

That night, December 19, a detail from the 30th Infantry Division's 105th Engineer Combat Battalion arrived in Stavelot. Working within a smoke screen under the noses of the Germans, our comrades planted and wired over a thousand pounds of TNT and blew the stone bridge that should have been blown the night of December 17. Before dawn, December 20, incredibly brave and dedicated SS panzer grenadiers attempted to wade the icy Amblève and lodge an infantry force around the bridge site, but the attempt failed.

There was little more than an engineer company holding Trois-Ponts under the command of Major Bull Yates, the exec of the 51st Engineer Combat Battalion. In addition to somewhat understrength Company C, 51st Combat Engineers, Yates counted upon two squads of Lieutenant Bucky Walters's platoon and Staff Sergeant Paul Hinkel's squad of Company A, 291st, Sergeant Angelo Magliocca's resident squad of Company C, 291st, and Lieutenant Warren Rombaugh and about twenty engineers from his platoon of Company C, 291st, who had made their way to Trois-Ponts from Château Froidcoeur late in the afternoon of December 18. A small number of American stragglers who trickled into town during the day were added to the defense force, but they did not amount to much. In all, about two hundred Americans were in and around the town.

After the bridges were blown on December 18, not much happened at Trois-Ponts. The engineers holding the town exchanged sporadic fire with the passing German road columns, but there were no heavy weapons available and certainly there was no inclination among the Americans to raise the ire of the Germans.

Late that night, December 18, with no reinforcements in the offing, Major Yates decided to attempt a ruse aimed at making the Germans think the town was amply defended. Gathering the eight trucks available and placing them in the hands of Sergeant Magliacco's squad, he sent them up a hill with no lights on, then down the hill with headlights blazing, then back up the hill with no lights showing, and so forth until dawn.

Fortunately for Bull Yates and his tiny command, the Germans had no immediate need to take the Trois-Ponts side of the Amblève or Salm rivers. Throughout December 19, the Germans obligingly returned the engineers' sporadic fire, but they remained at arm's length beyond the river barrier.

During the evening of December 19, an engineer combat patrol out of Trois-Ponts ran into a patrol of the 82nd Airborne Division's 505th Parachute Infantry Regiment, which had come from Werbomont by way of Haute-Bodeux and Basse-Bodeux. It was a mutually agreeable meeting, for the paratroopers expected to find Trois-Ponts in German hands and the engineers expected to find Germans on the road. At first light, December 20, the advance elements of the 505th Parachute Infantry Regiment moved to the heights west of Trois-Ponts. Just in time.

Casting about for a bridge to replace the lost span at Stavelot, Lieutenant General Hermann Priess, the commander of the I SS Panzer Corps—the 1st SS Panzer Division's parent unit—had located a rickety wooden structure across the Amblève, at Petit Spai, immediately to the north of Trois-Ponts. He ordered the 1st SS Panzer Division's Colonel Mohnke to grab the bridge, drive across the Amblève, take Trois-Ponts, and reinforce Kampfgruppe Peiper's drive toward the Meuse from La Gleize.

Though the 505th Parachute Infantry continued to concentrate along the commanding heights west of the Salm, the engineers in low-lying Trois-Ponts—including our troops from Company A and Company C, 291st—were subjected to heavy small-arms and machine-gun fire after the Germans seized the heights east of the Salm. Between 0900 and 1100, December 20, German artillery fired into the town, although with minimal effect.

The 505th's commander, Colonel William Ekman, arrived in Trois-Ponts at 1300 hours and immediately went to confer with Major Bull Yates—who rather impudently greeted him by noting, ''I'll bet you guys are glad we're here.'' As soon as the meeting was concluded, Colonel Ekman ordered his own engineer detachment to repair the Salm bridge our Sergeant Jean Miller had blown on December 18; the 505th was going to continue its counterattack immediately. The bridge was in adequate enough shape to carry foot traffic late that afternoon, so an unsupported company of the 2nd Battalion, 505th, walked across and advanced southwest in the direction of Wanne, the first step in outflanking the German MSR between Trois-Ponts and Stavelot.

In the wee hours of December 21, long after the American paratrooper company crossed the Salm at Trois-Ponts, the 1st SS Panzer Division was ready to begin crossing the Amblève at Petit Spai. Until then, for several days, the bridge had been employed solely by German light reconnaissance elements looking for new routes through the area. The very first vehicle in the German column, a self-propelled tank destroyer collapsed the bridge and settled into the shallow water. So another way across the Amblève was blocked firmly.

On December 19 and 20, the period of the 1st SS Panzer Division's exceptionally lackluster performance at Stavelot and Trois-

Ponts, Kampfgruppe Peiper attempted to break through to the Meuse by way of Stoumont, the Targnon bridge on the Amblève, and Stoumont Station. The 6th Panzer Army's armored spearhead was firmly held by mixed elements of the 30th Infantry and 3rd Armored divisions.

The loss of the Stavelot bridge, the failure to breach the Amblève at Petit Spai, and Peiper's thus-far failed attacks in the direction of the Meuse caused German attention to shift—as inevitably it had to—toward the only nearby road center through which the Meuse could yet be reached. That seemed to bode well for the troops at Stavelot and Trois-Ponts, but it was indeed a very bad omen for those of us waiting at hitherto quiescent Malmédy. We were the obvious target.

CHAPTER 16

December 18, 1944, passed rather quietly at Malmédy. After all the heart-stopping concern of the previous day and night, Lieutenant Colonel Harold Hansen and I had an opportunity to take a rational look at our situation. If the Germans attacked, it was not good; if they did not attack, our situation did not matter. Hansen and I spent a tense day strengthening our defenses—he among his infantry, armored infantry, and supporting arms and I among my Company B and Company C squads manning fifteen roadblock positions around the edge of the town.

Our first contact with Germans on December 18 came at a little after noon, when a German motorcycle with a sidecar stormed down the N-32, right at Sergeant Charles Dishaw's squad's roadblock. The squad machine gunner opened fire and both Germans were killed. The corpses were examined by the 99th Norwegian Battalion's intelligence officer and identified as being from the German 3rd Parachute Division. Unknown to us at the time, only a few hundred paratroopers had actually been dropped; the rest of the 3rd Parachute Division was in action on the ground near Butgenbach. I have no idea what the two paratroopers were doing around Malmédy, but their presence caused an immense amount of concerned speculation.

Late in the morning, my assistant S-3, Lieutenant Tom Stack, returned from driving several massacre survivors to Spa. To our amazement and delight, Tom had in tow the 30th Infantry Division's cavalry reconnaissance troop. The troop commander told us that the rest of the 30th Division was on its way down from the 9th U.S. Army zone and would be on hand during the night or by the following morning. At last, something to look forward to!

At 1645 hours, Sergeant Dishaw's roadblock on the N-32 was

approached by a jeep bearing markings of the 106th Infantry Division. Neither Lieutenant Wade Colbeck nor Sergeant Dishaw's men nor several 99th Norwegian Battalion infantrymen manning the block liked the looks of the jeep or the six men riding in it. Someone wondered aloud what a 106th Division jeep was doing so far out of its zone. Before anyone could act, one of the two soldiers perched on the hood of the jeep jumped to the ground and ran toward the roadblock, yelling, "They're Krauts!" One of the men in the jeep opened fire on the running man, at which point the other man on the hood jumped off and ran from sight. With that, the jeep driver jammed the vehicle into reverse and desperately tried to make a run for it. Sergeant Dishaw and his troopers recovered from their shocked amazement and sprayed the jeep. One of the passengers jumped to the ground and tried to evade the fire as he ran into the woods. He was shot in his tracks, killed. The other three occupants of the jeep surrendered. They were indeed Germans, members of Skorzeny's commando brigade. One of them told his 99th Battalion interrogator that he had been informed that Malmédy was in German hands. The two American soldiers riding on the hood of the jeep turned out to be authentic 106th Division men who, with the jeep, had been captured by the Germans in the overrun 106th Division zone.

During December 18, also, we discovered that some of the German-speaking citizens of Malmédy were in, of all things, commercial telephone contact with German soldiers in nearby villages and towns. We had known that there was little sympathy for the Allied cause in this former German-annexed city, but we had not expected anything like the depth of anti-American feeling the telephone caper revealed. Given the free flow of information to the Germans, I was stunned that no attempt had been made to seize Malmédy before the 99th Norwegian and the 526th Armored Infantry battalions arrived during the night.

Aside from some intermittent shelling, we were not molested during the evening. I attempted to get some sleep—my first since arriving in Malmédy—but that lasted less than two hours. There was simply too much going on that I had to be a part of.

Early on the morning of December 19, the headquarters and 2nd and 3rd battalions of the 30th Infantry Division's 117th Infantry Regiment began arriving in Malmédy with the 118th Field Artillery Battalion. The fresh infantrymen, whom the 291st had supported in Normandy and at Mortain, displaced the 99th Norwegian and 526th Armored Infantry battalions in the town.

Company B of the 99th Norwegian Battalion was broken up to help strengthen our engineer roadblocks while the rest of the unit took over zones of responsibility east of the town. The headquarters and two companies of the 526th Armored Infantry Battalion and its attached tank destroyer platoons remained in their original positions along the railroad embankment. The Norwegians and the armored infantrymen were temporarily absorbed into the 30th Division's command structure.

The arrival of all that infantry—plus artillery, all manner of antitank weapons, and who-knows-what-else—lifted our spirts to glorious heights, but it did not relieve us of one iota of our responsibility to block the roads and bridges leading into town. My engineers spent most of the day extending and perfecting minefields throughout the Malmédy zone. It also fell to us on December 19 to lay and wire demolitions charges in two railroad underpasses, the railroad bridge, and the Warche River timber trestle bridge. Then, as if there wasn't enough for us to do, we were ordered to build and man a network of machine-gun emplacements along the railroad embankment. I gave that job to Lieutenant Frank Rhea, of Company B, and Lieutenant Don Davis, of Company C. The demolitions work was placed under the supervision of Master Sergeant Ralph McCarty, the battalion operations chief.

During the day, the entire 120th Regimental Combat Team arrived and displaced the 117th Infantry units and 118th Field Artillery Battalion, which shifted westward, toward Stavelot, to support Lieutenant Colonel Robert Frankland's 1st Battalion, 117th. Lieutenant Colonel Peter Ward's 3rd Battalion, 120th, set up in town and tied in on its right (west) flank with the 117th Infantry. The 1st Battalion, 120th, filled in toward the east and made physical contact with the right-flank element of the neighboring 1st Infantry Division. The 2nd Battalion, 120th, remained in reserve north of town with headquarters near—wonder of wonders—Major General Leland Hobbs's 30th Division forward CP. Command of all the troops in and around Malmédy was transferred to Colonel Branner Purdue, the 120th Infantry's commanding officer. I was tickled to become a subordinate again.

As the Malmédy defenders shivered in their foxholes beneath the onslaught of incessant cold rain, low-level German bombers and fighters passed overhead but did not molest us. However, infantry patrols operating in advance of our lines experienced brief, violent clashes with German patrols. A patrol from Company B, 99th Norwegian Battalion, captured several scouts from the 1st SS Panzer Division and, later, one of our machine-gun outposts wiped out another German scouting party, also from the 1st SS Panzer Division.

German artillery fired at us from time to time through the day. The shelling was ineffectual, but one round did hit Lieutenant Colonel Ward's CP of the 1st Battalion, 120th, and wounded one soldier.

The most unusual occurrence of the day was when Sergeant V. L. Martin, the Company C mess sergeant, was approached by two bedraggled Germans in paratrooper smocks at the roadblock he was manning. The two Germans told interrogators that they had been members of Lieutenant Colonel von der Heydte's parachute force but had become separated from the main body during the jump. Alone and without food, the two eventually decided to surrender to the first Allied soldier they encountered. That was Sergeant Martin. The 291st had been chasing paratroopers—and rumors of paratroopers—for three days. Now, for the first time, we learned how few of them had actually been dropped. Two and two added up to four and our intelligence people soon figured out that the vast bulk of the German 3rd Parachute Division had not been dropped behind our lines but was trying to break in on the ground.

December 19 was not a great day for the American divisions arrayed around the point of the northern shoulder, to our east. A massive effort by the 12th SS Panzer and 277th Volksgrenadier divisions pushed our 2nd Infantry Division out of two key villages while elements of the 12th SS Panzer and 12th Volksgrenadier divisions finally wrested Büllingen from our 99th Infantry Division. Also, the 1st Infantry Division was under intense pressure around Butgenbach. If the point of the shoulder cracked, as we feared it might, we could very well have Germans in our rear within hours.

Late at night on December 19, Lieutenant Colonel Peter Ward and I conspired to locate a nice, quiet spot, far from our command posts, where we could bunk down and get some overdue sleep. I finally took Ward down to the former 44th Evacuation Hospital, where my battalion dentist, Captain Paul Kamen, was manning an aid station. Paul obligingly fixed us up with a pair of dry, soft beds and promised to do his best to let us sleep in peace. It was not to be. At around 0200 hours, December 20, German shelling and American counterbattery rose to a resounding crescendo that, though it did not quite drive us from our bunks, prevented Lieutenant Colonel Ward and me from sleeping.

At about 0830 hours, 1st Sergeant Earl Short, of Company B, stepped into my CP to relate details of the demise of a German reconnaissance halftrack. The vehicle had approached our southeast roadblock but had tripped mines before Company B troopers there could issue a challenge. First Sergeant Short told us that all four Germans manning the halftrack had been killed in the blast and that one had been hurled far up into a tree. It was a good story, but worrisome to me in that it indicated that the Germans finally were probing our defenses. As the morning wore on, I received additional information relating to German patrol activity around the town, and there was more word from troops inside the town that civilians were still phoning news to their German brethren in nearby villages.

Late in the morning, a squad from Company B, 99th Norwegian Battalion, wiped out a German foot patrol near one of our roadblocks. Word soon made the rounds that the dead Germans were panzer grenadiers from the 1st SS Panzer Division. Other Norwegian outposts traded shots with other Germans they caught patrolling along the fringes of our defenses. Under this rising pressure, preparation of the railroad viaduct and underpass and the Warche bridge for demolition was completed during the day by engineers under Master Sergeant Ralph McCarty.

Good news of a sort was obtained through my reading of the 30th Infantry Division's message traffic with neighboring units. Though the 6th Panzer Army continued to apply heavy pressure on the point of the northern shoulder throughout the day, the situation along the 2nd, 99th, and 1st Infantry divisions' fronts from Elsenborn to Waimes had been stabilized. Nevertheless, our divisions continued to face fanatical or at least determined attacks by the 12th SS Panzer, 12th Volksgrenadier, 277th Volksgrenadier, and 3rd Parachute divisions. It was obvious to me that a German breakthrough anywhere along the point of the shoulder would sweep into Malmédy.

I tried for another night's sleep, but, at 2300 hours, December 20, I was rousted from my bunk by a radio call ordering me to proceed at once to Spa. The order came from my boss's boss, Colonel Bill Carter, the 1st Army chief engineer, and apparently had been prompted by the 1st Army commander's assumption that my part of the 291st was no longer needed at Malmédy. I was stupefied by the order, but neither Colonel Carter nor Colonel Anderson could be reached by radio, so I felt obliged to comply.

With great reluctance, I gathered my staff and all the Company B and Company C troopers we could relieve on short notice. Leaving word that the rest of the 291st squads were to follow after sunup, I set off for Spa to see what the blazes was going on. We arrived in Spa at about 0100 hours, December 21, and proceeded directly to Lieutenant General Courtney Hodges's 1st Army headquarters.

There was no one home. No one had bothered to tell me that the 1st Army headquarters—Colonel Carter included—had shifted behind the new Meuse barrier line two full days earlier, on December 18. I was too tired and angry to make inquiries at that impossible hour, so I told everyone to get some sleep.

I did not know it then, but the 291st had been and still was at the center of some rather heated wrangling among several generals and their staffs. What had happened behind the scenes was that the 30th Infantry Division—of the 9th Army's VIII Corps—had assumed responsibility for our part of the old V Corps sector while 1111th Group and the rear echelon of the 291st had wound up in the new VII Corps sector. In effect, the 291st had become a VII Corps unit with a portion (the *largest* cohesive portion) operating in support of the VIII Corps. It must be said that Colonel Carter did not concern himself with these niceties; his foremost concern was that he needed every engineer he could muster to help establish the new Meuse line. He assumed—reasonably, but incorrectly—that there were enough 30th Division engineers on hand to relieve us at Malmédy. Hence the call. When Major General Leland Hobbs, the 30th Infantry Division commander, learned that the 291st was being pulled out even before his own division's 105th Combat Engineers reached Malmédy, he hit the roof. Hobbs simply pocketed the movement order for two days, until General Hodges got wind of our continued presence in Malmédy. We were ordered to move by Colonel Carter on the army commander's express order. However, as we were moving, General Hobbs shouldered his way onto the 1st Army command net. Heavy radio exchanges soon convinced General Hodges that my portion of the 291st, at least, was a key component in Malmédy's integrated defense plan and that the greater cause would be best served by sending us back to Malmédy.

I was somewhere along in my sixth hour of sleep in three days when I was again rousted, this time by the arrival of a 30th Division messenger who carried a dispatch from Colonel Carter. I was ordered to return to Malmédy. I had my officers and men awakened at 0300 hours and, at 0500 hours, December 21, we all groggily set off into the mist, bound once again for Malmédy.

We were into the S-turn at which the Spa road converged with the Malmédy-Stavelot road when German artillery based at Amblève fired directly into our path. In the distance, I saw flares suddenly burst along what I took to be the front line at Malmédy. My driver, Corporal Curtis Ledet, floored the gas pedal of my command car, but we virtually ran directly into a bursting shell. We were not stopped, but the body of the car and the windshield—and Corporal Ledet—were peppered with shrapnel. Thankfully, no one else was hurt, and it was with immense relief that we pulled up at the first of Master Sergeant Ralph McCarty's two roadblocks on the western approach to Malmédy.

I was a bit nonplussed to learn that McCarty and his engineers had turned the roadblocks over to infantrymen from the 120th Infantry, but it became clear that he and the others we had left behind did not yet know that we all were to remain in Malmédy. They were in town sleeping or preparing to meet us in Spa. Without giving much more thought to the infantrymen or the rather intense artillery fire, I led the way into town and went directly to the 3rd Battalion, 120th Infantry CP to tell Lieutenant Colonel Ward that we were back. He replied that he was glad to have us back—because the Germans were finally attacking Malmédy en masse.

CHAPTER 17

Our adversary on the morning of December 21, 1944, was Colonel Otto Skorzeny's 150th SS Panzer Brigade—the unused core of the German commando operation. It says much about the failed planning of the 6th Panzer Army that Skorzeny and his elite troops were in Belgium being used as cannon fodder in a frontal attack on Malmédy.

Though by December 20 the German high command in the West still hoped to eke out a victory of some sort in Belgium, the original plan had to be radically altered so as to coincide somewhat with objective reality. The Meuse was still the key objective, but there was little chance that it would be reached anywhere near Liège—*we* had helped see to that—so the German generals opted for any lodgment on the Meuse that their panzer armies could achieve. This alleviated a great deal of pressure on the American troops holding the northern shoulder; the best chance of reaching the Meuse lay in the zone of Manteuffel's 5th Panzer Army, though its chances were beginning to become remote.

In the north, when the 1st SS Panzer Division had failed to penetrate the Amblève at Petit Spai, the commander of the I SS Panzer Corps, Lieutenant General Hermann Priess, had asked permission to abandon costly efforts to relieve Kampfgruppe Peiper around La Gleize. Priess had wanted to simply cut his losses and shift the rest of the 1st SS Panzer Division against Malmédy, where there appeared to be a real chance to accomplish a breakthrough. This decision was particularly timely since, at the moment it was made, the 12th SS Panzer, 3rd Parachute, 12th Volksgrenadier, 277th Volksgrenadier divisions were making considerable gains at the point of the shoulder, around Elsenborn.

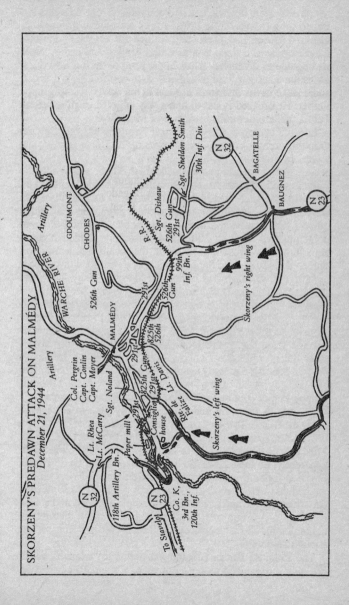

SKORZENY'S PREDAWN ATTACK ON MALMÉDY
December 21, 1944

General Sepp Dietrich, the 6th Panzer Army commander, issued a reply overruling Priess's very reasonable military decision. Dietrich had personally formed the original Liebstandarte Regiment, had led it in its earliest battles, and had overseen its upgrade to divisional status in the form of the 1st SS Panzer Division. Dietrich, one of Hitler's favorites, felt he had a personal stake in the division's use and in the fate of Kampfgruppe Peiper. He ordered Priess to find a way to get through to relieve Peiper while other units took care of Malmédy.

Into the center of this 6th Panzer Army debate fell Colonel Otto Skorzeny. As early as the evening of December 17, the towering Austrian, another of Hitler's personal favorites, had seen that his commando effort had failed. There was by then no point in sending more American-uniformed SS commandos into the void, and there would be no opportunity to send his 150th SS Panzer Brigade raging deep into the American rear in the guise of an American armored unit, as one potential scenario contemplated. Though Hitler had personally forbidden Skorzeny himself to cross into Belgium, the commando leader volunteered his brigade to Sepp Dietrich for a suitable conventional assignment. Dietrich had turned the Skorzeny brigade over to the 1st SS Panzer Division's Colonel Wilhelm Mohnke, and Mohnke had ordered Skorzeny to his new headquarters in Ligneuville. When General Dietrich had ordered the 1st SS Panzer Division to relieve Kampfgruppe Peiper, he apparently made no specific reference to the 150th SS Panzer Brigade, nor apparently did he object to General Priess's bending of the law in favor of sending Skorzeny against Malmédy. Indeed, the capture of Malmédy would offer a vast new road net over which Kampfgruppe Peiper could be sustained and massively reinforced.

At least in part, the makeshift Skorzeny plan to seize Malmédy evolved from a very early report from a team of Skorzeny's own commandos which indicated that Malmédy was lightly held. That was on December 17 or early December 18. Since then, apparently, no fresh news had been received at the 1st SS Panzer Division forward headquarters. The Germans had no idea that we had been reinforced to the strength of nearly four infantry battalions on line and one in reserve, ample artillery, and a wide range of supporting arms, including a reasonable number of antitank guns and tank destroyers. If we lacked anything, it was enough engineers.

The 150th SS Panzer Brigade was hardly a "brigade" at all, nor was it organized along the lines of a standard combat organization. Heavily task oriented, the groupment boasted only ten tanks—a mixture of Mk.IVs and Panthers, many of which had been disguised to resemble American M-4 medium tanks. Beyond several assault guns and a sprinkling of mortars, there was no organic direct support fire power available, nor was there anywhere near a brigade's worth of infantry troops on hand to deliver the assault. To get to Malmédy, most of the Germans had to travel aboard captured American Jeeps and trucks.

In some ways, the Skorzeny commandos were Hitler's first team. But not at Malmédy—not the way they were to be employed.

The December 21 attack on Malmédy was but a small part of the 6th Panzer Army's general offensive aimed at breaking through the point of the northern shoulder of the Bulge. However, it received serious initial artillery support from 1st SS Panzer Division artillery arrayed around Amblève. These were the guns whose shells we ran into on the Spa road. Apart from the initial fire mission, however, Skorzeny apparently received no artillery support other than that provided by several of his brigade's organic self-propelled guns. Relying on outdated intelligence and certain of a swift victory against light screening forces, Skorzeny did not even bother with an adequate preparation by his own infantry mortars.

The first element of Colonel Skorzeny's attack on Malmédy involved 120 SS commandos dressed in a motley array of German and American uniforms or bits and parts of both. Supported only by several halftracks, they charged up the N-32 from Five Points and ran straight into an ambush that had been prepared by the 1st Battalion, 120th Infantry, and detachments of 291st engineers.

At around 0330 hours, December 21, the lead German halftrack to emerge from the pea-soup fog ran into the forward edge of our minefield on the N-32 and was blown up. Sergeant Sheldon Smith's squad of Company C, 291st, and the many 120th infantrymen in the area put out a withering fire while supporting artillery—using the brand-new and still-secret variable time (VT) fuse for the first time in Europe—massacred the follow-on elements with incredibly effective air bursts. When the German company-strength unit finally pulled back, it left vehicle parts and body parts strewn all up and down the road to Five Points.

As soon as the German survivors withdrew, Sergeant Smith's squad helped rescue several Germans from the blasted halftrack.

These men were brought to my CP just after I arrived there myself. They told me that the attack up the N-32 was a diversion, that the main attack was due to commence west of town shortly. I sent them under guard to Dr. Kamen's aid station for treatment and passed what little news I had along the communications net. By then, however, the main attack had been long underway.

The main thrust was made by all ten German tanks and most of Skorzeny's commandos in the direction of the Malmédy-Stavelot-Spa crossroads. It began only minutes before I returned through that road junction on my way from Spa, but it was not particularly close by the time the last of my troops passed to relative safety.

The Germans' main objective was the road junction. Had they merely wanted to secure Malmédy, they need not have crossed to the north bank of the Warche, for most of Malmédy was south of the river. However, Skorzeny's brigade crossed far down the Warche by way of a timber trestle bridge far beyond our main line of resistance. In doing so, it outflanked the defenses of Company K, 3rd Battalion, 120th Infantry, had established on the west side of the Warche bridge, facing down the direct road from Stavelot. It was a very smart move because if we blew the bridge we would have trapped many of our men on the wrong side of the Warche.

We could not have blown the bridge anyway. It later came out that Master Sergeant Ralph McCarty's engineers manning blocks near the Warche bridge and the railroad viaduct had been relieved by infantrymen during the night and sent into town to get some sleep in anticipation of their displacement to Spa at dawn. McCarty had been very careful to explain the use of the detonators to the troops who relieved him, but apparently these devices were not particularly high on their list of things to remember in the event of an attack. In fact, for safety's sake, someone had disconnected both detonators. Particularly galling is the fact that a German prisoner taken the previous afternoon had tipped us off to the probability of the attack.

The moment Master Sergeant McCarty heard of the German approach, he rushed to the road junction in a jeep with three other engineers to set off the bridge and viaduct charges, but he was too late. The German tanks had crossed the Warche behind our backs and were massing to deliver an attack on the crossroads from our lightly held southern flank.

McCarty's jeep reached the underpass beneath the road and

railroad viaducts before the Germans did. There, McCarty met up with Technician 5th Grade John Noland, who was in charge of one of two engineer roadblocks guarding the underpass. McCarty decided to assume command of the viaduct roadblocks, so he ordered his three passengers to proceed on foot down to the paper mill in which the detonator for the Warche bridge charge had been left. If the Germans veered toward the crossroads instead of the underpass, they would need to cross the Warche from south to north. It was simple: If the bridge was blown before the Germans arrived, they would never be able to reach the crossroads. If they attacked toward the underpass and appeared certain to overrun it, McCarty would blow the highway viaduct and block the roadway.

The three engineers—Technician 5th Grade Vince Consiglio, Private William Mitchell, and Private Joseph Spires—trotted through the thick fog toward the paper mill, which overlooked the Warche bridge from the south bank. Private Spires, in the lead, was just turning toward the mill with the fog-obscured sky lit up as trip flares in a field to the south were set off by the approaching German infantry. (This must have been at the moment my convoy from Spa reached the road junction.) Instinctively, all three engineers ran for the nearest cover, a house across the street from the paper mill.

The first floor of the house was occupied by a .50-caliber machine-gun crew belonging to the 825th Tank Destroyer Battalion. The tank-destroyer company commander was hunkered down in a rear room to direct the fire of two tank destroyers dug in behind the building. Also, several other .50-caliber machine guns had been emplaced in makeshift bunkers surrounding the house, and a handful of infantrymen from Company K, 120th Infantry, arrived moments after the engineers. In all, there were thirty-three men in and around the building, and they were the front line facing Skorzeny's main attack.

As the occupants of the house struggled to build up firing positions, the vanguard German tank nosed into the edge of one of the minefields our engineers had spent days emplacing and one of its tracks set off a powerful antitank mine. The entire tank burst into flames that flared up to reveal the otherwise fogbound troops following close behind. The German assault faltered momentarily as following tanks gingerly maneuvered to find a way around the mines.

* * *

As the German attack developed, one of Skorzeny's Panthers—disguised to resemble an American M-4 tank—split off from the main body and attacked toward the underpass. Screaming "Surrender or die," these commandos attacked into the teeth of our engineer-manned emplacements and Company B, 99th Norwegian Battalion.

As soon as this side attack went off, Corporal Black Mac McDonald, the Company A machine-gun team leader, now in charge of a strongpoint on the railroad embankment, raced into the open to switch off the safety device blocking detonation of the daisy chain of mines strung in front of his position. At roughly the same moment, Technician 5th Grade John Noland, at the underpass roadblock, was thrown from his feet by the blast of a mortar round. Without pausing, Noland jumped back up and also raced into the open to close the road in front of his position with another daisy chain. By then, Norwegian infantrymen and engineers with rifles and machine guns at both positions and along the railroad embankment were firing full tilt into the German spearhead. The Germans, who were beset by VT-fused artillery fire, were unable to close on the engineer-manned roadblocks, but fragments from one of their mortar rounds that burst in a tree killed Private Wiley Holbrook, one of our Company A machine gunners.

The Germans made it as far as the slope of the embankment, but the engineers and Norwegians cut them down with machine guns and hand grenades while one of the 825th Tank Destroyer Battalion 75mm guns damaged the Panther and obliged it to withdraw. The heavy fire from the embankment and the deadly VT-fused artillery rounds cut many of the German foot soldiers down and forced the rest to retreat. That ended that.

The Company K, 120th Infantry, troops guarding the south end of the Warche bridge gave way before the main armored assault, which was hitting them from the rear. Nevertheless, one of the German tanks was destroyed from its rear when the infantry battalion's 81mm mortar forward observer fired a bazooka round into its lightly armored engine.

When a Panther disguised to resemble an M-4 approached the house across from the paper mill, Technician 5th Grade Vince Consiglio and Private Joe Spires ran up to the second floor and fired their rifles at accompanying German infantrymen. Then two more German tanks approached across a nearby field, their guns blazing. One stopped in the street between the house and the paper mill while the other headed straight for the bridge.

Consiglio ran back to the ground floor to get Private William Mitchell, the third engineer, who had found a bazooka. Just as Mitchell was leaning out a window to sight in on the German tank in the street, German machine guns sprayed the side of the house and killed him. He and the bazooka fell into the street.

Consiglio raced out the back door of the house to a machine-gun bunker. The gunner was dead, so Consiglio pushed him aside and fired at the German infantrymen in the field until a Panther nosed around the corner and by its mere dreadful presence sent him running back to the house. When Consiglio returned to the building, everyone on the first floor was dead. He ran upstairs, where Spires was still firing his rifle out a window facing south. The two fired on and on at a never-ending supply of targets until Spires was wounded painfully in the right arm. Consiglio helped him to the basement, where several medics were working over many wounded Americans.

The German attack had somehow caught the crews of the two nearest towed tank destroyers away from their guns. It was probably these men who raced into the house as Vince Consiglio emerged from the basement. Their sergeant immediately rallied them and led a charge right out the door. Virtually all the gunners were killed or wounded within minutes.

The German breakthrough across the Warche bridge and up the N-32 carried their tanks into a zone covered by three towed tank destroyers which were fully manned. Aiming down from the high ground overlooking the Spa road, the three 75mm guns opened fire while two self-propelled tank destroyers drove in from the flank. Two more German tanks were destroyed or disabled and a third German tank was disabled when two Company K infantrymen fired a bazooka point-blank at its turret.

The main body of Germans, now supported by only four tanks, fought on into the early afternoon, but it was plain to see within an hour of the initial assault that the 150th SS Panzer Brigade was not going to secure the vital road junction. Skorzeny's attack had certainly been more spirited than anything the 1st SS Panzer Division had attempted at Stavelot on December 19 and 20, but it was the ultimate example of too little too late. Leaving over five hundred of his men dead in the fields around Malmédy and caring for scores of wounded commandos, Skorzeny ordered the survivors to fall back to a defensible position in the hills south of our artillery fan. Many of the commandos engaged in heated fights with our troops disengaged and got out alive, but none of the tanks made it back.

CHAPTER 18

Near Trois-Ponts, in the dark predawn hours of December 21, the day after the 1st SS Panzer Division failed to cross the Amblève at Petit Spai, Major Bull Yates, of the 51st Combat Engineers, led a patrol across the Salm to see what the Germans over there were up to. Not far from the river, Yates's engineers discovered German engineers—the first any of us had seen in the Bulge—attempting to install a new bridge only yards upstream from the structure that had collapsed hours earlier beneath the weight of a German self-propelled tank destroyer. The American patrol was itself discovered as it attempted to withdraw, and a bullet from the heavy German fire struck Major Yates in the arm. He escaped only after plunging into the swift waters and swimming to the far bank while Sergeant Paul Hinkel's squad sprayed the Germans from its nearby roadblock position. As he had his wound treated, Yates made his report to Colonel William Ekman, the commander of the 505th Parachute Infantry, and Ekman ordered the area around the new bridge bombarded by an 82nd Airborne Division parachute artillery battalion that was deployed on the heights overlooking Trois-Ponts. The German engineers were dispersed by the devastating gunnery and the bridge-building effort floundered.

The evening before, late on December 20, Company E of the 505th Parachute Infantry's 2nd Battalion had crossed the Salm footbridge below Trois-Ponts and advanced to the village of Wanne to establish a blocking position astride a potential German route of advance. Among the many efforts of the 1st SS Panzer Division to bypass our dug-in defenses on the Amblève and Salm was an advance by an ad hoc force of German infantry and self-propelled guns down the hitherto unused road. By 1100 hours, December 21, Company E found its hilltop position sur-

rounded by Germans advancing directly toward the Salm footbridge. An eight-man outpost opened fire on the assault guns
with bazookas, and all the German vehicles were destroyed or
disabled. However, the German infantry launched an immediate
counterattack, and all eight American paratroopers were killed
or captured.

Within minutes, the main body of Company E reported the
sighting of German tanks and more infantry maneuvering off
the road, also in the direction of the Salm. The paratroop company radioman added that his unit was cut off. Back in Trois-
Ponts, Lieutenant Colonel Benjamin Vandervoort, the 2nd
Battalion commander, placed an immediate request for artillery
to support Company E. The parachute artillery battalion located
on the heights west of Trois-Ponts responded with a withering
thirty-minute fire mission that damaged but did not disperse the
advancing German tank-infantry force. During that time, Lieutenant Colonel Vandervoort tried in vain to obtain orders from
Colonel Ekman by means of apparently faulty radio equipment.
Finally, at about 1330 hours, Vandervoort acted on his own by
dispatching Company F across the Salm footbridge to try to link
up with Company E on the Wanne hill. By that time, members
of Company C, 51st Combat Engineers, had strengthened the
footbridge somewhat, so a jeep towing a 57mm antitank gun
was sent across with the paratroop company.

Meanwhile, near Wanne, the German tanks had become
bogged down in the muddy, slushy fields off the main road
through town. Thus, the German infantry attacked Company E
without tank support but nevertheless penetrated to the American position to wage a series of no-quarter hand-to-hand fights.
Company F and the 57mm antitank gun arrived on the scene
and engaged the Germans, thus alleviating some of the pressure
on Company E. The antitank gun knocked out several late-
arriving German tanks, but it was disabled and the lieutenant
commanding it was killed by the German counterfire. The German and American soldiers were locked in a mutual death grip
when Colonel Ekman ordered all of Vandervoort's troopers to
pull back across the Salm.

As the paratroopers began the extremely dangerous daylight
withdrawal, all the available engineers of the 51st and 291st
battalions were ordered to cover them from various defensive
positions along the west bank of the Salm. Holding an enfilade
position north of the footbridge, overlooking the blown railroad
bridge, was part of Lieutenant Bucky Walters's platoon of Com-

pany A, 291st. Bucky assumed—correctly—that the Germans
would be right on the heels of the retreating paratroopers and
that they would use their momentum to try to force their way to
our side of the Salm footbridge. He prepared his troops as well
as he could, marking off fire lanes through which he was certain
the Germans would have to advance down the heights toward
the footbridge.

The Company A engineers were ready by the time the American paratroopers began pouring down the steep slope of the
ridge on the east bank of the Salm. As expected, the Germans
were right behind them. Handfuls of hard-pressed Americans
jumped from high up the slope directly into the swift, ice-cold
water while others rushed toward the footbridge. It was clear to
the engineers that their countrymen were routed. Many German
soldiers stopped on the heights to open fire on the swimmers,
but many of them also followed the paratroopers straight over
the edge of the cliff.

For the longest time, the engineers, who were armed with
many .30-caliber machine guns, were unable to place effective
fire on the Germans for fear of hitting intermingled friends. At
length, however, a knot of Germans amounting to about two
platoons raced right out onto the footbridge. Bucky Walters ordered all his machine guns to open fire. At the same time, Sergeant Hinkel's squad opened fire from the west end of the
footbridge itself, and so did many nearby engineers from the
51st Combat Engineers. The main body of Germans was stopped
with extremely heavy casualties, but a handful surged all the
way across the bridge and ran smack into Hinkel's squad. These
Germans were thrown back following fierce hand-to-hand combat and, indeed, the bridge was swept clear of Germans within
several minutes. A German attack that made for the blown railroad bridge briefly engaged Lieutenant Walters's troopers, but
it was thrown back, too.

At about 1500 hours, as the battle at the bridges raged toward
a bloody conclusion, Colonel Wallis Anderson called the
wounded Major Yates to order all the 1111th Group engineers in
Trois-Ponts to turn their responsibilities over to the paratroop
engineers and withdraw immediately to the new Meuse defensive barrier. Bull told the colonel about the fight that was then
raging and assured him that he would try to sort things out if
the battle ended on terms favorable to our side.

At 1630 hours, by which time the German attacks had long
ago dissipated, Major Yates called Bucky Walters to his com-

mand post and told him of Colonel Anderson's order. Bull officially detached all the local 291st engineers from his makeshift engineer task force and advised Bucky to locate the main body of our battalion while he moved the group from the 51st to Marche to rejoin that unit's main body. Bucky took the advice and, after all the gear had been loaded aboard trucks, ordered his three-squad Company A contingent to Haute-Bodeux. Bucky's group left at dusk. Shortly thereafter, Bull Yates's group, consisting mainly of Company C, 51st Combat Engineers—blew the Salm footbridge and left town.

The Company A, 291st, group was extremely surprised and disappointed to find Haute-Bodeux abandoned, for all hands had been harboring dreams of reunions and a hot meal. Undaunted, Bucky led the way toward the former Company A command post at Werbomont. Surely, good news awaited the stragglers there.

By the time Bucky's group approached the former Company A command-post village, the 82nd Airborne Division's paratroop engineers had installed a new bridge at Lienne Creek to support the 505th Parachute Infantry's occupation of Trois-Ponts. Unfortunately for Bucky and his men, the bridge was outposted by some extremely tough-minded paratroopers wise to the ways of Skorzeny's American-uniformed commandos. Unhappily, Bucky was unable to prove his identity, so he and all his men were disarmed at gunpoint and marched off to the local prisoner-of-war stockade!

Bucky's furious indignation and vociferous arguments were meager salve. In the hour between their forcible incarceration and the arrival of an interrogator, nothing Bucky or his men said was heard with the least amount of interest. However, a brief official interrogation convinced the captors that our engineers were the true article. After only a few inquiries, Bucky and his troops were sent straight up the road from Werbomont toward the 1111th Group headquarters, at Huy.

By midnight, Bucky's column was advancing cautiously through the first snowstorm since the start of the German offensive. Cold, miserable, and nearly blind, the vehicle-borne engineers ground slowly toward Huy. At length, at about the time all hands were wondering if they were on the right road, a shouted challenge from dead ahead brought the trucks to a sudden stop. Bucky shouted his identity into the dark and was in turn ordered to advance up the center of the roadway with his hands held high. This order was met by an audible groan from all the cold, miserable troops, but the lieutenant had no choice but to obey with alacrity.

Incredibly, the roadblock confronting Bucky Walters's column was manned by the 2nd Squad of Walters's own platoon. The squad leader told Bucky that rumors had placed him among the dead. Minutes later, with fresh directions in hand, Bucky and his companions began the very last lap to rejoin the battalion rear echelon. By morning, following what amounted to a snack and a quick nap, the main body of Bucky's platoon and Sergeant Hinkel's squad were hard at work planting a new minefield in the frozen ground fronting the Meuse defensive barrier.

The 1111th Engineer Group was still something of a shambles when Bucky Walters finally made his way ''home'' in the wee hours of December 22. Between December 18, when Colonel Anderson was ordered to displace to Huy, the group headquarters had been unable to locate the *entire* 296th Engineer Combat Battalion or more than a few elements of the 202nd, which had been attached to the group on December 11. The 51st Engineer Combat Battalion was more or less complete, as were various bridging and engineer maintenance companies, but the 291st—the elements whose whereabouts were known—was spread across many hundreds of square miles of the war-torn Ardennes. Withal, despite the huge gaps in his organization, Colonel Anderson was obliged to handle the group-sized job of preparing the final engineer barrier in front of the strategically vital Meuse River.

On December 19, Major Ed Lampp had only the smaller rump portion of the 291st to offer Colonel Anderson. Captain Jim Gamble's Company A headquarters group was more or less intact and available, as was Lieutenant Arch Taylor's entire 3rd Platoon of Company A. However, of the rest of the Company A, only a handful of Lieutenant Al Edelstein's 2nd Platoon and a squad of Lieutenant Bucky Walters's 1st Platoon were on hand. Company C was represented by a handful of headquarters specialists and something less than a mixed line platoon of stragglers. Company B was not represented at all among the battalion-rear force; it was with me in Malmédy. What it came down to was that the bulk of the 291st men in Modave with Ed Lampp were officers, clerks, and specialists from H&S Company.

The two companies of the 51st Engineer Combat Battalion that were on hand before December 21 were deployed in a rather hot defensive sector centered on Hotton and, therefore, were

A typical timber trestle bridge constructed at Ettlebruck, Luxembourg by A & C companies.

Stavelot, Belgium. The vital bridge across the Ambleve River can be seen in the left center of the photo.

Petite Spa Bridge near Trois Points, collapsed beneath the weight of a German self-propelled gun.

One of several German tanks knocked out by the 291st's daisy chain mines as Colonel Otto Skorzeny attacks Malmédy on December 21, 1944.

Battling the flames after the first US bombing raid on Malmédy.

Civilian victims of the US Army Air Force's Christmas Eve raid against Malmédy.

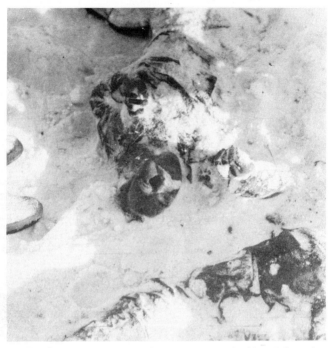

Lieutenant Tom Stack's engineers uncovered this victim of Kampfgruppe Peiper's bloody massacre beside Five Points.

The "impossible" 110-foot double Bailey bridge built on a curve at Heimbach, Germany, by the Company A platoons commanded by lieutenants Bucky Walters and Arch Taylor.

A completed float is lowered into the water by the Quickway crane.

A pair of treads is placed crosswise on the float by the Quickway crane and secured by a work party.

An engineer utility boat pushes the completed float into the stream so it can be placed at the head of the bridge.

Company A engineers on suicide point position the float and drive home the locking pin.

A Brockway truck was set on fire in an artillery bombardment of Lieutenant McCarthy's construction site at Remagen.

German artillery attacks went on day and night. Here a German shell lands on the east bank of the Rhine, opposite the 291st's work sites.

The Treadway bridge at Remagen after direct German fire wipes out three floats.

The twisted wreckage of the Ludendorff Bridge set against the forbidding Erpler Ley.

Colonel David Pergrin (to the right of sign) upon completion of the bridge at Remagen.

The 291st's 480-foot-long Treadway bridge on the Blue Danube, built to aid the assault into Hitler's redoubt area.

able to contribute little to the engineering tasks. Likewise, in the zone of the 84th Infantry Division, to which Lampp's portion of the battalion was attached, the bulk of Company A, 291st, was deployed in fixed defensive positions; Arch Taylor's 3rd Platoon was in Hamois guarding the Dinant-Huy highway and preparing to blow a bridge across the Bocq River; the squad of Bucky Walters's 1st Platoon was manning a roadblock in front of Modave (the same one that Bucky eventually ran into); and the Company A command group and an assortment of stragglers were sent to man a block at the crossroads in the tiny village of Barvaux Condroz. The mixed platoon of Company C was dispersed across the entire defensive sector, installing minefields across every possible German avenue of approach.

While not facing the level of danger their brothers were facing at Trois-Ponts, Stavelot, Malmédy, and Lienne Creek, the men of the 291st's battalion rear were involved in some incredible privation. The weather deteriorated to the point where simply manning the many Company A roadblocks was a nightmare of cold, freezing winds. Equipment and tools were in such short supply that the Company engineers charged with laying minefields were often on their knees in freezing water-logged pastures or digging into unyielding frozen earth with their fingers. However, despite the physical stress and the mind-numbing worry over the fate of countless missing buddies, the battalion rear element persevered and slowly overcame the elements and the pervasive fog of war. Slowly, as bleak day passed into bleak day, individual stragglers and small organized groups such as Bucky Walters's made their way home to Modave. Each blessed arrival was an excuse for raucous tale swapping and heartfelt, tearful reunions. And each new arrival added to the growing muster of bodies to be thrown into the teeth of the frantic, freezing defensive effort.

During the few days just prior to Christmas, the last remnants of Kampfgruppe Peiper were defeated near Stoumont and La Gleize, mainly by elements of the 30th Infantry and 3rd Armored divisions. In the end, following exceptionally bitter fighting, Lieutenant Colonel Joachim Peiper and a mere handful of survivors abandoned their fuelless trucks and tanks, made their way overland on foot, and waded the freezing Salm below Trois-Ponts. Fewer than eight hundred of the seven thousand Waffen SS men Peiper ultimately commanded reached the 1st SS Panzer Division German lines at Wanne on December 23.

The reasons for Peiper's failure are many and varied:

First among them, I believe, was my battalion's intimate knowledge of the Ardennes road nets, which had been built over the course of three months. This knowledge allowed us to move fluidly along roads about which the Germans exhibited zero knowledge. Next, I believe, was the immense technical skill of the 291st as a whole. We were experts at planting demolitions, laying mines, and deploying roadblocks. Every one of these skills proved vital during one or more phases of the struggle. Coupled with these straight engineering skills were the fruits of my long-standing insistence upon the maintenance of intrabattalion communication nets. Yes, we lost track of many battalion elements, but we never missed an opportunity to stymie Kampfgruppe Peiper or the rest of the 1st SS Panzer Division because our communications were not working. Above all, with respect to the skills of the 291st, my never-ending search for and development of the strongest, most highly motivated platoon and squad leaders paid dividends far beyond my most sanguine expectations; not one troop leader I know of hesitated when a wholly independent decision had to be made. Without the supreme skill and courage of the men of the 291st Engineer Combat Battalion, there would have been an excellent opportunity for the 1st SS Panzer Division to unseat the American northern barrier from Malmédy to Lienne Creek and to open the way to the Meuse for a massive breakthrough by the entire 6th Panzer Army.

As much as we did to defeat the Germans, their own shortcomings were of paramount importance. Peiper's failure to employ *any* of the bridging equipment in his column was a colossal *strategic* blunder. At Lienne Creek on December 18, for example, he could have struck all the way to the Meuse if he had been able to throw across even a rudimentary engineer bridge capable of supporting his tanks. At a higher level, the German high command failed to recognize the incredible mobility of the American infantry divisions, a mobility derived in large part from our very large investment in engineering assets.

Finally, at the highest strategic level, the Germans failed to marshal sufficient air support for their armored spearheads—a vital failure in their own blitzkrieg strategy—*and* they failed to factor in the effects of our own massive air-support assets.

Unfortunately, for myself and many of my companions at Malmédy, our side's massive air-support capability proved to be a little too much of a good thing.

CHAPTER 19

On the morning of December 22, the day after Skorzeny's attack on Malmédy, I received a message directing me to meet with Colonel Branner Purdue, the 120th Infantry's commander, at the command post of the 3rd Battalion, 120th Infantry. I was sure that Colonel Purdue was going to do something to recognize the efforts and sacrifices of the infantrymen, tank-destroyermen, and engineers who had defended the vital bridges on the west side of town against the German onslaught.

Colonel Purdue indeed began the conversation with a thank you, and then he asked me to accompany him on a walking tour of our defenses. He led me north through town, then along a narrow trail into the forest, and then halfway up a firebreak on a hill from which we could view the entire town. From there, we proceeded west to the field artillery position. The view was breathtaking; we could see the entire town, its valley, and far into the woods to the south. Directly below us were the paper mill and the three bridges around which the previous day's hand-to-hand combat had been waged. Far off, I could see the smoke from German artillery, followed within moments by the dull *thump* of their firing.

As we watched, Colonel Purdue finally got to the point. He told me that the 30th Infantry Division intelligence section had deduced that the Germans were building up for a renewed push into town, a stronger effort than the one we had weathered the day before. I nodded, not seeing at all where this was leading. Then the colonel dropped his bombshell: He wanted me to blow all three bridges.

I was dumbfounded, but I managed to respond with a protest, at least insofar as the old stone railroad viaduct was concerned. I pointed out that our armies would be on the move toward

Germany—in days, weeks, months, whenever—that replacing the viaduct would be a major engineering feat, and that until the structure was replaced there would be no way to get resupply trains east of Malmédy.

I was overruled. The colonel in charge of defending Malmédy wanted all three spans blown, so the lieutenant colonel in charge of Malmédy's engineers had no choice but to obey.

We blew the Warche River bridge and the old wooden railroad trestle with ease, but it took some serious thought and preparations to drop the massive stone railroad span. I turned the job over to Captain John Conlin, of Company B, and he turned the execution over to Lieutenant Frank Rhea's platoon.

It was an enormous job, and it had to be completed by sunset. A large crew of engineers working under Sergeant Charles Sweitzer staged cases of TNT on the top of the bridge, sixty feet above the highway, and rigged eighteen hundred pounds of the explosive around one stone pier and an additional five hundred pounds on the crown. Sweitzer also had placed over five hundred pounds of German mines and captured German explosives. When all the charges had been set, he ran out five hundred feet of cable and attached it to a detonator set in a safe hollow. When everyone was clear and safety had been confirmed, Sweitzer yelled the traditional ''Fire in the hole,'' and ignited the charges.

It was a monstrous explosion! Stones and pieces of railroad ties landed hundreds of feet out in every direction and huge gouts of gray dust and black smoke rose high into the slate-gray sky. Though we were watching from an immense distance, Frank Rhea and I were obliged to dodge a truckload of falling debris. The Germans added to the festivities by throwing in a cluster of rockets.

My only concern as I viewed the altogether complete demolition job was that my many friends among the railroad engineers should not learn of my role in this fiasco. I intended to earn a living after the war with the Pennsylvania Railroad, and I just knew that I eventually would have to face some of the men who would have to clean this mess up and build a new viaduct.

In addition to destroying those three bridges, we had to set charges and man detonators at several other bridges in the Malmédy area. I was certain that all the bridges would eventually be blown and that my troops would be the ones to replace them.

As it turned out, the Germans never again threatened Malmédy. No, Malmédy's worst enemy after December 21, 1944, was the U.S. Army Air Forces.

* * *

On December 23, beneath cloudy skies, twenty-eight B-26 medium bombers of the U.S. 9th Air Force's IX Bombardment Division got confused on their way to the German town of Zülpich, which was thirty-three air miles from Malmédy. Twenty-two of the twenty-eight pilots eventually realized they were off course and aborted their bombing runs. However, six of the medium bombers dropped a total of eighty-six five-hundred-pound general-purpose bombs on Malmédy.

All of the bombs detonated around and through the center of town. Though severely dazed and shocked, Captain Larry Moyer, Captain John Conlin, and I immediately went to work organizing rescue efforts by all of our available troops—including many we pulled off the defensive barrier.

The town center was devastated. Fires were raging among the many collapsed buildings, roads and streets were thoroughly blocked, and there was ample evidence—screams, mainly—that many civilians and soldiers were buried alive in the rubble.

Among the first help to arrive was an engineer fire brigade organized by three of the 291st engineers running our water purification plant—Technician 5th Grade John Chapman, Private First Class Camillo Bosco, and Private First Class John Iles. The makeshift fire brigade came complete with a fire truck and hoses.

As our line engineers converged on the ravaged area, Larry Moyer and John Conlin quickly organized rescue teams to sift through the rubble in search of survivors. Bulldozers arriving on the scene were deployed to begin road-clearing operations under the direction of Lieutenants Frank Rhea, Wade Colbeck, Don Davis, John Kirkpatrick, and Leroy Joehnck and Master Sergeant Ralph McCarty. This was especially ticklish work near the center of the bombed-out area, for the rubble blocking the streets was likely as not to contain buried survivors. At the far edges of the blasted area, Sergeant Charles Sweitzer's demolitions team blew fire lanes to contain the further spread of the otherwise uncontrollable fires.

Within minutes of the detonation of the last bomb, Captain Paul Kamen's makeshift battalion aid station was receiving the first of the many, many military and civilian casualties. Shortly, litter teams were organized by several of our squad leaders—Sergeants Sheldon Smith and Al Melton, and Corporal Black Mac McDonald. Unfortunately, the shortage of medics left the onerous task of separating the dead from the wounded to these three stalwarts. Too soon, lines of dead civilians and soldiers were being deposited in an open temporary morgue in the schoolyard near the aid station. By the time the last living victim had been freed from the rubble, Paul Kamen—our *dentist*—and his medics had treated about a hundred civilians and fifty GIs. Among the injured troops was Technician 3rd Grade Mack Barbour, an irrepressible medic who went straight to work as soon as his wounds had been bound.

My troop leaders and troops were magnificent. As I walked through the rubble, finding very little that needed my attention, there rose in me a sense of pride even the events of the past week could not surpass. Their reaction to the unbelievably frightening disaster had been so quick, so thorough, so giving. Almost without let up, these combat-hardened young men worked straight into the night, gingerly sifting the rubble of countless buildings for some sign of even the most tenuously maintained spirit of life.

Locating the living—and the dead—in the rubble was more difficult than it sounds. The mighty detonations of the five-hundred-pound bombs had ground many parts of many buildings to a fine, powdery gray dust which coated everything in sight. A living, unconscious body looked much the same as dead stone, and more than a few survivors were located only after they gave way beneath the boot-shod feet of would-be rescuers. There was no red blood visible—only less-dry blood-charged patches of the ubiquitous gray dust. And throughout the effort, the strenuous breathing resulting from heavy, frantic physical labor carried great volumes of the noxious fine powder and cordite-tinged air into the noses, mouths, and lungs of the rescuers.

Many of the tableaux we uncovered were simply pitiful. Master Sergeant Ralph McCarty and Technician 5th Grade John Noland lifted some heavy rubble from the ruin of one house and found several live children arrayed around the cold, stiff bodies of their mother and father. Children and adults whose clothing had been reduced to gray, dusty rags wandered aimlessly through the area of the worst destruction, all no doubt driven temporarily over the edge by the shock and grief that had burst upon their comparatively orderly lives. (It is one thing to see a war going on, and quite another to have that war explode in your family's sitting room.)

We eventually learned that the BBC had reported Malmédy as being in German hands, and we chalked the error up to that bad information. We had placed many huge marker panels on roofs throughout town, but the low clouds apparently obviated their being seen in time. However, a subsequent investigation revealed that it was a navigation error, pure and simple. I cannot imagine what would have befallen us had all or most of the B-26s dropped their bombs.

This was the second time in the war that the 120th Infantry had been bombed by friendly aircraft. Hundreds of casualties had been sustained by the regiment in July, during the carpet bombing that marked the beginning of Operation COBRA, the Normandy breakout. Accordingly, Major General Leland Hobbs, the commanding general of the 30th Infantry Division, raised holy hell with 1st Army Headquarters, and the 1st Army raised some hell with the 9th Air Force. All that produced was a rather bland pro forma message indicating that the flyboys would try to avoid such incidents in the future.

Adding considerably to our woes that December 23 was a particularly fierce German rocket and artillery bombardment against the lines of Lieutenant Colonel Harold Hansen's 99th Norwegian Battalion. Even before the bombardment quite ended, German infantry attempted to storm the 99th's lines, but they were beaten off—rather easily, I'm glad to report.

Well after sunset, I took measures to organize shifts so we could pull relays of my hard-working engineers off the job for hot food and sleep. However, the work never ceased. Late on the morning of December 24, I finally stumbled from the work site, intent upon catching a few winks at my command post.

I am sure I had no sooner nodded off than Sergeant Bill Crickenberger shook me awake so he could tell me that a rescue team directed by Captain Larry Moyer had located a 30th Infantry Division field kitchen buried close to the town square. I grabbed my driver, Corporal Curtis Ledet, and headed to the scene in my command car. By the time we arrived, Captain John Conlin had brought in an air compressor and Corporal Jesse McGhehee was busting his jackhammer through a concrete wall so we could gain access to the basement in which the cooks were entombed.

Progress was maddeningly slow. As soon as McGhehee had made some progress into the concrete wall, Private First Class Jim Coupe, Captain Conlin's driver, organized a small group of Company C engineers to begin lifting the jackhammered debris from the excavation. The fit was extremely tight, so the lifting and carrying went forward very slowly. As the men worked, news arrived from the 120th Infantry's CP that up to ten cooks might be trapped in the basement.

By around 1430 hours, McGhehee had jackhammered a hole barely large enough to crawl through, so that is exactly what Larry Moyer and I did, leaving John Conlin outside to direct the ongoing effort. Just as Larry and I squeezed through the opening—before we could make a move to locate the trapped cooks—eighteen IX Bombardment Division B-24 heavy bombers unloaded on Malmédy.

Little of what the B-26s had left standing on December 23 remained in the wake of the thoroughly efficient B-24 strike of Christmas Eve. Many of the 120th Infantry's companies and platoons were struck by the cascading bombs. Casualty figures went through the roof—or would have had there been a roof left standing anywhere near the central core of the town. By way of comparison, the December 23 B-26 raid was as an appetizer at the B-24 group's seven-course feast.

The bombs knocked me for a loop. The first thing I knew, Larry Moyer was lifting a beam that had pinned me to the inside of the concrete wall through which we had just crawled. Indeed, the top portion of the wall itself had collapsed on Larry and me. I was still dazed, barely conscious of being rudely shaken by my companion, when Larry forcefully suggested that we get the hell out of there. I thought that was a neat idea, but we appeared to be trapped, with no means for digging.

Say the magic word—Engineer!—and "Open Sesame!" Before I had an opportunity to clutch at all the good news my renewed senses were collecting, Corporal McGhehee jackhammered through the wall again. Homing on the dusty gray light, Larry and I made a painful, halting beeline for the breach and crawled through on aching, bruised knees and elbows. Someone was speaking to me, but I could barely make out the low notes through the ringing in my head.

I was still collecting myself and my scattered wits when we found John Conlin in a heap in the street. A long tear in one of his legs was bleeding freely onto the cobblestones. A tearful Private First Class Jim Coupe oversaw the tender lifting of his unconscious captain to their command car. For the moment, the last we saw of either of them was when Coupe roared off toward Dr. Kamen's aid station.

As the waterfall roar in my head subsided, I checked Larry Moyer out for injuries and, finding him in swell shape, turned the entire town-wide rescue effort over to his care. Then and there, I sent word of Conlin's apparent condition to Lieutenant Frank Rhea, appointing our only West Pointer acting commander of Company B. I was so certain that John would be separated permanently from the battalion that I decided to head Rhea's platoon on the spot with the best NCO in the battalion. That was an easy choice: I called Master Sergeant Ralph McCarty to me and told him that he was, from that moment on, a second lieutenant.

Having taken care of the most pressing business, I hobbled through the center of destruction to the command post of Lieutenant Colonel Peter Ward's 3rd Battalion, 120th Infantry. I was both amazed and gratified to find the building undamaged and Ward and his staff uninjured. At my express urging, Peter radioed the 30th Division CP and directly asked General Hobbs for help. Next, I returned to the town square to pick up my command car and driver. I was shocked to find that the vehicle had been blown up and that Corporal Ledet had been wounded and evacuated.

There was no work for me at the field-kitchen site, so I again hobbled through the debris, this time toward my own CP, which was on the eastern edge of town. I had my heart in my mouth most of the way, but even at a distance I could see that the building was still standing. No one in the building had been hurt, but terrible news awaited me: Private Edward Barker, of Company B, had been killed by a bomb, and Private John McVay had been seriously injured. I also learned for the first time that Private Edward Gutkowski had been seriously wounded by German artillery fire on December 23 while manning one of the roadblocks on the western edge of town. In all thus far, our battalion's casualties in Malmédy—from December 17 to Christmas Eve—had been three killed and nine wounded. It was not good, but I knew how very much worse it could have been.

The rescue effort doggedly went forward, an all-out offensive against the debris. The lines of civilian and military dead continued to stretch across the school playground as the first licks of snow heralded a thoroughly unwanted White Christmas. The temperature dropped to eighteen degrees, impeding progress in the rubble and adding immeasurably to the fatigue of our utterly possessed workers. Water from the fire hoses that froze in the streets had to be broken up to keep evacuation routes clear, and wet outer clothing froze on the backs of our hard-working engineers.

The officers and men were by then nerveless. Lieutenant Tom

Stack, my acting operations officer, teamed up with Lieutenant Leroy Joehnck, my acting intelligence officer, to fight a stubborn fire in a basement coal bin. Eventually, the persistent smoke dazed both men and Leroy was scalded painfully by steam gushing up from the red-hot coals.

I was of little or no use. By 1800 hours, my ears were ringing louder than ever, and I was nearly out of my mind from the noise and unremitting pain in my head. Nevertheless, I managed to give some thought to morale and thus ordered Larry Moyer to see to setting up a Christmas tree in the abandoned 44th Evacuation Hospital command post. When that little job had been completed and some rudimentary trimming had been done, I told Larry that he was to collect all the officers for a Christmas toast.

As soon as Larry left to complete his Christmas rounds, I realized how much pain I was in. I decided to have my head examined and made my way rather shakily to Paul Kamen's aid station. As soon as I told Paul how much pain I was enduring, he and Technician 3rd Grade Mack Barbour helped me lie down. Barbour started writing up an evacuation tag while Paul told me that I had been walking around for hours with one of the most severe concussions he had ever seen. He added that I had a punctured eardrum and severe contusions across my shoulders that could prove extremely dangerous if not properly treated.

I knew very well that many of my engineers had returned to duty after being treated for their cuts and bruises—Mack Barbour was a perfect example, decked out before me in his white bandage. I told Paul that what was good enough for the men was good enough for me. I might be known as the "Old Man," but I was a hale and hearty twenty-eight years old. The matter had not been settled when Mack Barbour informed me that another engineer had been brought in, and would I like to speak with him.

I gathered my strength, launched my weary, aching body to its feet, and followed Mack and Paul Kamen into the next room. There, arrayed around a makeshift tree that must have been in the making long before I told Larry Moyer to find one, were the stalwart leaders of the forward echelon of my brave, loyal 291st Engineer Combat Battalion. Using mess kits, canteen cups, a glass tumbler, and paper cups, we drank up several bottles of champagne the departed Curt Ledet had purloined long months before in France and feasted on cold K rations. When all had eaten, I asked everyone to stand while I recited a Christmas prayer. Then, with the last of the champagne, I held my cup high before this battered, exhausted, unbeaten group of heroes and offered a toast I am sure was on everyone's lips: "To Captain John Conlin, to our success in stopping the Germans, to our men who were killed defending Malmédy, to all those killed and wounded in Malmédy by our own air force, and, finally, to peace. To an early peace!" With that, my officers drank up and scattered from the room to resume their duties.

It was not a merry Christmas, but at least it was spent among my dearest, most loyal comrades.

On Christmas Day, nearly everyone in town was fed hot turkey and mashed potatoes. The chaplains from the 120th Infantry passed out sorely needed clean socks to the engineers working in the bomb-gutted town center. My Christmas present was a new command car, formerly Major Ed Lampp's, which he donated along with his driver, Technician 5th Grade Mike Popp. Mike also brought news from Modave that all was well with the battalion rear echelon.

I was finally just settling into the Christmas spirit when, for the third time, the IX Bomber Command tried to eradicate Malmédy. This time, at around 1430 hours, four B-26 medium bombers dropped a total of sixty-four 250-pound all-purpose bombs on us instead of the authorized target, German-held St.-Vith, in the center of the Bulge. Once again, the 291st was called out to locate and free the American and civilian victims and help succor those who were still alive.

The 291st suffered its last casualty in Malmédy on December 26. Technician 4th Grade Burnie Hebert, a Company B cook, had half of his right leg amputated by a German artillery shell while he was working in the open beside a field kitchen directly across the street from my CP. Fortunately for all the other troops standing in the open nearby, the shell was a dud; it plowed into a sandbank but did not detonate.

Shortly after Burnie Hebert was evacuated, Colonel Bill Carter, the 1st Army chief engineer, managed to get my battalion forward echelon sprung from Malmédy. Under orders to report directly to General Hobbs, whose 30th Division CP was in Francorchamps, I said my good-byes to Lieutenant Colonel Harold Hansen, of the 99th Infantry Battalion, and Lieutenant Colonel Peter Ward, of the 3rd Battalion, 120th Infantry. Both offered effusive heartfelt thanks and godspeed to me and my engineers. Next, I shaved and dusted off my uniform as well as

I was able and jumped into my new command car beside my new driver and set off for the 30th Division CP.

General Hobbs greeted me warmly and told me of his desire to have the 291st permanently attached to the 30th Division. Then, as he pinned a Silver Star medal on my chest, he handed me my copy of a recommendation for the 291st's Presidential Unit Citation. In the end, the battalion received not only the Presidential Unit Citation, but the French Croix de Guerre with Silver Star and a recommended Belgian Fourragère, all for our part in the defense of the northern shoulder of the Bulge.

Before allowing me to leave to rejoin my waiting troops for the trek to Modave, General Hobbs once again thanked me for our efforts in stopping Kampfgruppe Peiper and supporting his division. I thanked the general for his kind words and added that it had been an honor to support his 30th Infantry Division at Mortain, Aachen, and in the Ardennes. And then I left—to knit the two halves of the 291st back together, to prepare for our part in driving the Germans out of the Bulge and in finally ending this terrible, wasteful, life-consuming war.

PART FOUR

INTO GERMANY

CHAPTER 20

As my new driver, Technician 5th Grade Mike Popp, drove me back through the Ardennes, he filled me in on the state and deployment of the battalion rear echelon. According to Mike, the battalion rear was headquartered in Modave and was overseeing roughly fifteen roadblocks manned mainly by Company A engineers. Elements of Company C had also shown up at Modave and were at work laying minefields, but apparently elements of both Company A and Company C were still missing. Company B and a platoon of Company C had remained in Malmédy pending relief in place by the 30th Division's organic 105th Engineer Combat Battalion, but at least we knew where they were and that they were in the hands of good and trusted infantry commanders. The situation throughout the northern Bulge was still so fragmented and confusing that it was hard for Major Ed Lampp to know whether he should write off the missing troops or not; after all, many men who had been reported killed or seriously wounded had been dribbling into Modave under their own power for a week.

Before my little convoy arrived in Modave, I fell sound asleep in the front seat of my new command car. I was unconscious when Mike rolled up to the battalion rear command post, and he had carried me halfway indoors before I knew what was going on. I was greeted at the door by our trusty assistant personnel officer, Warrant Officer John Brenna. John smiled, told me he was glad to see me, and added that I looked like I had been dragged through a wringer with spikes on the rollers. That is about how I felt.

Ed Lampp, Bill McKinsey, and Big Max Schmidt, H&S Company commander, greeted me effusively, and Ed said that he would like to talk with me as soon as I felt up to resuming active command of the battalion. Meanwhile, he would see to quartering, feeding, and assigning the scattering of headquarters and Company A men I had brought in. I dumped my aching body into a cot in the personnel section's orderly room and immediately fell into a deep sleep. I could not have been asleep very long before I was startled awake by a presence. When my eyes snapped open, I was staring directly at the burr haircut sported by the 1111th Group commander, Colonel Wallis Anderson. The colonel's eyes were twinkling, so I knew that things were going well in his world.

My boss told me that his boss, Colonel Bill Carter, wanted me to submit papers supporting an effort to have a Presidential Unit Citation awarded to the battalion, as well as appropriate French and Belgian awards. I told him of General Hobbs's desire to do the same and he told me to write the backup paperwork.

Next, Colonel Anderson provided me with my first overview of the 1111th Group's unparalleled contribution to the containment of the German breakthroughs in the northern Bulge. He sketched in the activities of elements of the 291st about which I had no prior knowledge and explained how our brother engineers in Company C, 51st, Engineer Combat Battalion, had stood out in the defense of Trois-Ponts. The colonel also told me that the main body of the 51st under Lieutenant Colonel Harvey Fraser, had held the barrier line from Barvaux to Hotton and from south of Marche to Rochefort. "Scrappy" Fraser, as his men were already calling him, was a West Pointer who had taken command of the 51st on December 14. Since December 17, he had overseen the destruction of three footbridges, two highway bridges, and a railroad bridge while holding a twenty-five-mile front against German armored and infantry attacks. According to Colonel Anderson, the barrier lines shaped mainly by the 291st and 51st Engineer Combat battalions were now in the hands of *five* infantry and *three* armored divisions, from Malmédy all the way back to the Meuse River.

As he turned to walk away, the colonel ordered in a mock gruff voice, "Get your rest!" However, I was a little too excited to go right back to sleep, so I took the first bath I had had since December 17 and then slept for ten straight hours. When I awoke, I went to the headquarters field kitchen and gulped down a thoroughly restorative cup of hot black coffee.

I immediately called a staff meeting to determine the present status of the battalion. By then, even more of our missing men had found their way to Modave or had sent word that they were on the way. My first inquiry was about casualties—how many and who. My adjutant, Lieutenant Don Gerrity, reported four known fatalities and that a dozen officers and men had been wounded and evacuated. Don was quick to add that, given the circumstances of the battalion's service, this was absolutely minimal, no indication at all of what the troops had faced. A recent tally revealed that only seven of our men remained missing. (They all eventually returned.)

John Brenna reported that Group had asked for recommendations for personal awards and that he had passed the order on to the line companies to obtain submissions. John said that the preliminary list was quite lengthy. Captain Max Schmidt, the H&S Company commander, and Captain Jim Walton, the battalion supply officer, ruefully described the man-size job fulfilling orders from the line companies for replacement clothing and personal gear, weapons and equipment, explosives, mines, vehicles—you name it. He also had to find Ed Lampp a new command car to replace the one Ed had given me for Christmas. This prompted an inquiry from me about the condition of my injured driver, Curtis Ledet. Ed said that Ledet was on the mend and that he would take him on as his new driver as soon as he returned.

Once the housekeeping decisions were out of the way, Captain Bill McKinsey briefed us on our situation at that moment. The plan I had worked out for the gradual release of the line platoons still in Malmédy was a bit more gradual than I had planned. Apparently, turning over the roadblocks and minefields to the 30th Division's 105th Combat Engineers was very slow going. However, at last word, Lieutenant Don Davis's Company C platoon was on the way to Modave, as was a Company B platoon. Bill certainly expected the last of our troops from Malmédy to arrive by December 31. McKinsey, who had missed all the action because I had sent him on a much needed leave just before the Germans attacked, reported that he was just back from Malmédy. According to Bill, the town, which was blanketed by six inches of snow, looked like a graveyard and would take years to be rebuilt in the wake of the three devastating bombing raids.

The overall situation described by Bill looked promising. The northern shoulder, which had come under the control of Field Marshal Bernard Montgomery's 21st British Army Group, was holding easily against the by-then pitiful attacks of the 6th Panzer Army. There was still a lot of action in the center, where the eminently more successful 5th Panzer Army still appeared to be full of fight. In the south, the 101st Airborne Division was holding out at Bastogne and German advances everywhere else had been blunted or even driven back. Behind the divisions containing the Bulge were a great many more U.S. Army divisions preparing to eradicate it, and some British formations were arriving along the northern shoulder.

Bill next showed us on his current situation map where elements of the 291st and 51st Engineer battalions were holding sections of the so-called Meuse barrier line. Word was that the engineers manning line positions were due to be relieved soon by armored and infantry units. McKinsey's map also showed the location and extent of the many minefields our engineers had laid, and it was an impressive picture.

According to Bill, the bulk of the 1st U.S. Army was maneuvering so it could begin pushing the 5th Panzer Army back from the nose of the Bulge, to drive the Germans as far back from the Meuse as possible. The 3rd and 9th U.S. armies, to the south and north respectively, were to try to cut through the Germans on the two shoulders and bag as many German divisions in the resulting pocket as possible. (Unknown to us, however, the extremely cautious Field Marshal Montgomery was driving the 9th Army staff mad with delays and overcautious build ups, and the critical edge in timing that might lead to the entrapment of most of the 5th Panzer Army was being frittered away.) Closer to our immediate interests, the 84th Infantry Division was on the move toward Marche, which was in our zone of responsibility, and relief of our units on the barrier line appeared imminent. Soon, Major General J. Lawton Collins's VII Corps—the veteran 84th Infantry Division, 2nd and 3rd Armored divisions, and the newly arrived and utterly untried 75th Infantry Division—was about to establish its headquarters east of the Meuse astride the Huy road. We had been nominally and temporarily attached to the 84th Infantry Division.

McKinsey's blockbuster news was saved for the end of his briefing: As soon as elements of the 51st, 300th, and 308th Engineer Combat battalions had relieved elements of our Company A and Company C along the Meuse barrier line, the entire 291st was to move back to Malmédy, Trois-Ponts, and Spa to support the projected attack into the German rear.

The relief of our troops on the Meuse barrier line was accomplished on schedule and the last of our troops from Malmédy—2nd Lieutenant Ralph McCarty's platoon of Company B—arrived at Modave on December 31. As had all the other line platoons, Ralph's was reequipped from the soles of the men's combat boots on up, and all the broken and marginal equipment was replaced. On January 1, 1945, following two days of frantic work, the refurbished 291st was ready to undertake its new assignment.

I took the opportunity of our pre-New Year respite to reorganize the battalions's officer contingent. The need to replace immediately the wounded Captain John Conlin in Malmédy had pointed up a serious gap in our organization, namely my failure to replace earlier my executive officer, who had returned to the States months before. While we were at Modave, I confirmed Frank Rhea's appointment as the Company B commander and promoted Frank to captain. I also confirmed Ralph McCarty's battlefield commission and appointed him Rhea's successor as Company B's 3rd Platoon commander. Next, I offered the vacant exec billet to Ed Lampp, but he turned it down in favor of remaining the battalion operations officer. I didn't blame Ed and, indeed, was relieved that he chose to do so. I then offered the exec job to Captain Larry Moyer and, when he agreed to give up Company C, I saw to his promotion to major. Larry's departure from Company C resulted in my appointment of Warren Rombaugh to the rank of captain, and he took over Company C right away. Warren's former platoon billet was assumed by Lieutenant Tom Stack, the assistant operations officer who had been of such value in Malmédy. I also conferred battlefield commissions on the battalion's three warrant officers: John Brenna in Personnel, Coye Self in Supply, and Robert Bryant in Motor Transport.

We were well organized and had earned the supreme confidence of successful combat veterans when we left Modave for Spa on January 1 to undertake the first in what was to be an unbroken chain of major contributions in support of our side's final march to victory in Europe.

CHAPTER 21

Our move back to the Malmédy–Stavelot–Trois-Ponts area, while pleasing in many of its aspects—we would literally be completing the huge job we had started—had a down side that nearly offset the joy and potential sense of accomplishment. The new arrangement of corps and divisions poised along the northern shoulder of the Bulge necessitated our detachment from the 1111th Engineer Group. We would be working for the XVIII Airborne Corps and, thus, the 1186th Engineer Group. As it developed, we had been transferred upon the express recommendation of the 82nd Airborne Division's Major General James Gavin, who had seen a tiny portion of the 291st in action at the Lienne Creek bridge. In addition, Major General Leland Hobbs's 30th Infantry Division had been attached to the XVIII Airborne Corps, and that undoubtedly had a further impact upon our transfer. In fact, as soon as I reported to my new group commander, I was told that the 291st would be providing *close* combat engineer support for the 30th Infantry Division.

The first order of business was plotting the huge restoration job that faced us across our former and immediate area of operations. Following Captain Bill McKinsey's thorough survey of the 30th and 82nd divisional zones, Major Ed Lampp and his staff plotted in on a master map all the bridges we would have to replace or build anew in support of the XVIII Airborne Corps projected attack into the central Bulge area. Having developed strong views since Normandy about the critical role of engineer assault bridging—and knowing even what little we knew then about Kampfgruppe Peiper's failure to bring along bridging—I spent a lot of time bothering higher headquarters with requests and demands for adequate bridging support assets. As a result, as Bill McKinsey's reconnaissance teams prepared to move out with the infantry, Captain Max Schmidt, now our supply officer, went into perpetual motion lining up and deploying every bridging company our superiors would let us have.

In my preassault briefings, I told the line company troop leaders to anticipate the placement by the Germans of extremely heavy artillery, mortar, and rocket fire on the assault bridge sites. I frankly expected the battalion to sustain heavy casualties during the break-in phase of the counterattack into the Bulge. The Germans were the world's masters of defense in adverse situations. They were stubborn, resourceful, and tactically brilliant with the best instincts for exploiting defensible terrain.

The offensive in our sector began on the evening of January 10, 1945. Jumping off through two feet of snow, Captain Jim Gamble's Company A built a Bailey bridge to replace the structure blown across the Amblève at Trois-Ponts by the 51st Combat Engineers. While our engineers worked, the lead element of the 82nd Airborne Division assaulted across the freezing river and established a shallow bridgehead in the face of die-hard German opposition. Directly alongside the paratroopers, clearing mines, was Sergeant Joe Geary's squad of Lieutenant Al Edelstein's platoon.

The night was cold and crisp and, even with gloves on their hands, our men had an extremely hard time horsing the cold steel bridge panels into position. Yet they worked as perhaps they had never worked before, egged on by the specter of the two elderly Belgian civilians whose frozen bodies lay beside the building where they had apparently been executed by Peiper's Waffen SS thugs. Despite the difficulties borne by the cold night wind, Company A completed the 120-foot double-single Bailey span in near-record time. As soon as the bridge was ready, the armor supporting the 82nd Airborne's attack surged across into the shallow bridgehead and began the long drive back to the German frontier. Following the assault elements closely, the Company A engineers went to work clearing mines ahead of a bulldozer rigged out to scour the roadway of its coating of snow. The temperature hovered around zero degrees, causing our freezing troops to wonder how the infantrymen out ahead were firing their weapons.

Lieutenant Don Davis's platoon of Captain Warren Rombaugh's Company C went to work on a 140-foot Bailey bridge to replace the timber trestle bridge across the Salm below Trois-Ponts that Lieutenant Bucky Walter's troops had blown. It took

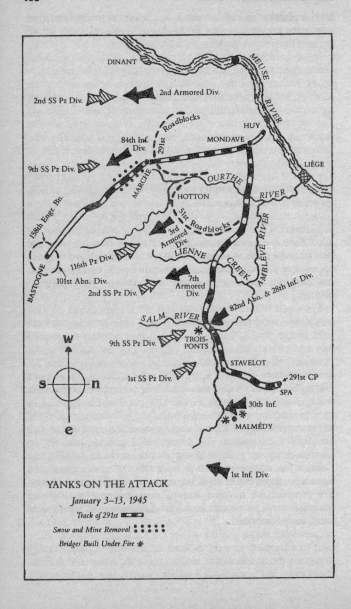

YANKS ON THE ATTACK

January 3–13, 1945

Track of 291st ▰▰▰▰

Snow and Mine Removal •••••

Bridges Built Under Fire ✳

Davis's platoon just three and a half hours to bridge the river despite the presence on the far heights of elements of the 9th SS Panzer Division. A number of cold, miserable Waffen SS men were rounded up by our infantry as soon as they crossed the new bridge, and they told their interrogators of their mission to plant mines to cover the retreat of a much larger force.

At Malmédy, Captain Frank Rhea's Company B worked on the west side of town, rebuilding the Warche River bridge and clearing the underpasses around which Skorzeny's attack met its end on December 21. This was Company B's third bridge installation at this one site. First, on our arrival in the area early in the autumn, the company had installed a Bailey bridge. In November, the Bailey bridge had been replaced by a timber trestle, which Rhea's former platoon of Company B had blown, per orders on December 22.

On January 13, at Malmédy, the 30th Infantry Division was preparing to jump off following ten full days of relative inactivity. Our gruesome mission this time out would be locating the bodies of the men of the 285th Field Artillery Observation Battalion who had been butchered at Five Points by Peiper's armored spearhead on December 17. Two feet of snow now blanketed the killing field, but I was certain we would be able to locate the bodies based on information I had collected from the battered survivors we had aided in the immediate wake of the barbaric massacre.

As the 120th Infantry's attack was about to get underway toward Geromont, Mike Popp drove me down that way so I could follow the assault close behind the infantry. As we neared the little village, we ran into Colonel Branner Purdue, the 120th's commanding officer, who was also aiming to move close behind the infantry assault elements. As I climbed out of my command car to greet the colonel, he jokingly asked if I would like to liberate the village with my troops. I responded in a dead serious tone that we had no time to fight as infantry, that we would have enough to do opening the road, clearing mines, and building bridges under fire so his tank support could get to the front. I was still smarting over the regimental commander's short-sighted panic-driven refusal to put off blowing the Malmédy railroad viaduct on December 22.

As feared, the Germans had had an opportunity to lay tons of mines along the roadways and in the fields around Malmédy, particularly in Company B's sector, west of town. Perhaps it

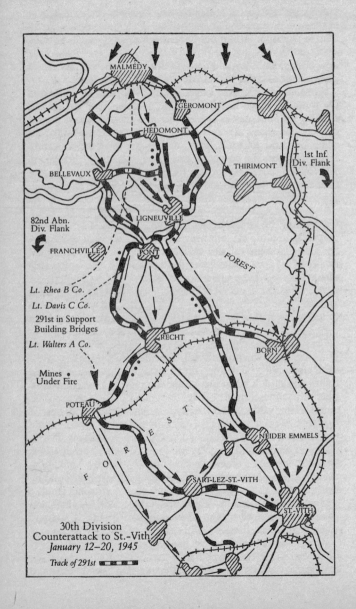

MALMEDY

GEROMONT

HEDOMONT

THIRIMONT

1st Inf.
Div. Flank

BELLEVAUX

LIGNEUVILLE

82nd Abn.
Div. Flank

FRANCHVILLE

PONT

FOREST

Lt. Rhea B Co.

Lt. Davis C Co.

291st in Support
Building Bridges

Lt. Walters A Co.

RECHT

BORN

Mines
Under Fire

POTEAU

NEIDER EMMELS

F O R E S T

SART-LEZ-ST.-VITH

ST.-VITH

30th Division
Counterattack to St.-Vith
January 12–20, 1945

Track of 291st

was the devious minds of the SS commandos or only the finger-numbing cold, but the Company B troops seemed to have more trouble with these minefields than any of our units had experienced since Normandy.

The 30th Infantry Division's general assault went off through two feet of snow in zero-degree weather where the wind chill factor measured out at minus-twenty degrees. As Colonel Purdue's 120th Infantry moved to seize Geromont and Five Points, the adjacent 117th Infantry crossed the Amblève at Petit Spai on a new treadway bridge installed by the 30th Division's organic 105th Combat Engineers. At the same time, also, the adjacent 28th Infantry Division's 112th Infantry moved across the Petit Spai treadway and our Trois-Ponts bridges to attack the heights south of Stavelot before linking up with the 82nd Airborne Division's drive from west of our Salm bridge below Trois-Ponts.

The 30th Infantry Division's objective was the city of St.-Vith, in the center of the Bulge. Before it—and us—lay the rugged terrain of the Ardennes, a seemingly endless series of narrow valleys cut by swift, meandering streams. It was country very similar to that faced by Kampfgruppe Peiper, and it was defended by wily Germans every bit as determined to stop our push as we had been to stop theirs. Nevertheless, the abominable weather and rugged topography plagued the 30th Infantry Division's attack far more than the dogged Germans, including all the mines and blown bridges. In places, the snow confronting our infantrymen was armpit deep. The main roads were narrow and slippery, and often in execrable condition. Mines aside, the road conditions all but stopped our modern wheeled and tracked army. Lateral roads that might have been used to skirt or bypass tough defensive cordons were often rendered impassable by snow too deep for our vehicles to breast.

Captains Gamble, Rhea, and Rombaugh's engineer line companies employed all their bulldozers to cut fresh attack and supply routes through the heavy snow. Often, bulldozers with their makeshift armored cabs had to precede the infantry assaulting snowbound German blocking positions.

Much of what we faced was the fault of Field Marshal Montgomery, whom General Eisenhower had to place in command of the American-manned northern Bulge shoulder because the Germans had cut off most of the 1st and all of the 9th U.S. armies from General Bradley's 12th Army Group headquarters. Montgomery was a vexatious, unimaginative leader who was openly disdainful of his American subordinates. Far from bring-ing pressure to bear on the collapsing 6th Panzer Army assault, he had frittered away decisive opportunities in order to, as he called it, tidy up the haphazard result of days of unavoidably unruly defensive battles. In one of its uncountable galling as-pects, Montgomery's delay had forced the crack 30th Infantry Division to rest on its haunches for the ten inactive days leading up to the January 13 jump-off out of Malmédy and Trois-Ponts. The Germans had used that time to dig in deep and mine all the routes in front of their lines. Nature had added, literally, the icing on that cake. Within an hour of our 0600 jump-off, three tanks supporting the 120th Infantry were knocked out by mines our engineers could not detect through the snow.

The Germans on our front—comprising the 293rd Volksgren-adier Regiment—were thinly spread, but they tenaciously held the best ground and overlooked all the avenues of approach. The terrain and the snow tended to canalize our assaults across ground that had been mined to excess by the former tenants, the 1st SS Panzer Division. The mines we faced were largely invis-ible to our magnetic mine-detection equipment because, by the time we attacked, they were sheathed in ice. The weight of heavy vehicles, particularly tanks, was sufficient to set them off.

The direction of the 120th Infantry's attack forced us to take a slightly roundabout path from Malmédy to nearby Five Points. Before we could locate the massacre victims, we had to take the village of Hedomont, which was atop a defended ridge with a commanding view of the killing ground. Hedomont was stoutly defended through January 13 despite two attempts to outflank it by the 3rd Battalion, 119th Infantry Regiment. The Germans skillfully employed their *Nebelwerfer* multibarrel rocket projec-tors, artillery, and mortars to hold off the attackers. Lieutenant Wade Colbeck's platoon of Company B was operating in direct support of the attacking infantry, bolstering a similar platoon of the 105th Combat Engineers. In addition to locating and remov-ing mines and clearing paths with bulldozers, the two engineer platoons fashioned and sent forward the many two-pound TNT charges the infantrymen required to blow foxholes for them-selves and emplacements for their mortars and machine guns. Without the explosives, the infantrymen would not have been able to dig in, for the ground was utterly impervious to shovels. Our engineers also had to remove several mine-disabled tanks which were blocking routes over which fresh ammunition had to flow.

Fighting in freezing cold is extremely difficult and wearing. In addition to being burdened with cumbersome clothing and having one's fingers and limbs quickly become too numb to feel, the cold weather warrior is easily fatigued and his mind often becomes robbed of its keenness simply because the body naturally puts its best effort into burning up an enormous amount of energy in its incessant struggle to maintain its own internal temperature. Even defenders sitting in static positions are robbed of their physical strength and mental acuity by the body's need to burn its natural fuel, but the attacker, who must exert more physical power and project vastly more mental energy, is by far the greater victim. As much as anything, the 3rd Battalion, 119th Infantry's failure to overrun Hedomont swiftly was a result of the debilitating aspects of the cold. Nevertheless, in the end, at 2330 hours, the 2nd Battalion, 119th Infantry, launched a flank attack that routed the defenders. This gave us free rein over the high ground overlooking the Amblève and secure access to the site of the Malmédy massacre.

Early on the morning of January 14, Lieutenant Tom Stack's platoon of Company C carefully worked its way down from the Hedomont ridge to the field below Baugnez and Five Points. There, stepping gingerly through a layer of snow that was about eighteen inches thick, Sergeant Albert Melton's squad deployed its mine detectors and advanced into the killing field. One by one, the detectors indicated the position of the metal accouterments on the bodies of murdered GIs who had lain in that field for just under a month. As each body was located, 1st Army graves registration technicians stepped forward to begin removing the snow so they could, at first, copy the names from dogtags into a registration book.

The dead GIs were found frozen in a variety of grotesque attitudes, just as they had died. No bodies were removed yet from the positions in which they were found. A placard bearing a number was placed on each body in the order in which it was found and Signal Corps photographers took pictures as evidence for lawyers and future generations that a ghastly crime had been committed there.

As American men went about their grim duties, a squad of 30th Division military policemen marched a group of about fifty German prisoners through the adjacent Five Points crossroads. All work in the killing field ceased and a great wave of hatred rose from our ranks and reached out to the passing Germans. It is a wonder that none of our troops opened fire. When the last German had passed, the grisly work resumed. At length, after the last body had been located and after the last photograph had been taken, the graves registration technicians began lifting the bodies into trucks. Eventually, except for the eerie stillness, a passing stranger would never have known that this was a place of death.

Despite the rigorous defense and the disadvantages of the weather, the 30th Infantry Division ground slowly forward with two regiments abreast and one in reserve, battalions attacking in columns of companies because of the canalizing nature of the broken terrain. There were some good roads to be found, but they were few in number, did not necessarily run in the desired direction, and invariably ran afoul of Germans holding ridges as many as six or seven hundred feet above the narrow valley floors. It stood to reason that the roads paralleled the low-lying valley streambeds, but even as engineers we wished otherwise. Often, our thrust up one valley outflanked—or was in effect outflanked by—Germans defending the next valley over. On one memorable occasion immediately after we left Baugnez, Mike Popp and I were negotiating the ridgeline above Ligneuville in our command car when we spotted a lengthy German column, complete with horse-drawn artillery, on the river road between Bellevaux and Pont. Before I could pass along news of my discovery, American artillery forward observers in the area also spotted the Germans and called in a fire mission that obliterated the enemy soldiers and their horses. Long after the actual scene ended before my eyes, I was stunned by the ferocity of the death struggle and sickened by the carnage, even though it was meted out against the countrymen of the scum who had murdered my countrymen in the field below Five Points.

The Germans failed to blow the bridge at Ligneuville and our 117th Infantry rushed across it and siezed a three-hundred-yard corridor on the south bank of the Amblève. Behind this fortuitous screen, other elements of the 117th Infantry captured the town at 1830 hours, January 14. This victory all but ended the resistance of the 293rd Volksgrenadier Regiment and weakened the adjacent defensive sector of the German 3rd Parachute Division.

Late on January 14, also, a quick bombing and strafing raid thrown in by the Luftwaffe left three of our Company C troopers wounded on the hotly contested approaches to Born. This raised ample new fears, for the Luftwaffe had been quiescent for the entire month since the start of the Wehrmacht's Ardennes offensive. One important aspect of our bridge-building plan had been based upon our anticipation of a strong appearance of the Luftwaffe: We planned to build two vital bridges at night to obviate their being discovered and interdicted by German air. It would be difficult enough to build those and other bridges under German artillery, mortar, and rocket fire; we were afraid it might be impossible in the face of a concerted air attack.

The first of the two key bridge sites to fall into our hands was at Pont, just south of Ligneuville. Work began at literally the moment the near approaches to the bridge fell into the hands of our infantry. In fact, our Company B engineers went to work while intermingled with the first wave of attacking infantrymen. The Bailey bridge, begun on the night of January 15, was supporting the 119th Infantry's attack down the Pont-Recht road early the next morning.

Out ahead of even our forwardmost line squads and platoons, Captain Bill McKinsey and his intelligence reconnaissance teams often went into the assault with the infantry so they could instantly assess the condition of recaptured bridges that appeared to be intact. Bill and his troops were feeding a steady stream of vital information to Major Ed Lampp, who had to marshal our assets and schedule our work. Every minute we gained in getting news from the front was a minute gained in building and repairing bridges over which the infantry and armor could attack and be supported and resupplied. Minutes meant lives.

As the 119th and 117th Infantry regiments were plowing southward up and over the hills overlooking the Ambléve, the 120th Infantry had became embroiled on January 13 in what was to be a three-day battle royal to secure Thirimont, the ridge town controlling the 30th Division's left (eastern) flank. Crack troops from the German 9th Parachute Regiment, supported by plenty of artillery, had skillfully dug in before and through the town. Until Thirimont fell on January 15, our old comrades of the 120th Infantry lost 450 killed and wounded. However, their sacrifice gave the 30th Division control of a long section of the vital highway leading south toward St.-Vith.

On January 16, the 119th Infantry attacked out of Pont toward Recht across Company B's new Bailey bridge. Our troops helped the infantry regiment's vanguard clear an abatis roadblock comprised of thirty-eight trees that had been felled across the highway. On the 119th Infantry's right flank, the 117th Infantry

reached the heights of Wolfsbusch by nightfall, again with the
help of our engineers. At that point, the going became sluggish
because the Germans threw in their relatively fresh 326th Infantry Division along with the remnants of their 18th Volksgrenadier Division. However, despite the infusion of new regiments,
the 30th Division maintained pressure toward Recht and was
rewarded for its persistence on the night of January 18-19 by a
German withdrawal from the objective. The 117th Infantry's
vanguard sprang forward into abandoned Recht early in
the morning of January 19.

On the evening of January 19, Bill McKinsey radioed the
battalion CP to tell us that the bridge at Poteau was out. The
infantry had not yet captured the bridge site, Bill said, but he
could see from his vantage point with the forwardmost troops
that the span was down. This was bad news, for the Poteau
bridge, at the west end of the 30th Division zone between Vielsalm and St.-Vith, was one of the two key bridges in our zone.
Its immediate replacement was absolutely vital for the 117th
Infantry's continued progress toward the XVIII Airborne Corps
objectives. Ed Lampp called Captain Jim Gamble, of Company
A, and Jim dispatched Lieutenant Bucky Walters's platoon.

Early in the evening of January 19, I witnessed the 120th
Infantry's capture of Born and then rushed over to Poteau to see
how well Bucky's platoon was doing in support of the 117th
Infantry. Mike Popp drove through battered Recht, which was
so quiet and still that we both commented on it, but our approach
on Poteau revealed an opposite scene. The town was dead black,
but its environs were in flames. When we arrived at the bridge
site, Bucky's platoon was already at work in the near-daylight
glow of a burning barn about two hundred feet north of the
chasm into which the Germans had dropped the former bridge.
I arrived just as Sergeant Elio Rosa's squad was launching the
nose of the Bailey bridge.

I quickly found Bucky Walters and asked if his platoon had
sustained any casualties. He told me that the German artillery
fire had been heavy, but the only damage it had done was to the
barn. Level-headed Bucky had asked the infantry to relay a request for artillery counterbattery fire to keep the German guns
off his back, but he had overlooked an important matter of safety;
I suggested that he get some of his men formed up to fight the
fire, for the German artillery would have less chance of hitting
what its forward observers could not see. Paradoxical to a fault,

the Germans resumed their artillery fire after the flames had been quenched.

Sergeant Rosa and his troops were past masters at ducking incoming artillery fire, so the bridge site was virtually clear before the first rounds detonated. A cat-and-mouse game ensued in which our engineers undertook frantic building efforts between intermittent shellfire, but the Bailey bridge was declared open for business by 0200, January 20.

The fall of St.-Vith was already ordained by the time the 30th Infantry Division resumed its virtually flawless advance at first light on January 20. By then, the 7th Armored and 1st Infantry divisions, attacking out of the adjacent V Corps zone, on the 30th Division's left flank, were pressing down past Born. All of the attacking divisions in both corps zones made good progress against stiff but nonetheless failing opposition. All the advances continued steadily through January 21 as well. On January 22, the 117th Infantry followed a brief artillery barrage into Sart-les-St.-Vith and captured a large group of German soldiers before breakfast. One zone over, the 119th infantry took in quick succession Hinderhausen, Ober Emmels, and Neider Emmels.

Late on the morning of January 22, Bill McKinsey told us at least one good reason for the Germans' rather unreasonable ongoing defense of their by-then untenable St.-Vith position. The east-west roads through the central core of the Bulge were locked up with bumper-to-bumper traffic, all of it heading east, toward the German frontier. Hammered by American artillery and struck repeatedly by our 9th Air Force P-47 fighter-bombers, the roadbound Germans were being slaughtered. However, the road through St.-Vith remained vital if they were to salvage anything of the 5th Panzer Army from the inner Bulge, so they had to hold us as far back from the town as they could for as long as possible. Those of us who had helped contain the northern Bulge during our defensive struggle understood the enemy's problem and even were mildly sympathetic to their plight, but nothing was to be held back with victory so near at hand.

St.-Vith fell to the 7th Armored Division on January 23. That in itself was fitting, for the division had been ejected from the town by the 5th Panzer Army a little over a month earlier. Carried forward by the 30th Division's momentum, the 291st continued on right through St.-Vith, clearing mines and repairing roadways, until we came to rest about two miles south of the demolished city. Having weathered the demolition of Malmédy and overseen the salvation of its rubble-buried victims, I could only wonder at the number of human lives that had been extinguished beneath the rubble of St.-Vith, which had to be one of Europe's most destroyed cities.

The enemy's feverish struggle to pull his depleted divisions back into Germany without the St.-Vith crossroads cost him countless dead. In addition, our divisions had captured an average of a thousand prisoners of war per day since we jumped off on January 13.

On January 27, as we were in the midst of strengthening the 30th Division's local road net, we were ordered to secure and provide close support for a pending operation to be undertaken by the 82nd Airborne Division. We turned all our job sites over to the 105th Combat Engineers and immediately bid yet another fond adieu to our comrades of the 30th Infantry Division.

CHAPTER 22

The objective of the 82nd Airborne Division at the end of January 1945 was achieving a breakthrough of the Siegfried Line at Losheim, the same place the Germans had broken through in the opposite direction at the start of their Ardennes Offensive. For the new attack, Colonel H. Wallis Anderson's entire 1111th Engineer Combat Group was attached to the XVIII Airborne Corps, so the 291st was transferred from the 1186th Group back to Colonel Anderson's direct command.

At 0600 hours, January 29, Major General James Gavin's 82nd Airborne Division jumped off through the 7th Armored Division into the Losheim Gap. Occupying an initial front line between Born and Amblève, the 82nd Airborne attacked northeast across the high ground overlooking Wereth with the 325th Glider Infantry Regiment on the left, the 504th Parachute Infantry on the right, and the 505th and 508th Parachute Infantry regiments in reserve. Attacking beside the 82nd, on the left, was the crack 1st Infantry Division.

The men of the 291st Engineer Combat Battalion did not follow the lead companies of the 82nd Airborne into the Losheim Gap as we had followed the lead companies of the 30th Infantry Division toward St.-Vith. No, mostly we *led* the paratroopers through the hip- and thigh-deep ice and snow, scraping paths through trackless minefields with our armored bulldozers so the lightly armed and largely unsupported paratroopers and glider infantrymen could move at all. From the outset, we faced a howling blizzard and minus-degree temperatures through a dense forest that lacked all but rudimentary footpaths. The problems and hardships we faced were surmountable, but only by battle-hardened troops with stout hearts and iron determination. Fortunately, the 291st had those in abundance.

201

Particularly noteworthy were the heroic efforts of Technician 5th Grade Herbert Helgerson, a Company B bulldozer operator, near Wereth on January 29. Helgerson distinguished himself as he was clearing heavily drifted snow from a supply road directly along the front lines. Often working ahead of the infantry, he was once pinned down by a German machine gun and was almost constantly exposed to mortar and artillery fire called by German forward observers who seemed to have him under observation throughout his mission. Despite the unnerving proximity of the fire, Helgerson nevertheless got the road cleared so the infantry could receive vital support from the rear.

Another noteworthy performance was turned in by Corporal Edward Woertz, who became so wrapped up in his work that he worked eighteen hours or more at a time for four consecutive days. In fact, Woertz kept working at one point even though German machine-gun fire was hitting the body of his bulldozer.

Not surprisingly, some of the most stout-hearted men were those who had already proven themselves in close combat with the enemy. One such, who constantly drove his armored bulldozer directly into the face of enemy emplacements, was Technician 4th Grade John Noland, whose exemplary leadership had done much to save the day against the Skorzeny brigade at Malmédy. Eventually, though, John was seriously injured by a flurry of German rifle fire as he cut a trail for the troops of the 325th Glider Infantry in front of an active German defensive position. Also working far above and beyond his expected performance, Lieutenant Wade Colbeck took miserable, life-threatening turns in the cabs of the armored bulldozers when his platoon's cold-dazed operators needed respite or relief.

In addition to the bulldozers and road graders we directly committed to supporting the infantry, we had as many as ten bulldozers and five road graders in constant operation behind the lines, laboriously opening or cutting supply and evacuation trails. The Germans had mined every possible route through the forest, but our mine-sweeping teams seemed to have found every mile along the routes we opened and used.

Despite the formidable natural obstacles and hardships, the 504th Parachute Infantry advanced seven thousand yards on January 28, capturing Herresback after killing 65 and capturing 201 Germans without sustaining any losses. The 325th Glider Infantry faced stiffer opposition in its zone and suffered losses accordingly. However, it also wound up the day far ahead of its line of departure.

The 82nd Airborne Division's attack continued on a northeasterly heading on January 29, but abominable weather conditions—a fullscale blizzard—restricted the 325th and 504th regiments to gains averaging two thousand yards. A subsidiary attack by the 505th Parachute Infantry southeastward on the high ground toward Honsfeld eked out only fifteen hundred yards. The 291st thus found itself still within the same area of Belgium in which we had operated prior to the German offensive, which had begun about six weeks earlier.

On January 30, the 325th Glider Infantry jumped off to the northeast at 0500 hours. By 1500 hours, elements of the regiment had reached Bucholtz, abreast the Honsfeld-Losheim railway line. By nightfall, patrols of glider infantrymen were reporting back from the German side of the frontier. On that day, also, the newly committed 508th Parachute Infantry captured Lanzerath and the damaged highway bridge over the railway line. American troops were thus in possession of Kampfgruppe Peiper's original jumping-off position, a significant gain. On January 31, a day of consolidation in the 82nd Division's zone, the 505th Parachute Infantry bullied its way forward to Losheim-Ergraben against moderate resistance.

As Technician 5th Grade Mike Popp and I toured the frontier area visiting my operating platoons, we noted how many German vehicles and horse-drawn artillery units had been knocked out by our tactical air. Also, many of the villages had suffered extensive damage at the hands of our fighter-bomber pilots, and there was no evidence of German civilians in the region. Apparently, a decree from Hitler that the civilians defend the Fatherland unto death was being rigorously ignored.

Captain Bill McKinsey reported that the Lanzerath bridge, which the 82nd Airborne was counting on to get its mobile artillery and armor forward, was impassable. Based on Bill's frontline survey, we prepared to build a 180-foot Bailey span across an 80-foot-deep railroad cut through the Lanzerath ridge. The location of the new bridge would be precisely on the Belgian-German border, our first construction assignment in the Nazi homeland. The job was a typical rush. General Gavin's division headquarters wanted to bolster the 508th Parachute Infantry's positions on the high ground between Losheim and Manderfeld with the self-propelled guns of the 629th Tank Destroyer Battalion. As it was, the 508th had already repulsed one German counterattack with its light infantry weapons and, though Bill McKinsey reported seeing German infantry in re-

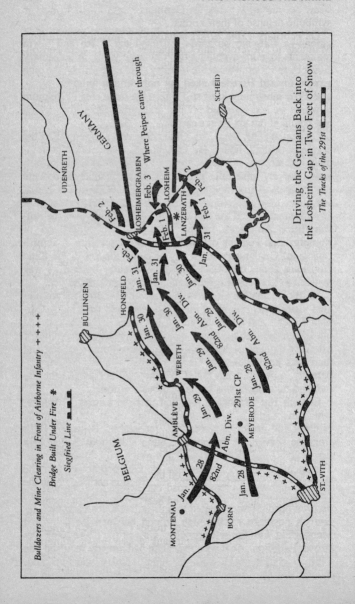

Bulldozers and Mine Clearing in Front of Airborne Infantry + + + +

Bridge Built Under Fire ✳

Siegfried Line ∎∎∎∎

Driving the Germans Back into
the Losheim Gap in Two Feet of Snow

The Tracks of the 291st ∎∎∎∎∎

GERMANY

BELGIUM

UDENRETH

SCHEID

Where Peiper came through

LOSHEIMERGRABEN   Feb. 3

LOSHEIM

LANZERATH

Feb. 2

Feb. 1

Feb. 1

Feb. 1 Feb. 2

Jan. 31

Jan. 31

Jan. 31

Jan. 30

Jan. 30

Jan. 30

Jan. 29

Jan. 29

Jan. 29

82nd Abn. Div.

Jan. 29

82nd Abn. Div.

Aqu Div.

82nd

Jan. 28

Jan. 28

Jan. 28

BÜLLINGEN

HONSFELD

WERETH

291st CP

MEYERODE

AMBLÈVE

MONTENAU

BORN

ST. VITH

treat, no one knew what the Germans might throw in next in symbolic defense of their border.

On February 1, the 291st's battalion CP moved forward from Malmédy to Meyerode and Companies A and C were consolidated to build the Lanzerath bridge. Before advancing to the bridge site, however, our mine-sweeping teams had to probe forward and clear all the approaches. As expected, the Germans had mined all the shoulder areas with antitank and antipersonnel devices and, as expected also, had wired in numerous booby traps whose only purpose was to kill or maim engineers clearing the mines. As usual, we suffered no losses, but working in the snow and ice made matters extremely ticklish.

Major Ed Lampp's plan was to begin work on the bridge at 0030 hours, February 2. Long experience had imbued Ed with the belief that a bridge as critically important as this one would be under observation by German artillery forward observers, so his typical response was to do as much work as possible under cover of darkness. Beginning at sunset, the two engineer companies and all their equipment moved into holding areas within a mile of the bridge site. For the next six hours, all the troops worked feverishly to prepare for the massive, miserable job ahead. Then, at 0030 hours, right on schedule, Captain Warren Rombaugh's Company C advanced to the bridge site en masse to begin the first continuous twelve-hour shift. Because it was so cold, Warren could work his platoons for only four hours apiece, which we had learned is about as long as human beings could endure the superhuman task of wrestling the unbelievably frigid five-hundred-pound steel bridge panels into place.

The night was foggy and sleet fell steadily upon all the men whose duties prevented them from seeking even rudimentary cover. Progress was dampened a bit by the sleet because it obliged all the workers to pull their woolen watch caps down across their ears and faces. Sporadic artillery fire added considerably to the delaying action of the weather but fortunately resulted in no casualties. One of the greatest dangers lay in the potential for slipping or sliding off the glazed steel bridge panels into the eighty-foot-deep railroad cut. Again, no one was injured, though there were repeated heartstoppers throughout the ordeal. All this was done with the knowledge that the lightly armed and relatively unsupported troops of the 508th Parachute Infantry were waiting for their tank destroyers in vulnerable infantry fighting positions about a mile in front of the bridge.

Mike Popp wrestled our command car to the bridge site at

about 0300 hours, February 2, in the immediate wake of one of uncountable numbers of artillery barrages. As I watched the miserably cold battle-hardened Company C troopers wrestle the five-by-ten-foot panels of the double-triple Bailey bridge across an eighty-foot-deep chasm in the midst of a vertical ice storm, I became convinced that these were men who would finish anything, literally anything, that anyone could conceivably dream up to be accomplished by combat engineers.

The bridge, which would be two panels thick and three panels high with a single-span treadway floor required the placement of 216 five-hundred-pound panels. When completed, with one end in Belgium and the other end in Germany, the 180-foot span would be able to support a forty-ton load moving at six miles per hour.

We opened the bridge to traffic at 1700 hours, February 3, forty and a half hours after work began. We did so following an around-the-clock effort by two complete engineer combat companies and without suffering a single casualty or injury despite the incessant German artillery fire and incredibly dangerous working conditions. Our first customers were all the self-propelled tank destroyers of the 629th Tank Destroyer Battalion. And the payoff, soon to arrive, was a coordinated attack, amply supported by way of the Lanzerath bridge, in which the 325th Glider Infantry and 504th Parachute Infantry regiments quickly and decisively cracked the Siegfried Line between Neuhof and Udenreth, just north of the Losheim Gap.

As soon as possible, the 291st followed the 82nd Airborne through the dragon's teeth and formidable array of bunkers and pillboxes comprising the Siegfried Line. Behind us lay the long-sought breach in the enemy frontier and ahead of us lay victory, but not without privation and struggle, hope and glory as we had never seen them before.

CHAPTER 23

On February 7, 1945, Colonel Anderson contacted me with orders to move the entire 291st Engineer Combat Battalion to a new jumping-off point in the Hürtgen forest. The news was unwelcome and immediately became the cause of deep-seated anxiety among those of us who had followed the largely unsuccessful pre-Bulge efforts by up to 120,000 Americans to secure this vital, densely wooded, frontier region. Unfortunately for the many Americans who had tried and failed and the many more of us who would try again, the capture of the Hürtgen forest was absolutely essential to the contemplated broad-front Allied attack across the Cologne plain to the Rhine River, the last important natural barrier keeping us from Germany's western heartland. The essential features within the forest region were two massive hydroelectric dams, the Urftallsperre and the Schwammenauel, that controlled the water level of the north-flowing Roer River. If the Allies could not capture the dams intact, the Germans could flood the Roer valley and deny us the broad-front access to the Rhine that appeared essential to our strategic concept.

The previous fighting in the Hürtgen had been about the grimmest of the war in Western Europe. Not only had the Germans made a special effort to plant mines and booby traps—they knew how important the region was to us—they took special pleasure in firing their artillery into the densely packed treetops in order to create exceptionally deadly sprays of shrapnel and wood splinters against which infantrymen advancing in the open could in no way defend themselves. Together with many extremely complex, extensive, continuous, interlocking, and hardened defensive sectors on the ground, these features had resulted in over nine thousand casualties prior to the Bulge.

We were doubly annoyed with the news of our commitment to the renewed Hürtgen drive because we felt we had narrowly evaded a December commitment due to the onset of the German Ardennes Offensive. I had already traveled through the American-held Hürtgen region in the days immediately prior to the German offensive to review the manner in which the 291st was to be employed in the effort to capture the Roer dams. I had frankly hoped in the weeks after the Bulge that the higher headquarters responsible for reducing the Hürtgen defenses had forgotten about the 291st's prospective commitment. As it turned out, my wishes came to nothing.

To get set for the new Hürtgen drive, the entire battalion caravaned from Meyerode to Walheim, a German town east of the Siegfried Line in the vicinity of Schmidt. We remained attached to the 1111th Engineer Group, but we now came under the control of Major General John Millikin's III Corps, which was in the center of the 1st U.S. Army zone, directly facing the Hürtgen forest. On our left was the VII Corps and on our right was the V Corps. Unless the III Corps was able to secure the Roer dams intact, the 9th U.S. Army, adjacent to the 1st Army in the north, could not attack into the Roer valley for fear of being flooded out by the Germans, who after all could see the shape of our strategy. If the 9th U.S. Army could not advance, neither could Field Marshal Montgomery's entire 21st Army Group, to which it had been attached. And, if the 21st Army Group could not advance, neither could the four Allied armies arrayed in the center and the south—the 1st and 3rd U.S. armies in the 12th Army Group zone and the 7th U.S. and 1st French armies in the 6th Army Group zone. When all was said and done, then, an Allied advance to the strategic Rhine barrier came down to III Corps' hoped-for success in the Hürtgen forest.

The corps-wide preparations for the assault on the Roer dams gave us some time to clean up and take care of overdue housekeeping chores—and to settle down after our harrowing weeks in the forefront of the assault into Germany. The billets we took over for the troops were only fair, but they were warm and snug compared to the places in which we had been hunkering down for weeks. Everyone had an opportunity to heed my command to shave daily, and showers were set up to handle everyone's needs. Only marginally less important than the care and feeding of the troops was the opportunity the break afforded us to maintain, refurbish, and replace our sorely abused equipment.

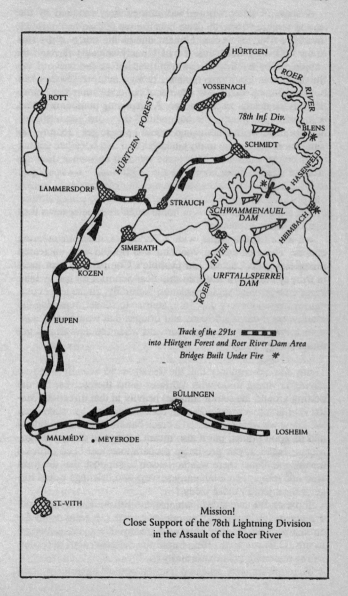

ROTT

HÜRTGEN

HÜRTGEN FOREST

VOSSENACH

ROER RIVER

78th Inf. Div.

BLENS

SCHMIDT

LAMMERSDORF

STRAUCH

SCHWAMMENAUEL DAM

HASENFELD

SIMERATH

ROER RIVER

HEIMBACH

KOZEN

URFTALLSPERRE DAM

EUPEN

Track of the 291st
into Hürtgen Forest and Roer River Dam Area
Bridges Built Under Fire ✳

BÜLLINGEN

MALMÉDY • MEYERODE

LOSHEIM

ST.-VITH

Mission!
Close Support of the 78th Lightning Division
in the Assault of the Roer River

A spate of letter writing was immediately requited by the arrival of a ton of mail that had been following us around through the battle zone for weeks. This included hundreds of responses to the 650 Christmas cards the battalion headquarters staff had mailed to the families of our men just before the onset of the Bulge. It was gratifying reading, though some responses had been mailed by relatives of several of our dead comrades before news of the deaths reached home. A surprising number of letters and cards addressed to me complained that sons and husbands had not been writing home and would I please get "Johnny" to write more often. The many packages that had been late getting to us before Christmas brightened our respite with a dizzying array of goodies from home. As the "Old Man," I was obliged to sample more sweets than any human being should have. Given our fears regarding the battalion's next battle, the caring attitude of our relatives and friends at home came as sweeter news than I can possibly express.

We kept up our skills with a variety of local engineering chores. The area around Walheim was riddled with uncleared minefields, and Captain Jim Gamble's Company A kept itself in trim by building a small airstrip near Schmidt for use by light Piper Cub artillery spotting planes. Naturally, all the letter companies were out every day, from sunrise to sunset, repairing the muddy, shell-damaged roads and bridges that would carry supplies forward and casualties rearward when the new assault got underway.

There was no certainty that the 291st would actually wind up having anything to do with the Roer dams themselves, but the betting around the senior staff ran heavily in that direction. Major Ed Lampp was extremely forceful in such prognostications. We knew we were considered a crack battalion. Being so judged had its good points, but it also meant facing the dirtiest assignments. Besides, our pre-Bulge preparations had been directed toward the dams; there was no reason to suppose that the folks who had remembered our early surveys and briefings would forget the subject of those plans.

To be on the safe side, I had Captain Bill McKinsey send out a recon team on February 9 to look over the dams from the closest possible vantage point and to assess the overall situation in the III Corps zone. Bill briefed the battalion staff and company commanders late that evening.

The 78th Infantry Division had jumped off against the dams

on February 5 following its series of unsuccessful attacks against Schmidt. (The mission of capturing Schmidt had been turned over to Major General James Gavin's 82nd Airborne Division on February 2 and Gavin had proceeded toward the city by a new route—directly down the main highway through Lammersdorf rather than overland through the often-used and stoutly defended steep-sided Kall Gorge.) Also on February 5, the 9th Armored Division's Combat Command R (for Reserve) went in south of the 78th Division, in the vicinity of Wahlerscheid, in the Monschau forest, a region of the Hürtgen. It came as considerable relief to learn that the second-largest of the Roer dams, the Urftallsperre, had fallen intact to the 9th Armored on the first day of its assault. As Bill McKinsey gleefully pointed out, "That's one dam we won't have to rebuild!"

The main assault, that by the 78th Infantry Division, met light opposition on February 5 and 6 but nonetheless proceeded at a cautious pace. On February 7, the division commander decided to put all three of his infantry regiments into an effort to leap forward to the unsecured Schwammenauel Dam. A company of the division's organic engineer battalion, the 303rd, was placed at the front with each of the attacking infantry regiments. In the ensuing action, the engineers alone destroyed or directly helped destroy over two hundred concrete pillboxes in the defended sector between Lammersdorf and the Roer.

Bill McKinsey saved the best news for last. The 9th Armored Division had been sent to the aid of the 78th Infantry Division on February 9, permitting the 78th Division to redirect its 309th Infantry Regiment cross-country against the Schwammenauel Dam. By day's end, only hours before Bill conducted his briefing, the vital dam had fallen into the hands of the 309th Infantry. Better than that, the dam was intact. And, best of all, the fall of the dam had allowed the 9th Infantry Division's 60th Infantry Regiment to spring forward right into Schmidt. All of the III Corps objectives had been taken and the entire SHAEF assault to the Rhine could commence—without the 291st's having been committed to the bloody fighting in the Hürtgen forest.

Early on the morning of February 10, Colonel Anderson called the battalion CP and asked me to get over to Group immediately with Major Ed Lampp. There, Major Harry Webb, the group operations officer, briefed Ed and me on Operation GRENADE, the projected assault across the Roer River.

First Webb told us that although the Germans had not destroyed the dams they had accomplished several acts of mischief. In particular, they had destroyed the powerful dam machinery and discharge valves on the Schwammenauel and had diverted the water from behind the Urftallsperre to behind the Schwammenauel. The effect was not, as feared, an unstoppable torrent of water, but we were faced with stopping a relentless flow that, unchecked, would flood the Roer valley for about two weeks. If that happened, the 9th U.S. Army's drive toward the Rhine would be seriously delayed and that would have a ripple effect across the entire SHAEF front. According to Webb, it looked as though the assault would be delayed for about two weeks.

In addition to wrecking the machinery, the Germans had blown part of the spillway, leaving a big gap on top of the dam. The eighty-foot gap prevented the 78th Infantry Division from getting any armored support across the dam to the thin infantry screen defending the bridgehead on the east bank of the Roer.

Major Webb next directed our attention to his situation map. He told us that when Operation GRENADE commenced, we were to directly support the 78th Infantry Division by building a bridge across the gap in Schwammenauel Dam and thus assure the free flow of armored vehicles and supplies toward the east. As Webb spoke, Ed Lampp caught my eye and smiled as if to say, "I told you so!" Indeed he had, many times over the past few days.

After telling us that the effort undoubtedly would be made under direct German fire, Webb ended the briefing with a rather too chipper, "You guys got the contract."

Before returning to my CP to mount out the battalion, I was taken aside by Colonel Anderson. He told me that the 291st had been selected for the job by senior 1st Army officers because of the sterling regard in which we were held.

Ed and I returned to the CP and called a meeting of senior staff and line officers to discuss the new and challenging mission. Bill McKinsey immediately dispatched patrols to survey the entire 78th Division rear and report back about any damaged or destroyed bridges and stretches of roadway that needed to be swept for mines or repaired. By then, the early thaw had left many long stretches of vital roadway in utter disrepair following the passage of our army's steel-cleated tracked vehicles. As soon as Bill left to dispatch the patrols, Captain Max Schmidt got on the phone to Group to line up our fair share of the available engineering supplies.

* * *

The overall plan for Operation GRENADE was to start the assault at the northern end of the battlefield by building bridges in the zone of the northernmost assault divisions—in the zone of the 9th U.S. Army's XIX Corps. Once a bridgehead had been established east of the river, succeeding divisions would cross the same bridges and hook south through the preceding units.

Thanks to the slow flooding by way of the Schwammenauel Dam, the Roer had swollen from thirty yards to over a hundred yards in the zone of the XIX Corps. This caused an incalculable delay while engineers tried to figure out if they should try to bridge the wider-than-anticipated river or wait for the water to recede, in which case they would face a wide muddy bog across the entire flood plain. It was decided to wait.

While the battalion CP moved from Walheim to Rotgen, due west of Schmidt, the letter companies of the 291st used the delay to clear mines and restore the road net in our zone. We also dug in the heavy field pieces of the 78th Division's general support artillery battalion.

On February 18, Group called to say that it had just received a dispatch from III Corps that had apparently passed through the headquarters of the 1st Army, the 12th Army Group, and SHAEF on its way from the White House. President Roosevelt had signed the Presidential Unit Citation for which the 291st had been recommended for its wide-ranging service during the Bulge. Colonel Anderson asked me to drop by Group headquarters to add my endorsement to a section of signatures that included Roosevelt, Eisenhower, Bradley, and Hodges. Every man in the battalion—and those who had been wounded and evacuated during and since the actions in which we had earned this honor—was given a copy of the citation and authorized to wear the ribbon. However, we had no time to undertake a formal ceremony, for we were too busy preparing for our next great adventure.

On February 19, a damaged B-24 heavy bomber came down in a smallish field south of Rotgen. Those of us at the CP heard the plane go in so I jumped into my command car with Technician 5th Grade Mike Popp and rushed to see what was going on. The makeshift landing field, part of an extensive minefield, was the zone of Lieutenant Don Davis's platoon of Company C. By the time I arrived, the crew of the heavy bomber was climbing out of the airplane amidst shouted pleas from Don and his men that they stay put until a safe path through the mines had been cleared with the aid of mine detectors. The entire fresh-faced bomber crew—they all looked to be about eighteen years old—disregarded the instructions and trudged across the muddy field toward us. When they got to the road, we pointed to the many signs that warned of the presence of mines in the field, but those cocky boys laughed and boasted, "If we can crash-land a heavy bomber in a small field like this, there's no minefield that can do us in." With those foolish flyboys looking on, Davis's men immediately went to work plucking mines from exactly the route they had followed from the bomber. When the airmen saw the mines, they became so agitated that they refused to return to the bomber to collect their personal effects.

By February 22, the flood waters in the Roer valley had receded sufficiently for Operation GRENADE to commence the next day, February 23. As planned, the assault began in the north, toward Jülich, in the zone of the 9th U.S. Army's southernmost XIX Corps. German air and artillery knocked out the assault bridges in the zone of the 102nd Infantry Division, but engineers employing a massive smoke screen in the adjacent 29th Infantry Division zone breached the river. By day's end, tanks were advancing into Jülich. In the next zone south, elements of the 30th Infantry Division conducted an assault river crossing in boats, but no bridges were completed in its zone and, thus, no armor could be sent to support the bridgehead.

In the northern 1st Army sector, the VII Corps got no bridges across the Roer on February 23, but, next day, engineers built a Bailey bridge on the piers of the blown main highway bridge into Düren. This was the only bridge built to support the VII Corps assault that day. A treadway pontoon bridge that was to be thrown across the river on February 24 was delayed by a fierce defensive effort on the part of the 12th Volksgrenadier Division. This bridge was eventually completed, but the Germans continued to harass the units crossing there.

By February 28, parts of six divisions on the XIX and VII corps zones were across the Roer, advancing into the Cologne plain toward the Rhine. During the morning, our battalion liaison officer, Captain Lloyd Sheetz, called from the 78th Infantry Division CP to tell us that all three regiments of the 78th were safely across the river and preparing to attack across the Cologne plain next day, March 1, alongside the 9th Armored Division.

Among other jobs, the 291st was to support the III Corps attack by building a Bailey bridge at Blens.

As soon as we got the news from Lloyd Sheetz, Ed Lampp sent Bill McKinsey to Blens to survey the bridge site. Toward evening on the 28th, Bill returned—overdue—from the last-minute reconnaissance with an uncharacteristic haunted expression on his face. As the story developed, Bill's recon team had approached the blown Blens bridge so it could confirm the measurement of the length of the Bailey bridges we were to throw the next day. Germans on the east bank of the Roer had apparently spotted Bill and his team and had put a great deal of effort into keeping them pinned. The scouts had spent the entire day crouched behind an abutment and had escaped only after the onset of darkness.

Major Lampp assigned the Blens bridge to Captain Frank Rhea's Company B. In turn, Frank assigned the Blens job to Lieutenant John Kirkpatrick's platoon.

Frank moved the Company B CP into a building near the bridge site at about noon, March 1, so he could oversee the staging of the bridging equipment. Almost as soon as Frank arrived, however, the Germans opened with a vicious artillery barrage. The shelling was still going on when Kirkpatrick's platoon moved into the open to launch the bridge nose out over the turbulent Roer.

The Blens bridge was to be a 130-foot triple-single span. We had built dozens of such bridges across France and Belgium, but the layout at Blens presented us with several unique challenges. Chief among our headaches was the fact that the far-shore abutment sloped downhill, thus causing the launching nose to be high above the ground. This was solved by holding the bridge in alignment and level by means of a stout cable affixed to a bulldozer winch while the structure was being shoved across rollers set on the near shore.

The initial artillery barrage abated, but the German guns opened with renewed fury at around 2300 hours. One of the heavy-caliber rounds struck the bridge itself and the resulting spray of shrapnel wounded five engineers. Though German rounds continued to fall all around the bridge site, Lieutenant Kirkpatrick stayed out on the span with the wounded men and helped the medics administer aid and dress wounds. Then, through more artillery detonations, John helped carry the wounded men to safety. As soon as the shelling abated, John calmly reorganized the platoon and led his engineers back out onto the span. Sporadic artillery fire ensued, but Kirkpatrick's platoon completed the job at 0310 hours, March 2—a record-setting performance of fifteen hours and ten minutes.

As soon as the bridge was completed, tanks and assault guns already lined up behind cover in the town pushed across to join up with the 78th Division's waiting infantry components. Before long, military policemen were herding German captives back across the Blens bridge.

While Company B was wrestling with the tricky, dangerous Blens bridge, Captain Jim Gamble's Company A was preparing to undertake different but equally challenging headaches at Heimbach. The objective, placed in the hands of Lieutenant Bucky Walters's and Lieutenant Arch Taylor's platoons, was the construction of a 110-foot triple-single Bailey span to replace a destroyed stone arch bridge that had been built on a curve.

Working against established procedure, Jim Gamble wanted to get the bridge started in full daylight because of the severe difficulty his platoons would face as they attempted to install a straight bridge on a curve. Thus, construction work began at 1430 hours, March 2. Because the existing part of the bridge was too narrow to set base plates, Lieutenants Taylor and Walters had their men emplace transoms to extend the width of the existing structure.

When I arrived to survey progress, the bridge was creeping out slowly above the river despite some very inaccurate shelling. After the troops added each new ten-foot section, the entire structure was angled slightly on the baseplate rollers, the only solution available for building a forty-ton assault bridge at such a tough location. The work was not only strenuous, it was hazardous. Perfect timing was required to prevent the entire structure from tumbling forty feet into the river.

The commander of the 78th Division's 303rd Engineer Combat Battalion, Lieutenant Colonel John Cosner, arrived shortly after me. He had just come from having his first look at the Blens bridge, and he was effusive in his praise. After Cosner had had a good look at what Company A was doing there, at Heimbach, he described feelings of awe. As we continued to watch, the 310th Infantry Regiment, which was screening the bridge site, sent back about fifty German prisoners—a real tonic for the engineers, whose backs were breaking from the grueling effort. They got the job done by 0900 hours, March 3—in eighteen and a half hours.

As soon as I returned to Rotgen on the morning of March 3 to check in at the battalion CP, I was given a message that Colonel Anderson wanted me to return his call. I dutifully complied, but the colonel was not in. Major Webb, the 1111th Group operations officer, told me that the colonel wanted to know how the bridge-building was shaping up. I told him that the Blens bridge was in and the Heimbach bridge had been completed an hour earlier. Next up was the Schwammenauel Dam bridge, which Captain Warren Rombaugh's Company C was slated to begin in a matter of hours. I told Webb that we had heard through 78th Division sources that the infantry had advanced far beyond the dam bridgehead and that they did not expect much artillery fire to be directed against Company C. Before ringing off, Webb told me that the colonel wanted to meet with me at the site of the dam bridge within the hour.

I immediately left the battalion CP and drove over to pick up Lieutenant Colonel Cosner at the 303rd Engineer Combat Battalion CP. We had agreed earlier to visit all three bridge sites and to discuss plans for supporting the 78th Division's drive across the Cologne plain. Cosner had infomation that all of the 78th Division's three infantry regiments were advancing rapidly in company with the 9th Armored Division against weakening opposition. According to Cosner, the 9th Armored Division's Combat Command B and the 78th Infantry Divison's 310th Infantry were already about fifteen miles east of the Roer. As we drove, we ruminated about breaching the next great barrier, the mighty Rhine. We were both certain that the Germans would blow every span across the mighty river from the Swiss frontier to the North Sea and that they would commit every available soldier, gun, and airplane to keeping all the Allied armies from crossing.

Everything was in order at Heimbach and Blens. Maintenance teams were working over both bridges and my engineers were out policing up the last of the mines. Speed-limit signs had already been posted on both bridges, which were in heavy use.

We arrived at the Schwammenauel Dam at 1330, March 3, and found Lieutenant Don Davis's and Lieutenant Tom Stack's platoons of Captain Warren Rombaugh's Company C having a ball. The vistas to the east and west were utterly breathtaking, with rich pine forests stretching into the haze of the Roer valley

and snow-capped hills marching beyond sight. We heard the
rumble of artillery, but it was far east of the dam, far beyond
range.

The open breach where the Germans had demolished the
spillway was seventy-five feet wide. It must have taken several
tons of explosives to do the job. Work had begun at 1245 hours,
right after lunch, and it was expected to be completed before
dinner, say around 1830 hours. The bridge was an eighty-foot
double-single Bailey span and the job was an absolutely straightforward affair in which Company C sustained only one casualty,
a sprained back.

The line platoons were about two thirds through the job when
Colonel Anderson finally arrived. I knew things were going well
as soon as I saw the twinkle in the Old Man's eyes. As he stood
with Cosner and me watching the completion of the very last
act in the long and bloody battle of the Hürtgen forest, the colonel reminded us that the ordeal had begun with an assault by
the 28th Infantry Division, the Pennsylvania National Guard
unit with which he had fought in World War I and whose engineer regiment he had commanded when the division was activated before America's commitment to World War II. Maybe
because I was a fellow Pennsylvanian, the colonel waxed nos-
talgic about the many scores of Pennsylvania infantrymen and
engineers who had died on their way to this dam.

That evening, when he got back to his quarters, Colonel Anderson wrote in his nightly letter to his wife: "I didn't sleep
well last night. Pergrin was involved in building three bridges
across a river where the danger was extremely in evidence from
all the hazards of war. When I didn't hear from him this morning, I went to the sites and saw three masterpieces of engineering skill and courageous leadership. I will sleep well tonight."

PART FIVE

FIRST ACROSS
THE RHINE

CHAPTER 24

As soon as the Schwammenauel Dam bridge was in, we moved up to Rheinbach to support the III Corps drive to the Rhine. Along the way, we helped knock down several roadblocks, cleared mines, and built three bridges—a Bailey span at Vlatten and a treadway and a Bailey at Euskirchen, which had been blown flat by our bombers. As we worked, 12th Army Group headquarters handed out assignments for the final big push to the Rhine. In the 1st Army zone, the VII Corps remained in the north, moving toward Cologne while the V Corps, in the south, pushed toward the river while maintaining firm contact with Patton's 3rd Army. The III Corps, to which the 1111th Engineer Group was still attached, remained in the 1st Army center with objectives along the Rhine from Remagen to Bonn.

On the evening of March 7, 1945, I arrived back at the battalion CP following a full, energy-sapping day watching the two bridges go in at Euskirchen. I was weary and hungry when my assistant adjutant, Lieutenant John Brenna, met me and anxiously reported that he had been hearing rumors that there was an intact bridge across the Rhine in the zone of the 9th Armored Division. John had no definitive word as to whether the bridge was already in our hands or if the 9th Armored Division was still trying to take it. I decided to pass up dinner in favor of getting more definitive information, so I ran straight to the schoolhouse in which the battalion operations center had been set up.

At my excited urging, Major Ed Lampp and Captain Bill McKinsey spread out our maps of the 9th Armored Division zone and we began poring over them in hopes of somehow divining where the bridge was. It took us no time at all. The only bridge we could locate in the 9th Armored Division's path

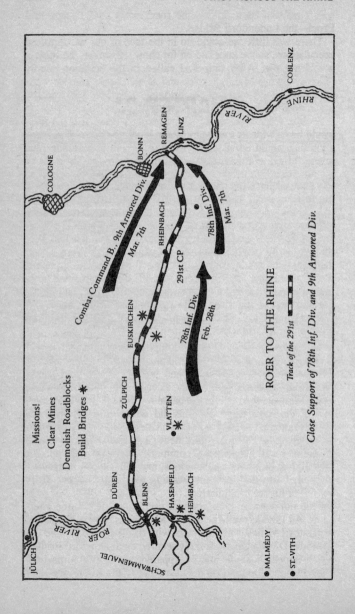

Missions!
Clear Mines
Demolish Roadblocks
Build Bridges ✳

ROER TO THE RHINE

Track of the 291st ▰▰▰▰▰

Close Support of 78th Inf. Div. and 9th Armored Div.

was a railroad span linking the river towns of Remagen and Erpel—the Ludendorff Bridge.

There was little we could do in the face of our unsupported speculations, so we knocked off for chow. However, the subject would not die. After dinner, I called in the battalion supply officer, Captain Max Schmidt, and asked him to tote up what we would need in the way of bridging materials if indeed the Ludendorff Bridge needed to be restored or replaced.

A close inspection of our Rhine maps revealed that the river would be as wide as twelve to fifteen hundred feet at Remagen, a job that would entail deployment of the entire battalion plus several bridge companies. This realization brought on a lot of good-natured wishes that the Remagen bridge had or would indeed fall into the hands of the 9th Armored Division intact and undamaged. If so, we would cross the Rhine with the 78th Infantry Division on dry soles. No one at headquarters that night said anything about *wanting* to bridge the wide, deep, swiftly flowing Rhine. Of one thing we could be certain, however. As Ed Lampp put it just before we turned in, "If there's a hot job, we'll get it."

Rumors and more rumors; March 8 was spent in a state of constant anxiety. I received orders at sunup to disperse the entire battalion throughout the Euskirchen area in order to cut through and maintain an access for the 78th Infantry Division's final drive on the Rhine. We were doing a dozen different jobs—clearing mines, building and maintaining bridges, knocking down abandoned roadblocks, and pushing rubble and debris back from roadways. I kept busy, as usual, jumping from worksite to worksite throughout the battalion zone. The wide dispersion of the squads and platoons did not seem to dampen the effective grapevine telegraph to which all the troops seemed to be attached; news of the imminent capture of a bridge across the Rhine raced ahead of my command car and was the subject of unending inquiries, speculations, and suggestions wherever I stopped. I was tied in knots, waiting for definitive news from my CP or higher headquarters.

I did not learn anything new or useful until late in the afternoon. As I made my way back to Rheinbach, one of the squad worksites I visited was all abuzz with the latest word: The 9th Armored Division had definitely secured the Ludendorff Bridge, which appeared to be intact. Apparently, the III Corps possessed a solid foothold on the east bank of the Rhine, the only one anywhere along the entire SHAEF front. I headed straight back to my CP.

When I arrived at the battalion operations center at 1730 hours, the expected message awaited me; I was to report to 1111th Group headquarters immediately. I leaped straight back into my command car and told Mike Popp our destination. "Don't stop for anything."

All the way there, though my heart was racing, I struggled to keep my mind in neutral. But I knew it, I knew we were as good as on our way to Remagen. The speedy half hour drive to Bad Neuenahr was interminable. As Mike pulled up in front of the 1111th Group CP, I jumped out of the not-quite-stopped command car and made straight for the door of the operations center.

In one of the war's uncountable ironies, the Ludendorff railroad bridge was about the last Rhine span SHAEF headquarters considered for achieving the first foothold on the east bank of the Rhine since Napoleon had crossed the river nearly a century and a half before. This was completely understandable to me, given the bridge's location and the surrounding topography.

The double-track Ludendorff railroad bridge spanned the mighty Rhine between Erpel, on the east bank, and Remagen, to the west. Recently, the Germans had decked over one of the tracks to allow retreating vehicles and footborne troops to get across. On the east bank, immediately after crossing the bridge, the double set of tracks disappeared into a tunnel beneath the six-hundred-foot Erpler Ley, a craggy hill, ideally suited for defense, that dominated the bridge site and the western approaches. Over the past weeks, the bridge had been routinely attacked by U.S. Army Air Force bombers and fighter-bombers. The span certainly had been weakened by such attacks—it was regularly reported as having dropped into the Rhine—but the Germans always seemed to reopen the railroad right of way. Apparently, throughout February, the traffic on the bridge had been mainly hospital trains. Lately, however, aerial reconnaissance had indicated major use by troops and vehicles retreating across the Cologne plain from the Roer.

Like us, the Germans had not given much consideration to a major push in the vicinity of the Ludendorff Bridge, so they had failed to fully exploit the terrain advantages offered by the commanding Erpler Ley. Moreover, frequent changes at higher levels of command—brought on by the Germans' rather panicked reaction to our many Roer crossings—had left the local defense commander operating pretty much on his own authority. The latest such change occurred shortly after midnight, March 7. During the wee hours, with the 9th Armored Division's leading battalions closing on the Rhine, the new corps commander sent a representative to Remagen to find out what was going on there and to oversee the destruction of the bridge if necessary. That officer arrived at about noon on March 7, just as Company A of the 9th Armored Division's 27th Armored Infantry Battalion was probing toward the heights on the west side of the river.

The German corps representative attempted to beef up the locally conscripted defense force by impressing retreating Wehrmacht stragglers into a makeshift infantry company. However, as quickly as he commandeered troops, they melted away. By the time the officer ordered the local defense company to the east bank, it had already been overrun in Remagen by the American armored infantrymen.

As the little battle raged on the west bank, the German engineer officer charged with blowing the bridge tested the firing circuits for charges that had been set out days before. Everything seemed to be working; all he still needed to blow the bridge was a firm order from someone in authority.

As fighting in the streets of Remagen continued, German observers atop the Erpler Ley sent word that American tanks were closing on the river from west of neighboring Remagen. The senior engineer wanted to blow the bridge, but the senior corps representative wanted to wait until an artillery battalion had completed its crossing.

The engineer and four assistants were on the west bank of the river when the Americans approached the bridge in earnest. The Germans had earlier planted a delaying charge designed to damage the western approach without damaging the bridge itself. When the leading Americans came into sight, the German engineers touched off the delaying charge and rushed back across the bridge to the tunnel, in which the detonator for the main charge had been set up. The delaying charge gouged a thirty-foot crater across the western approach to the bridge, obviating the use of tanks or other vehicles in the final rush to seize the span.

American artillery opened fire on Erpel and the Erpler Ley as the marooned American tanks fired white-phosphorous rounds to lay smoke and thus obscure the approach on the bridge itself by the dismounted armored infantrymen. Sensing the imminent end of the meager struggle, the German senior observer gave the expected order: Blow the bridge. It was 1720 hours, March 7.

At the western end of the railroad tunnel, which was packed with local defense conscripts and civilians, the senior engineer turned the firing key in his hands. Nothing happened.

Something had gone wrong. Undoubtedly, the split command chain and the confusion of battle had resulted in someone not having done his job. The engineer officer wound the firing key once again—and again, and again. Nothing. The wires had not been connected properly.

There was one remaining opportunity. An emergency charge had been laid, but it needed to be ignited by primer fuse. Someone would have to leave the safety of the tunnel to light the fuse. The engineer officer asked for volunteers. One man stepped forward, a sergeant. He was given hurried but detailed instructions, then he ran into the open to light the fuse. Moments later, a large explosion appeared to lift the center of the railroad span into the air. The Germans were convinced that the Ludendorff Bridge had fallen into the Rhine.

The smoke cleared, revealing the incredible fact that the span had settled back down onto its foundations. The bridge was intact, and there was no other means at hand for destroying it.

The leading platoon of Company A, 27th Armored Infantry Battalion, cautiously stepped out onto the span. With them were an officer and several troopers from the 9th Armored Engineer Combat Battalion who were on hand to clear any explosives they could find. The armored infantrymen probed their way across the bridge while the armored engineers located wires to the undetonated charges and cut them. To be on the safe side, all the German explosives were recovered and dumped straight into the river.

Over the next twenty-four hours, eight thousand American soldiers crossed the Ludendorff Bridge on foot, in trucks and jeeps, and aboard tanks. By the time I reached the 1111th Group CP on the evening of March 8, the 9th Armored Division was in possession of a battered but intact bridge and a reasonably secure bridgehead on the east bank of the Rhine, Germany's last formidable defensive barrier in the west.

I could feel the tension before I even entered the group operations center. Colonel Anderson was deep in thought alongside a map that evidently had just been tacked to the wall. When he became aware of my entrance, he took off his helmet and said, "Hi, Dave. We've got a little job for you."

The group executive officer was sitting in a chair and Major Webb, the operations officer, was standing alongside the Old Man. Webb, a dark-haired little guy, spoke up in his surprisingly deep voice, "Dave, your battalion has been selected to throw a treadway bridge across the Rhine as near the north side of the Ludendorff Bridge as possible. There's not much more I can tell you except that it's all hurry-up stuff, so you'll have to play it by ear. We received the contract from Colonel Carter this afternoon. You know, with your experience, you really don't have to be told how to do it, just that it's got to be done and done fast. You'll have help from the 998th Treadway Bridge Company and one other treadway company as soon as we've contacted it. They'll supply the equipment and anything else you need. Okay, Dave?" I nodded. "The 291st has the contract."

Major Webb then went on to provide a maddeningly sketchy outline of the seizure of the bridge, our side's defensive measures, and the plan for exploiting the windfall. If he asked if I had any questions, I didn't hear him.

As the colonel walked me to the door, he looked at me with his twinkling eyes and said, "Good luck, Dave. You and your men have the most important and dangerous bridge assignment in the history of the Corps of Engineers. We know you can do the job because the 291st has proved itself many times over."

"Thanks, sir," I mumbled. "Count on us."

The meeting had ended alomost before I knew it had begun. Still somewhat dazed, I made my way straight to the group communications center and asked the sergeant operating the radio to contact my battalion CP. As my rising euphoria became entangled with my understandable anxiety, I heard Lieutenant John Brenna's voice on the line. "John, we've got the contract. We're to put a treadway across the Rhine as near the railway bridge as possible, to the north, downstream. That's as much as you need to know until I get back, but get the company commanders on deck immediately and get the staff working on the plan. We don't have a lot of time to lose, and I want things developed as quickly as possible. One treadway company has been ordered up to get there with us and another will be on its way. Okay? Now get started. I'll see you in less than a half hour."

I had to talk to someone, so I shared my excitement with Mike

Popp as we barreled down the road to Rheinbach. When I ran out of words, Mike looked at me, his face hidden behind a huge grin. "God, Colonel, this is big, ain't it? I hope we don't run out of gas!" Any other time, I would have laughed, but my mind was racing; I was too preoccupied. I did not yet know many of the details of the capture of the bridge nor how many troops and tanks were guarding its eastern approaches. My engineers had built many spans under fire, but none as vital as this next one. I was worried that the Germans would throw the proverbial "everything they had" into efforts to take back what had been theirs.

My entry into the battalion operations center was met with stony silence. I could plainly see the strain on the faces of my staff officers and company commanders as they stopped talking and looked up at me in unison. I briskly strode through the gathering, turned, and faced them.

"You're about to face an awesome-looking scene for several days at Remagen, Germany. We all know that the Krauts failed to blow the Ludendorff Bridge across the Rhine. The 9th Armored has a toe-hold on the east bank and the 78th Infantry Division has been ordered to expand it to a bridgehead, hopefully as far as the north-south autobahn, which is about ten miles east of Remagen. We've got to get an M-2 treadway across, fast. Colonel Lyons [the III Corps chief engineer] believes the Ludendorff Bridge will collapse soon and that the Germans will bring up reinforcements to wipe out our guys already on the east side of the river. The brass is sure that Hitler's going to go nuts and do everything possible to break up this situation, so you can expect all hell to break loose. I hope—no, I pray—that we come out of this in good shape. We're in a tough position."

I had to pause to collect myself. Until then, every dire prediction regarding losses we might face in combat had been wrong, even during the darkest days of the Bulge. We had been a spectacularly charmed combat engineer battalion, given our area of expertise. But we had never before been the central characters in a play with strategic implications; we had never before been committed to the ultimate bull's-eye.

Crowding such thoughts from my mind, I turned to Ed Lampp. "Ed, I expect you have finished the primary overall plan for the battalion mission?" Ed nodded. "Will you review it, please?"

We had never been a unit long on show, but Ed replied with a crisp, "Yes, sir" and took his place at my side. "It is 8 March, 2130 hours, and the company missions are as follows: Captain

Gamble's Company A is to construct and assemble treadway rafts. Captain Rhea's Company B is also to construct and assemble the same. Captain Rombaugh's Company C is to prepare approaches, guylines, and cables. The 998th Treadway Company and another treadway company will operate some of the machinery and also keep equipment flowing to the site as we extend the bridging."

Ed paused to cast a by-then-familiar "I-told-you-so" glance in my direction. Naturally, he had been operating ahead of events. "Bill McKinsey was in Remagen this morning, looking over the situation as to where we can put our bridge. He can tell you more about that. How about it, Bill?"

With that, Bill stood to join Ed and me in front of the group. Motioning to the map board, Bill began, "You might look at this map again. I've marked the places that I think we might use. I put the number 'one' on the best location. It's about two hundred yards downstream from the standing bridge and is being used now as a ferry site. I hope we can move the ferries, but there are other places if we can't.

"The river flows north at about seven miles an hour, which might give us some problems. It's also kind of deep, so make sure you practice your swimming strokes, just in case. The length of the bridge, by the way, will be about eleven hundred feet at that spot. I can't remember hearing about any treadways being built that were that long; maybe one of you knows for sure."

Bill ended by telling us that Colonel Anderson had arrived at the primary bridge site at the same time he, McKinsey, had been looking it over. As soon the colonel's jeep appeared, mortar and machine-gun fire from the east bank hills overlooking the river had driven it and our recon team to cover behind buildings fronting the waterway. There had been no casualties, but Bill nevertheless warned us all that the job at hand would be no picnic. With that, he turned the conference back to Ed, who closed with an admonishment that time was short and the traditional, "Any questions?"

Max Schmidt's hand shot up. "Where do we get one-inch guy cable?" the supply officer asked. "I know we'll need it and I'm sure we don't have any."

"That'll be your job, Max," Ed answered, "and you'll have to get anything else we need any way you can. I don't want to leave anything to chance. Follow up with Rombaugh on all the kedge anchors, bridle cables, and fastenings we'll need to anchor the bridge against the current.''

Frank Rhea was next. ''What about the Krauts, Colonel?'' Typically, our West Pointer had his mind on the tactical situation. ''From what you're saying, we'll be the target of every gun on the east side.''

Frank's was a critical question, for the performance of the entire battalion depended upon how well we were able to protect ourselves if the Germans counterattacked. ''Set up your own machine guns and we'll request artillery support from the 9th and 78th divisions. We'll also ask Group to request antiaircraft guns to be set up around our sites. Anything the big bridge gets, we'll get the same. Expect plenty of bombing and strafing.''

Frankly, the enormity of our mission had not given me the freedom of mind to realize that we were naturally going to get whatever we asked for, no matter what. SHAEF itself would see to that, and all the subordinate headquarters would follow suit.

John Brenna asked if I wanted to move the battalion CP to Remagen. I thought that over for an instant and told him to set up a minimum forward CP near the bridge site but to keep the larger rear CP where it was, in Rheinbach, until further notice. I wanted to expose the smallest possible number of people to German retaliation.

Sensing that the questioning had about run its course, Jim Gamble approached me and half turned to face the others before announcing in a determined voice, ''Colonel, Company A is ready for this big bash and you can count on us!'' Immediately, similar sentiments were loudly expressed by everyone else in the room. I thanked them all for their enthusiasm and ended the meeting by telling them that we would start work in the morning and suggesting that they all get as much sleep as possible because, ''God alone knows when we'll be getting any rest again.''

The room emptied in a flurry of excitement and I found myself alone. My mind was abuzz instantly with details I had forgotten to bring up, but it was too late to reconvene the meeting. I felt myself becoming emotional, so I began thinking of my wife, Peggy, who would certainly have words to calm me down. I went out to the hallway and shouted for a cup of coffee, which appeared miraculously before I sank into my chair and lit a cigarette. As I sat with my head against the wall behind my desk, I cleared the war from my mind with memories of my brief married life and by conjuring up the many more married years I hoped would start soon, as quickly as we could feel the effects of our greatest contribution to closing out the war.

CHAPTER 25

The tension of knowing what lay ahead robbed me of my sleep that night, so I decided to head up to Remagen early to see what the bridge site looked like. I called out Mike Popp and we set out sometime after midnight, March 9. I was sure it was going to be an easy fifteen-mile drive, but it turned out that the Ludendorff Bridge was at the small end of a huge funnel that was pouring thousands of troops and just about as many vehicles across the Rhine. The road net was on the brink of collapse and the best driving Mike had in him got us no nearer than five miles. When we became totally bogged down in unmoving traffic, I told Mike to turn around and head back to the 1111th Group CP so I could at least check on the status of all the bridging materials we had ordered.

There was more news about the early engineering headaches at the railroad bridge. Apparently, on March 7, it had taken the lead elements of the 9th Armored Engineers several hours to clear and mark a path for the first tanks to get across. There were many holes in the bridge decking as a result of the abortive demolitions attempt and it was necessary for the first available company of tanks to negotiate a tortuous path marked by white engineer tape. This was accomplished in the dark, in the wee hours of March 8. Later, one of the several tank destroyers sent to bolster the east-bank toehold went astray and became wedged in one of the many large holes. That stopped the flow of vehicular traffic until about 0530 hours, March 8, when it was finally dislodged. Shortly thereafter, an infantry battalion of the 78th Infantry Division crossed on foot and began in earnest the job of expanding the bridgehead.

After daylight, as the initially sluggish German reaction to the seizure of the bridge developed into incessant and increasing artillery fire, a platoon of the 9th Armored Division's military police company moved out onto the bridge and its approaches to try to create some order from the chaotic influx of hurriedly redirected troops and vehicles that were being shoved, willy-nilly, across the groaning span. The MPs sustained heavy casualties as they worked to unsnarl the immense traffic jam and prevent the damaged structure from becoming overloaded. The 9th Armored Engineers also braved the fire as they filled in the thirty-foot crater on the western approach, cleared debris and disabled vehicles from the roadway, and surveyed and began patching the structural damage.

I also learned, to my relief, that the 998th Treadway Bridge Company was well on its way, with all its equipment, to Remagen and that there was at least a nascent effort underway to restore order along the roads leading there. Major Webb also had news that the 988th Treadway Bridge Company had been notified of its assignment to Remagen and that it was preparing to follow the 988th. I had had no news from Major Larry Moyer, my exec, who was with the first convoy of the 291st to set out for Remagen. Major Webb told me that he had spoken with Larry by radio and that the convoy was making fitful progress.

The best news Webb had to offer, as far as I was concerned, was that the group supply officer had located a cache of the one-inch steel cable that was absolutely essential to the successful completion of our new treadway pontoon bridge. Better still, the first shipment was on its way toward Remagen and was expected to arrive well before we would need it.

I was wound up and Webb was wound up. By the time he told me about the cable, we were both pretty much bouncing off the walls. He urged me to get some coffee, food, and above all, rest. I thought of inviting Mike Popp in to share the meal, but I found him fast asleep in the front seat of the command car, I ate sparingly, drank a calming cup of hot coffee, and tried to sleep on an empty cot. My mind would not shut down, so I finally got to my feet, went outside, and roused Mike. It was only about 0300 hours, but I felt it was time to make another try for Remagen.

If anything, traffic was worse than it had been at midnight. Mike's skillful driving was of no avail and we finally gave in and simply followed the truck in front of us through endlessly merging traffic along the narrow roads leading to Remagen. It took us ninety minutes to travel less than ten miles.

When we reached the outskirts of Remagen, I had Mike follow newly installed signs to the CP of Lieutenant Colonel John Cosner's 303rd Combat Engineers, the 78th Division unit we had supported in the Roer drive and crossing. Cosner, whose unit was slated to oversee mine clearance on the east bank and the new light ferry line, updated me a bit on the condition of the Ludendorff's roadway, adding news that Brigadier General William Hoge, of the 9th Armored Division's Combat Command B, had permitted engineers to dismantle wooden buildings in Remagen to provide planking to deck over both sets of rails and all the holes in the bridge roadway. Hoge, a trained engineer whose Combat Command B had captured the Ludendorff Bridge, was a former commandant of the Engineer School at Fort Belvoir. Cosner also told me that our intelligence had placed two panzer divisions on their way to counterattack our bridgehead.

Everything I had heard since the previous afternoon convinced me of the vital—strategic—importance of getting in our treadway pontoon bridge as quickly as possible. There was no telling when the Ludendorff Bridge might collapse. General Hoge, Colonel Anderson, Colonel Bill Carter, and Colonel F. H. "Rusty" Lyons (the III Corps engineer) had all examined the Ludendorff in the face of extreme personal risk, and all agreed that its life was very short.

As Cosner continued to fill me in, a section of the leading 291st convoy pulled in to ask directions. This immediately and profoundly raised my spirits, for everything of substance and rumor I had heard and seen until then had been essentially negative. Now, finally, I had some tools with which I could personally enter the fight to maintain our Rhine bridgehead.

Bidding good luck to Cosner, who himself had a big job to accomplish, I swung out with Mike Popp to lead the first of the 291st line engineers down to our own worksite. As we entered Remagen, the flow of traffic all but stopped. We proceeded at less than a crawl while, out ahead, thundering salvos of German artillery fire detonated among the buildings of the town and, I feared, on the wobbly Ludendorff span itself. Adding to my renewed sense of gloom was an unstoppable quaking inspired by my recollections of my near death in the Christmas Eve bombing that had destroyed the core of Malmédy. I forced my mind to focus on the distinctive sounds of outgoing artillery from our own batteries set up around Remagen. I also noted the occasional antiaircraft gun in the column or set up alongside the main road we were following. If there was an air attack—by their bombers or ours—Remagen at least would have some means to beat it off.

Finally, just after the rainy, dismal new day dawned, we reached the turnoff to the new bridge site. Mike led the tiny column around the many shell craters in the roadway until he had to stop in front of a grinning Captain Bill McKinsey and several of his reconnaissance scouts. "Hi, Colonel," Bill nodded in his enthusiastic manner, "Glad you could make it, sir. We're all set up and waiting for you to give us the word."

I felt my own characteristic grin spread to match Bill's. The relief was about complete as Mike pulled over and Bill gave me a rundown on what was going on.

The 86th Engineer Heavy Pontoon Battalion was already on the site with five pontoon boat reinforced rafts it had been employing as ferries to help get vehicles and men across the river. As Bill had briefed us earlier, the road net leading to the ferry site was about the best to be had on the north side of the Ludendorff Bridge, though it would need some widening, clearing, and improving. According to information provided by the local combat forces, the bridgehead on the east bank opposite the ferry site was shallow and did not extend very much farther to the north than the east-bank ferry site. The Germans controlled many of the riverfront buildings on the east bank and all of the heights that dominated the eleven-hundred-foot-wide river.

The engineering news was mixed. According to Bill, who had surveyed both sides of the river, there was cobblestone revetted in the banks on both sides, sloping about forty-five degrees to a height of just under twelve feet. We would have to get the cobbles out before we could begin building, and that would take a mighty effort by our bulldozers, which would have to cut the slope to the twenty degrees Bill thought would be adequate for tracked and wheeled vehicles alike. On the positive side, there was no end of materials for resurfacing the banks and roadways—endless rubble, more than enough gravel, and the cobbles we needed to remove.

I congratulated Bill on a job extremely well done. Since our first days ashore at Normandy, this young man had earned the equivalent of an advanced degree in engineering, and I told him so then and there. But it was all my responsibility, and I had the actual degree, so I left him to scout the area on my own.

I was first of all gratified to see how much had already been done by the 86th Pontoon Battalion. Working on their own behalf to get the ferry running, they had actually begun our work

for us. As I surveyed the west-bank ferry site, the first of my
own Company B bulldozers arrived to begin leveling the approach to conform to our own needs. Of equal importance,
Captain Gene Hancock's 998th Treadway Bridge Company
rolled in and got straight to work. I exchanged salutes and greet-
ings with Captain Hancock and gave him leave to pitch right
into work with his eager engineers. The general opinion
throughout the 1111th Group was that the 998th was the best unit
of its kind in the 1st Army.

Much to my surprise, as I gazed across the awesomely wide
and swift Rhine, I chanced to see a bulldozer with flails clearing
mines and working on the east-bank approach. I asked Captain
Warren Rombaugh whose engineers they were and he proudly
explained that Lieutenant Don Davis and Sergeant Bill Miller
had purloined a ferry and had taken their platoon across at 0400
hours. The first unit of the 291st to cross the river had been
working constantly under fire since then.

We took our first casualties at Remagen at 0830 hours, March 9,
right at the start of the job. Machine-gun mortar fire from the
buildings directly across the river—it was so accurate that I believed it was directed by a hidden observer on our side—began
falling among the troops at the bridge site. I happened to be in
the open with Bill McKinsey at the moment of the sudden onset,
but Bill and I managed to jump back to safety. I immediately
ordered Bill to get us some covering fire from our own machine
guns and then to go see if he couldn't rustle up an infantry
platoon to search the nearby buildings to locate the observer.
(No observer was found. Years later one of the German artillery
commanders told me that he knew of no such observer on the
west bank, that the accuracy was derived from the perfect view
from atop the Erpler Ley.)

Bill disappeared and, moments later, several of our machine
guns began spraying the far shore. The Germans had not used
tracers—the better to conceal their positions—but their firing
seemed to die off as ours picked up, so I imagine our guns hit
or hit close to theirs.

When the German gunfire had ceased completely, I peered
out from around my cover. Already, I saw, several of our medics
were loping into view. I joined them in the open as they worked
over eight wounded engineers from Sergeant Lee White's squad
of Lieutenant Wade Colbeck's Company B platoon. Four of the
seven needed to be evacuated for care by a doctor, but Sergeant

White and the two others went back to work after having their minor wounds dressed. It was a sobering first encounter with a foe more determined than ever we had found him.

As we were helping the wounded, word reached me that virtually all of Company B had arrived, as had leading elements of both Company A and Company C. I confirmed an earlier directive that all the companies set up billets on the lower floors of buildings along the river promenade near their worksites. That brought to mind my own need to find a building to house our battalion forward CP. I wanted to be close to the bridging operation, in a good, solid structure able to withstand bombs and shells. I finally found exactly what I wanted directly across from the bridge site, on the right hand side of a narrow street leading down to the river. Already in operation directly across the street was the battalion forward aid station. The new command post was a concrete canopy that looked like a garage with the doors off. I threw my bedroll inside to lay claim and returned immediately to the riverfront.

I had used the interval of escape to think through the implications of the direct fire we had faced and the casualties we had sustained right at the outset of our new mission. It would be tough enough to build the eleven-hundred-foot treadway pontoon bridge in a swift current without all the fighting going on around us. Despite all I had seen of the war since June, I frankly had no idea how we were going to succeed in the face of such deadly accurate machine-gun and mortar fire, not to mention artillery and air attacks once the Germans figured out what we were doing. The bridge was too urgently needed to cut our progress in half by working only during the dark hours; we needed to work in the open in broad daylight also if we were to have any chance of getting our bridge completed before the expected collapse of the adjacent Ludendorff span.

I looked up at the Erpler Ley and felt the icy grip of the central matter of our plight: We were sitting ducks!

I realized with a start that I had to pull myself together. There was no doubt that the troops were looking to me to exhibit the confidence they themselves needed at that critical moment. I consciously pulled myself as erect as I could and strode with a bearing of confidence straight down to the bridge site to offer words and signs of encouragement. Not for the first time, the troops inspired me when I meant to inspire them. They appeared almost defiant in their attitude as they consciously ignored the dangers of German shellfire while breaking their backs to accomplish the great physical labor of the enterprise. Here I found only veterans, the men who had stopped Peiper and Skorzeny in what history since has labeled the most important delaying action of the war in Europe.

The German fire started anew just after 0900 hours, this time against the assembly sites behind the riverfront, where two of my letter companies were prefabricating the pontoons (also called bays or floats) for the bridge. Fortunately, this fire appeared to be fallout from the main artillery effort against the Ludendorff. We suffered no losses and, indeed, these battle-hardened young men hardly flinched.

The German fire never quite abated. At 1030, shortly after we started floating the pontoons out into the river, it was still falling, though inaccurately. However, shortly thereafter, the first Luftwaffe fighters and light bombers to appear over Remagen swooped in to bomb and strafe both bridges. No sooner had the warplanes receeded than the Germans' guns on and behind the Erpler Ley placed several smoke shells right on our assembly site. This, as everyone knew, meant big trouble directly ahead. Immediately, we were subjected to a rising crescendo of artillery detonations. Work had to be abandoned as all hands ran and dived for the nearest cover.

During the first brief lull, I stood up with many others to survey the damage. The little section of the bridge we had completed had been struck dead on. Five pontoons had been knocked out, and so had an air-compressor truck and a Quickway crane. One of the assembly sites was on fire and, worst of all, more of my men were down, one from Company A and three from Company B. None were dead, but I found myself strangling on my grief.

Was the 291st losing its charmed existence? I wondered, I truly wondered.

During the days of the battalion's trips to England, my wife, Peggy, had gone to see the Carmelite nuns in the sanctuary near her home. The daughter of extremely religious Polish immigrants, Peggy had every bit as much faith in the powers of prayer. She had asked the nuns to remember me and the men of the 291st in their perpetual prayers, and every letter from Peggy carried reassurance that the prayers were continuing. Peg's faith was infectious, particularly as I faced the terror of combat and the crushing responsibility of command. By the time I arrived in Remagen, ample evidence had convinced me of the efficacy of the prayers offered up by the Carmelite sisters, I did not know what sort of a future we all faced as the focal point of German attention, but I knew in my soul that the power of my faith would somehow minimize the far worse fate we might face, that no matter how bad it became, the prayers of our loved ones and the Carmelite sisters would prevent it from becoming as bad as it might otherwise have been. If I was to go on, I had no choice but to believe.

I stood on the bank beside towering Captain Max Schmidt and asked my supply officer the obvious question, "Max, where are we going to get all the treadway stuff we'll need for this job?"

Not quite shrugging, Max looked down at me and replied, "Colonel, I don't know. We're going to need eighty or ninety bays to span the river and, if the Krauts continue to knock out this many, God knows how many more we're really going to need. I'll check with Group—tell them what's happening and see if they can keep replacements coming."

I told Max to do just that and to ask Group to contact Colonel Bill Carter, the 1st Army chief engineer, so he could get into the act with whatever he could conjure up. I doubted if there were enough available pontoons in Germany to do the job.

I needn't have worried. By then, the vital port of Antwerp was open and supplies were flowing to the SHAEF army groups over much shorter lines than had previously been the case. Unknown to Colonel Carter or his counterpart in the 3rd Army headquarters, both were vying for limited bridging materials by means of nearly identical subterfuges. Both colonels had agents at a vital regulating station through which the majority of the supply trains from Antwerp passed on their way to the front. The 3rd Army chief engineer's agent apparently was getting to the trains first and changing markings on the 1st Army equipment to get it on its way to the 3rd Army. However, Colonel Carter's agent had the last chance, and he changed the markings on *all* the trains bearing bridging materials. Thus, though lowly battalion commanders did not know it, there were enough pontoons in the 1st Army zone to build about eight floating treadway bridges at Remagen. All we needed to do to tap into the supply was ask.

Without knowing what was going on behind the scenes, Max and I decided to prepare for the worst, to overorder by a factor of at least two—more if we could get it. Charged up with a new vitality of purpose, Max hurried to find a phone so he could place his order with the 1111th Group supply officer.

Both sides were struggling mightily to build up their arrays of defensive and offensive weapons. German artillery of every size was on its way to battery sites beyond our east-bank bridge-head—even including a 540mm railway mortar weighing 130 tons and capable of firing a frightful forty-four-hundred-pound shell. Atop the Erpler Ley, within easy range of our bridge, German antiaircraft units were laying in more and more of their unbelievably accurate 88mm guns—not so much to knock down our fighters and bombers as to blow us engineers out of the water. Our side was matching the Germans gun for gun, at least. A battery of our own 90mm antiaircraft guns had already weath-ered the tricky Ludendorff crossing, and the rest of the antiair-craft battalion was scheduled to follow. Lighter antiarcraft units manning many halftrack-mounted quadruple .50-caliber ma-chine guns or stationary automatic 37mm antiaircraft cannon were already in position in the town, on the Ludendorff Bridge, and across the high ground on both sides of the river. In addi-tion, many 105mm and 155mm field pieces, including the entire 78th Infantry Division artillery group, were being dug in behind Remagen and neighboring river towns.

The canny Germans persisted in throwing in single-plane bombing and strafing attacks, not only at the bridges but against traffic on the congested roads leading to the Ludendorff. Every time their fighters or light bombers succeeded in closing the roads, the flow of troops to the east bank and guns to both banks was further delayed while the Wehrmacht struggled to achieve fire superiority. Of course, our air force was doing the same against the Germans, with about the same result—chaos.

All the confusion on both sides was compounded by the fact that neither side had remotely contemplated this confrontation within scores of miles of Remagen. This meant that both sides had to redraw their respective strategies completely and redirect any and all available units, many of which were already in mo-tion toward distant places. The result was a pair of messes that, for the moment, appeared to be canceling one another out.

If that was the case, it had little practical effect on our efforts to throw the new bridge across the Rhine. Working through what remained of the gloomy, rainy morning, the 291st and attached engineering units faced a fresh German artillery salvo about every two minutes. First, there was the fall of smoke shells to mark the target—us—and then there was the salvo by a battery or two of German field pieces. Often, but not often enough, the German fire was answered in kind by our supporting artillery. At infrequent intervals, the German guns engaged in counter-battery exchanges with our guns, but, mainly they kept their attention riveted on the two bridges. We tried laying smoke from generators to obscure our efforts, but all we succeeded in doing was pinpointing ourselves for the German artillery forward observers.

Throughout, the odd German plane streaked in to strafe the bridge or our assembly sites. Many of the troops had braved artillery fire going all the way back to the Tucker Bridge in Carentan. They were respectful of the consequences but generally at ease while working in it. After all, we had suffered few casualties in the face of German artillery. But we were virtually without experience in the face of German air. We all knew the stories of the vaunted Luftwaffe early in the war, but we had never seen it with our own eyes until March 9, 1945. Whereas there is something impersonal about artillery fire—something a fateful attitude could weather—there is something in being strafed that is stunningly personal, for the pilot's eyes and reflexes control the fall of bullets against visible targets. While the fall of artillery shells can be divined by the practiced ear and thus ignored in most cases, the approach of a German warplane, heralded by the eruption of antiaircraft fire, never failed to get the desired result—everyone scattered for cover. The only positive aspect of the experience was seeing several German planes trailing smoke as they streaked from sight or, far better, crashed in flames.

CHAPTER 26

The M-2 steel treadway bridge gave the U.S. Army a rapid means of getting tanks and other heavy vehicles across a river or stream. It could be built of floating spans, fixed spans, or a combination of both.

The roadway of the M-2 bridge consisted of continuous tracks of steel treadways formed of twelve-foot lengths connected rigidly at each joint by two pins. The treadways were supported on pneumatic pontoons spaced twelve feet apart, center to center. The pontoons, also called floats or bays, had steel saddles mounted and fastened on top. Shore connections were made by resting the end of the treadways on abutment sills on the banks or by using one or more spans. The type of shore connection usually depended on how close to the banks the shoreward pontoons could be placed, the slope of the banks, and how much weight the banks could support. The capacity of the M-2 steel treadway bridge was forty tons or less, depending on length and use. A bridge capable of supporting forty tons was known as a Class 40 bridge, as indicated on signs placed at either end.

The average time it took to construct a given treadway bridge depended upon the length, number of floats, and whether the work was done in daylight or blackout conditions. For example, a 216-foot bridge on eighteen floats would take two hours in daylight or three hours in blackout. A 362-foot treadway on thirty-two floats could be emplaced on five daylight hours or seven and a half blackout hours. Of course, all this depended on whether or not you were looking down the throat of a German 540mm railway mortar or other assorted terror weapons.

In somewhat more ideal conditions than we faced at Remagen, a single combat engineer company bolstered by the personnel of a treadway bridge company unit could easily construct a midsize bridge without help. One "unit" of steel treadway equipage, with which a treadway company was outfitted, provided up to 864 feet of bridging. One treadway unit included everything from canvas bags to the big rubber floats, 2,469 items in 45 separate categories.

Treadway bridge companies maintained a variety of vehicles for use in transportation as well as construction. There were the standard six-by-six trucks, Brockway air-compressor trucks, dump trucks, Quickway crane trucks, and the standard treadway crane trucks specifically designed to function with the M-2 bridge.

The eighteen-ton capacity pneumatic float was eight feet three inches wide, thirty-three feet long, and thirty-three inches deep. It was made of rubberized canvas tubing and had an outer tube, a floor, and a removable center tube. Each tube was thirty-three inches in diameter and weighed 975 pounds. The ends of the float were turned up to lessen the effect of the currents pushing against it. Deflated, a tube could be compacted into a bundle only four feet by three feet by nine inches.

The steel saddle placed atop the float was a plate of six interior sections with two end bearing sections, each with two steel beams over the plates. Secured by means of various devices, the entire saddle distributed the weight of the load-bearing function. Completed, the saddle weighed 2,200 pounds.

The steel treadway was the roadway of the M-2 bridge. It consisted of parallel treadways with grid flooring. One treadway section weighing 2,350 pounds had two parallel steel channel beams tied together laterally by I beams, channels, and pipe sleeves. At one end, the main channels were blunt; at the other end, tapered engaging plates with hook ends provided an interlocking connection with the adjacent treadway. The blunt end had two pipe sleeves running through holes in the treadway channels while the hook ends had one hole and a notch in the engaging plates. Two connecting pins joined the blunt end of one treadway rigidly to the hook end of the next treadway to form a continuous beam. Connection was made by inserting one connecting pin through the inner pipe sleeve on the blunt end of one treadway and the notches in the hook end of the next treadway. The second pin was inserted through the pipe sleeve at the blunt end and the holes in the adjoining hook end. The treadways were placed across the saddles on the floats so they could be engaged by retainers in the saddle beams.

Treadway connecting pins were used to join the treadways

longitudinally. The pins were two and seven eighths inches in diameter, four feet six and a half inches long, and weighed sixty-five pounds. There was a handle at the blunt end and a hole in the tapered end in which to insert a safety pin.

Kedge anchors weighing a hundred pounds were used to secure the bridge against the currents and wind. These were simply dropped over the edge of the bridge and allowed to secure themselves on the bottom of the stream.

A power utility boat was also part of the treadway company's equipment. It was used for general utility functions and to push the assembled bays from the assembly site to the nose of the bridge. Built on a molded, seamless plywood hull, the boat weighed eighteen hundred pounds and had a fifty-seven-horsepower marine engine. It was capable of carrying about four thousand pounds.

The job of placing and connecting the treadways, once the west bank had been prepared, went to Captain Jim Gamble's Company A. Jim assigned First Sergeant Bill Smith to place himself on the lead pontoon float to supervise the connection of the succeeding floats by means of the steel connecting pins. Lieutenant Al Edelstein's 2nd Platoon was assigned this most difficult task, as the powerboats brought the completed floats out to the uncompleted end of the bridge. Al's three squads—commanded by Sergeants Joe Geary, Black Mac McDonald, and Robert Billington—were to have alternated this back-breaking job, but ongoing casualties and the rough conditions made it difficult to maintain strict formal assignments. Beginning almost at the outset of the job, Edelstein's men, under the supervision of the platoon sergeant, Staff Sergeant Edwin Pigg, filled in on an as-needed basis without respect to squad designations. As things would turn out, this one platoon assembled the entire bridge, from bank to bank. By the end of the first few hours, also, the completed end of the lengthening bridge was referred to by all hands as Suicide Point.

Suicide Point was aptly named. As the nose of the bridge eased out toward the east bank, German forward observers were presented with a better, more distinct target. As the morning's work progressed, the fall of German shells came closer and closer to the exposed bridge nose, forcing the engineers out there to crouch more frequently in the saddles between the treadways.

The nose of the bridge was only 150 feet into the stream when a German shell found the bull's-eye. While engineers on the river-bank were hurt, the troops on the nose were unscathed, but they were also helpless to prevent five pontoons from sinking and thus dragging down much of the morning's efforts. By the time I arrived at a spot from which I could see the damage, First Sergeant Smith and the men of Sergeant Joe Geary's squad were on their feet, staring in apparent disbelief at the destruction. I heard no words from the two troop leaders, but I saw what amounted to a collective shrug as everyone started back to work. Their attitude seemed to render the overcoming of disasters a routine job for the war weary. As indeed it was.

That's when I sent Max Schmidt to ask the 1111th Group supply officer to try to double our allotment of pontoons and tread-way sections. There was no telling how many we would expend in the course of this treacherous mission.

Supporting the troops on Suicide Point were a total of five line platoons—the remaining two from Captain Jim Gamble's Company A, under Lieutenants Bucky Walters and Arch Taylor, and all three from Captain Frank Rhea's Company B, under Lieutenants Wade Colbeck, Ralph McCarty, and John Kirkpatrick. All five platoons were engaged in the grueling work of assembling the bays.

Captain Warren Rombaugh, the Company C commander, assigned the platoons of Lieutenants Don Davis and John Perkins to anchor the cable and align the bridge while Lieutenant Tom Stack's platoon constructed the east-bank abutment and cleared mines, debris, rubble, artillery shrapnel, and disabled vehicles from the bridge approaches.

Though the troops had started work virtually at sunup, it was not until 1100 hours that Captain Max Schmidt finally returned to the worksite with a weapons carrier hauling the big wooden reel bearing twelve hundred feet of one-inch steel cable. John Perkins's entire Company C platoon had to drop what it was doing to lend a hand wrestling the cable reel to the ground. Max Schmidt looked up at one point to see me worrying myself silly over the possibility of the reel becoming damaged, so, when the lifting job was over, he bowed in a mock courtly manner and announced, "There's your cable, sir, safe, sound, and on the site." I could not help but crack a smile as Perkin's men moved the monster reel into place to begin the job of anchoring the west end of the bridge.

The five platoons assigned to assembly jobs were spread across three separate assembly sites. At these, the troops placed steel treads upon the saddles, which had already been strapped to the inflated pontoons. When completed, each finished bay was pushed out to the end of the bridge by means of the utility boat. Once there, the squad manning Suicide Point grabbed it and jockeyed it into position so it would fit, tongue in groove. Then they took turns pounding in the long, heavy connecting pin with a sledgehammer. Kedge anchors would be deployed to anchor the new section in the stream until, later, the one-inch steel cable could be deployed from bank to bank to take most of the strain.

As successive bays were affixed to the end of the bridge, it became increasingly difficult to hold the span in alignment. Then the pressure of the current made it harder to pound in the steel connecting pins. The sledgehammer had to be wielded at an awkward angle, so the work was doubly exhausting and the job had to be shared in frequent rotations.

We soon passed beyond the realm of our own practical experience and that of other engineer units in the vicinity. As the pressure from the current mounted on a span that had grown unwieldy in its length, the point squad attempted new techniques for moving and pinning each new bay. In one such effort, they tried pushing the bay upstream with the utility boat in such a way, they hoped, as to ease the connecting pin through. No hand was light enough on the throttle, so that effort failed. Next, they tried using the utility boat to ease the pressure by hauling on the anchor lines of the adjacent float. No luck there, either. Getting brute power behind the sledgehammer was the only method that consistently worked.

CHAPTER 27

A shell from a heavy artillery barrage at about 1300 hours, March 9, scored a direct hit among the troops manning Suicide Point. The blast threw Sergeant Black Mac McDonald over the side of the utility boat, five of the Company A men on Suicide Point were wounded, and one other, Private Marion Priester, died instantly when his body was ripped open by shrapnel. I was on hand at the shore end of the bridge when a tearful First Sergeant Bill Smith carried in Priester's body.

I was still certain that a German observer with a radio was holed up somewhere on our side of the river, so I ordered Captain Frank Rhea to organize a squad from his Company B to search our part of town, possibly for a German soldier dressed in civilian clothes and mingling with the townsmen who had not evacuated the place. By then, we knew of the many German ploys during the Bulge, so it was not just paranoia that motivated me. However, the Company B engineers turned nothing up in the course of a thorough house-to-house search.

As the early afternoon wore on, we received several different kinds of important support. Colonel Anderson had arrived in Remagen at around 1000 hours but had remained out of our hair, silently watching our progress from a remote vantage point. Even after I learned of the colonel's proximity and went up to greet him, he never took an active part in doing my job for me. He never had before, but even I was ready to admit that this bridge was the most important job we had ever tackled, and technically the most taxing. However, knowing the Old Man was there, silently approving my actions, was an indescribable tonic.

When Captain Towner Webster's 988th Treadway Bridge

Company rolled in, we knew we probably would have enough equipment and bridging materials on hand to complete the job. The extra manpower Captain Webster's company represented provided an important morale lift for those of us who had been in Remagen since sunup.

When I called Major Webb at the 1111th Group CP to confirm the arrival of the 998th Treadway Company, Webb told me that a specially trained platoon from the 299th Engineer Combat Battalion was en route to help take care of replacing damaged floats. This was good news, but we could not wait; we had to get moving on our own if we were to beat the inexorable clock. At about 1530 hours, Frank Rhea and Captain Gene Hancock, of the 998th Treadway Company, organized a platoon-size scratch team to make the needed repairs. They prepared to move a Quickway crane out onto the bridge to begin lifting the damaging treads so the punctured pontoons could be replaced.

The shelling and air strikes never abated, and nothing we owned or operated was immune. At about 1600 hours, I trudged up the narrow little street to my CP and was shocked to see that the upper story of the building had taken a direct hit. The dirt floor on which my bedroll lay was ankle-deep in stucco and concrete. As I pondered the scene and swigged water from my canteen, I turned toward the river to view the progress of the bridge. The five-pontoon gap was painfully visible, but so were the undamaged sections on either side. I could see that the pontoon replacement effort was just getting underway. However, farther to the side, another one of our Quickway cranes was afire from a recent direct hit, and so were two Broadway trucks. I soon learned that the same artillery strike had demolished thirteen complete but unemplaced bays on the worksite at which they had been assembled.

It was an open question whether we would get the whole bridge in before German fire expended our resources and manpower. So far, we had sustained one man killed and eight men wounded and evacuated, plus about two dozen men who refused to turn themselves in to have their minor wounds treated. Two Quickway cranes and two Broadway trucks had to be written off so far along with at least eighteen completed bays. I had earlier estimated that we would need to emplace eighty-four floats between the two banks and that we would need about forty extras for replacement purposes. Now, I wasn't sure that forty extra would be enough or that we had enough trucks, cranes, or even men on hand to weather the constantly increasing volume of German fire.

What it all came down to, I realized, was the success of our infantry, tanks, and tactical air in pushing the Germans far back from the crossing. However, since the Ludendorff Bridge was still expected to collapse at any moment, *we* were in the best position to provide a lasting means for getting enough troops and tanks over to save ourselves and our effort. We would just have to take our beating, get the bridge done by one means or another, and support others who would be in a better position to settle our bridge's ultimate fate. The faster we built our bridge, the more troops, tanks, and artillery pieces our generals would be able to send into the attack that would ultimately provide the best security for our bridge.

In my mind that afternoon, everything—everything— depended on us.

The growing battles out along the bridgehead east of the Rhine were not going particularly well for our combat troops. On March 7, the first day of the Remagen bridgehead, the only troops to get across the Rhine were from the 27th Armored Infantry Battalion and the 1st Platoon of Company B, 9th Armored Engineer Battalion. After midnight, they were joined by most of the rest of the 9th Armored Division's Combat Command B, including the rest of the Company B, 9th Armored Engineers.

In the wee hours of March 8, the 1st Battalion, 310th Infantry Regiment of the 78th Infantry Division received the famous order, "Cross the Rhine. Turn Right. Attack." At 0500 hours, March 8, the battalion did exactly as ordered. No sooner had it turned to launch its assault to the south, however, than a powerful German force beat it to the punch with a strong assault toward the bridge from the south and southwest. It took immense effort for the freshly arrived infantrymen to hold what little had been turned over to them, for the German thrust was spirited, to say the least. In the end, the same broken terrain that thus far had hemmed in the American troop broke up the cohesion of the German attacks, but, as before, the Germans— and particularly the German artillery—continued to dominate the heights overlooking the river and the tiny American bridgehead.

As the morning of March 9 progressed, the 9th Infantry Division's 47th Infantry Regiment crossed the Rhine, and the 78th

Division's 311th Infantry Regiment followed, beginning around noon. As the 311th Infantry delivered an immediate northward assault, the 9th Infantry Division's 1st Battalion, 60th Infantry crossed the Ludendorff under heavy fire, followed by the 78th Division's 309th Infantry Regiment.

At 1435 hours, Brigadier General William Hoge turned over command of the bridgehead to the 9th Division's Major General Louis Craig, who had just set up his CP in Erpel. As the afternoon wore on, elements of the 9th and 78th divisions relieved Hoge's Combat Command B, which was not built for working in the broken, hilly terrain it had seized.

As March 9 wore on, the 78th Division's 311th Infantry Regiment fought through in the northern bridgehead to Unke land was battling the 11th SS Panzer Division for possession of Bad Honnef. Meanwhile, the 78th Division's center regiment, the 309th Infantry, in the northeastern bridgehead, attacked eastward with its three battalions abreast and was in possession of Rheinbreitbach and Brüchhausen. The 309th Infantry also reported the seizure of several key German artillery observation positions. After halting the German counterattacks toward the two bridges, the 1st Battalion, 310th Infantry ended the day in possession of the high ground around Ohlenberg, southeast of Erpel. By the late afternoon, the 78th Division had penetrated as deeply as two miles from Erpel in some places. The news was that more units from the 9th Infantry Division were crossing into the bridgehead and that General Hoge's Combat Command B of the 9th Armored Division was reconsolidating behind the east bank lines.

Against these gains, the Germans were marshaling fresh crack divisions behind the scenes. In addition to the 11th SS Panzer Division, the Germans were rushing in the 3rd Parachute Division and the 9th SS "Panzer Lehr" Panzer Division. More troops—and more artillery—were on the way.

I returned to the bridge site to observe Lieutenant Wade Colbeck's scratch working party as it struggled to replace the five damaged floats. It was a tricky proposition and, though the troops worked extremely hard, the effort was overtaken at about 1630 hours by a murky twilight.

Downstream, north of our bridge, the 86th Engineer Heavy Pontoon Battalion, which we had displaced in Remagen in the morning, had just reinaugurated its cross-river ferry with a run that carried five vitally needed tanks to the east bank bridgehead.

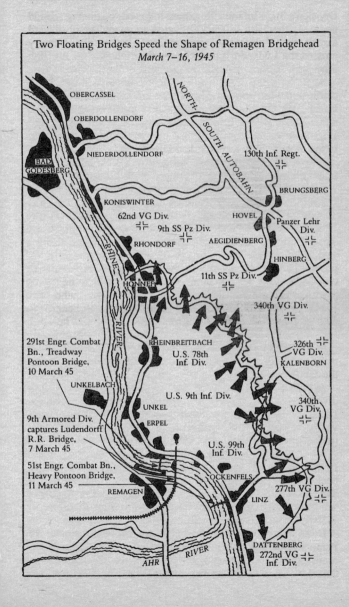

Two Floating Bridges Speed the Shape of Remagen Bridgehead
March 7–16, 1945

OBERCASSEL

OBERDOLLENDORF

NORTH

NIEDERDOLLENDORF

SOUTH AUTOBAHN

130th Inf. Regt.

BAD GODESBERG

BRUNGSBERG

KONISWINTER

62nd VG Div.

HOVEL

Panzer Lehr Div.

9th SS Pz Div.

RHONDORF

AEGIDIENBERG

HINBERG

RHINE RIVER

HONNEF

11th SS Pz Div.

340th VG Div.

291st Engr. Combat Bn., Treadway Pontoon Bridge, 10 March 45

RHEINBREITBACH

U.S. 78th Inf. Div.

326th VG Div.

KALENBORN

UNKELBACH

U.S. 9th Inf. Div.

340th VG Div.

UNKEL

9th Armored Div. captures Ludendorff R.R. Bridge, 7 March 45

ERPEL

U.S. 99th Inf. Div.

51st Engr. Combat Bn., Heavy Pontoon Bridge, 11 March 45

OCKENFELS

REMAGEN

277th VG Div.

LINZ

DATTENBERG

AHR RIVER

272nd VG Inf. Div.

On the return trip, the ferrymen brought back a number of ambulances carrying soldiers wounded in the day's fighting. The ferries made a small but important dent in the backlog of troops, tanks, and guns that were urgently needed to hold the bridgehead and, in so doing, alleviated a little of the enormous pressure on the 291st.

As I watched Wade Colbeck's troops working in the fading light, Max Schmidt bustled up and reported that the eastern bridge approach had been completed by Lieutenant Tom Stack's platoon of Company C and that the one-inch steel cable had been secured on the west bank. It only awaited the completion of the bridge to be run across the river.

Max was still extremely concerned about the ongoing loss of assembled floats. His brow was furrowed with evidence of his concern. "Colonel, we've never had anything like this. The Krauts are knocking the hell out of the floats. I keep checking to see if we have replacements and somehow we seem to have them coming. I hope we can keep supplied. It looks like we'll need enough to build two bridges."

Max had no sooner finished speaking than it seemed the air around us was sucked someplace else. From the new expression on Max's face, I could see that he felt it, too. Then we were nearly bowled over by an ear-splitting explosion. Belatedly, in unison, we instinctively ducked our heads and looked around.

"Whoa," Max bellowed, "What was *that*?"

All we could see was flying debris and a huge cloud of smoke rising from a spot about a block away from my little CP billet. I could think of nothing to do except state the obvious: "*That* is something new; I never saw anything like *that* before."

Naturally, Max and I were drawn to the area of the explosion. However, as we started walking, I heard someone call my name and went back to see who it was.

It turned out that I had been called by Lieutenant Colonel James Kirkland, the 1111th Group executive officer. He had just arrived in Remagen and wanted to know the status of our efforts. We pondered the nature of the big explosion, but we had no idea what had caused it. When that purely speculative part of the conversation ran out of steam, he began telling me about the terrible time he had had getting to Remagen because of the terribly chaotic traffic situation along the regional road net.

Lieutenant Colonel Kirkland's arrival was the lastest example of the keen interest my superiors in the engineer chain of command had in the Remagen crossings. About an hour earlier, I had heard of the arrival of Colonel Rusty Lyons, the III Corps engineer, who had opened a forward CP in a deep cellar about three hundred yards north of our bridge site. Colonel Lyons's arrival provided me with a link to the infantry units fighting across the river, for he was in direct contact with the III Corps commander and thus privy to information flowing in from the 78th and 9th Infantry division command posts. Colonel Anderson was joined by several of his key staff officers and a small group of clerks and communicators. My own battalion forward command group had also arrived by then and our communications chief, Sergeant John Scanlan, was already seeing to the establishment of a viable telephone net.

As we exchanged information, Lieutenant Colonel Kirkland and I slowly walked in the direction of my CP. On the way, he told me that Colonel Lyons had just told him that Lieutenant Colonel Harvey Fraser's 51st Engineer Combat Battalion and two heavy pontoon *battalions* were beginning to arrive at the riverfront as a preliminary to starting a heavy pontoon bridge upstream—south—of the Ludendorff, between Kripp, on the west bank, to Linz, on the east bank. Unfortunately for our old comrades in the 51st, the Linz side of the river had not yet fallen into the hands of the 78th Infantry Division's southward-advancing 310th Infantry Regiment. In addition, I learned that Lieutenant Colonel Clayton Rust's 276th Engineer Combat Battalion, of the 1159th Engineer Combat Group, had relieved the 9th Armored Combat Engineers on the damaged railroad span. Assisting the 276th Combat Engineers was a large team of specially trained welders and steel workers from the 1058th Engineer Port Construction and Repair Group. However, the betting was still running heavily in favor of the weakened Ludendorff falling into the Rhine "at any moment."

The fall of the German artillery rounds seemed to be picking up to a new crescendo as we gabbed and nibbled on parts of a K ration I had opened. The rise in the tempo of the artillery naturally gave rise to the subject of how well my men were holding up. I mentioned that we had been taking a real battering. "But still," I added, "hurt, dirty, and exhausted, they get bandaged up, get an aspirin, and jump right back to building the bridge—at least, those who are not too badly wounded do."

Kirkland was something of a character. A former Texas peace officer with an impenetrable drawl, he was an older man, somewhat distant, who wore a hearing aid. Altogether, he was a real curiosity. As we talked in the midst of the artillery barrage, I kept searching his face for signs that he was able to hear what I was saying. I also found myself speaking louder and louder, to the point of yelling each carefully enunciated word. I even moved my lips in an exaggerated manner so, if all else failed, he could see what I was saying. At length, as the artillery fire softened, I offered him a high-energy D-ration chocolate bar and suggested that we walk down to the bridge so he could see it for himself.

We left the shelter of the CP building and I yelled into the fresh lull, "Stay close to the wall and be ready to take cover when you see artillery and mortar rounds creeping along the river bank. Sometimes they fire smoke shells for target designation and then really open up. Watch it!" He nodded his comprehension and we stepped off at a fast pace.

As we approached Lieutenant Ralph McCarty's pontoon assembly site, Sergeant Floyd Wright was just replacing one of the Brockway air-compressor trucks that had been knocked out earlier by enemy fire. Suddenly, I heard McCarty yell, "Here they come. Take cover, quick!"

I hunched down in time to see a spattering of shell bursts within fifty yards of the worksite. Seconds later, three rounds detonated right on top of us. One of the detonations threw Lieutenant Colonel Kirkland to the ground and pushed both of us into the wall behind which we had sought refuge. When we recovered, we found that McCarty's early warning had precluded any personnel casualties, but one of the rounds had scored a direct hit on another Quickway crane truck, and it was burning.

I was lamenting the loss of the truck when I noticed that Lieutenant Colonel Kirkland was on his hands and knees, frantically scrabbling around on the ground. I asked him what the matter was, but he did not respond, even when I shouted a repeat of the question. It quickly dawned on me that the near miss had popped his hearing aid out of his ear. Ralph McCarty and I joined the group exec on the ground, but a thorough sifting of all the little debris proved fruitless.

We were still searching when the enemy guns renewed their firing on the bridge site. This time, we saw the German shells walking across the river toward the bridge. Actually, causing damage to the bridge was harder than it seemed, for the water dissipated the effects of all but a direct or very near hit. It was detonations on solid ground that caused most of the casualties and equipment losses. Once again, as the fall of the rounds approached McCarty's worksite, everyone scattered for cover. Everyone, that is, except poor Lieutenant Colonel Kirkland; he continued his frantic search for his lost hearing aid, no doubt quite unaware of the approaching danger. Finally, at the last instant, McCarty and I grabbed him and pointed in the direction of the artillery detonations. His eyes grew to an enormous size and he meekly allowed us to lead him to safety. As soon as the shelling stopped—forty-five terrible minutes later—I detailed one of McCarty's men to put the deaf man aboard my command car and drive him up the hill to the group CP. McCarty and I agreed that Kirkland was a brave man but rather foolishly inclined toward danger in light of his disability.

Each new wave of artillery assaults shut us down. During the humdinger forty-five minute evening barrage, First Sergeant Smith's crew on Suicide Point was pinned down by the fire, unable even to run to the relative safety of the riverbank because of the unrestored sixty-foot break in the roadway. Sergeants Frank Dolcha and Black Mac McDonald were likewise trapped in midstream in the utility boat.

The shelling finally subsided at about 1800 hours. When we came out from our cover and had seen to Lieutenant Colonel Kirkland, Ralph McCarty and I viewed a virtual moonscape littered with broken, twisted, and burning equipment. If anything, this had been the most accurate shelling of the day, and I still believed—more than ever—that the Germans had an observer with a radio posted on our side of the river. I again ordered Frank Rhea to scour the town around us with patrols, but to no avail, so I later asked 1111th Group to see to the forced evacuation of all the civilians still living in the town.

The specially trained platoon of the 299th Combat Engineers arrived at about 1830 hours and immediately relieved our makeshift pontoon-replacement crew out on the damaged bridge. In addition to handling the rugged work, the platoon gave us back a few dozen members of Lieutenant Wade Colbeck's Company B platoon—more hands for fabricating replacement floats.

Sometime during the early evening, I heard a preliminary assessment of the monster blast that had hit the town at around dusk. Semiknowledgeable speculation had it that we had been the target of a German V-2 rocket, a wonder weapon about which we had heard only the most distant rumors. Later evidence bore out the speculation; this had been the first of eleven V-2s that were eventually expended on us.

We received firm news that the Ludendorff Bridge had been reopened to light vehicle traffic at 1900 hours, following a lengthy closing during which only foot troops had been permitted to cross on the shell-damaged wooden decking. Fortunately, the pontoon ferries to the north continued to run without let up despite German efforts to hit the small waterborne targets.

Somewhere behind the heights west of Remagen, the last of the 9th Infantry Division's three infantry regiments was waiting to cross the river by any available means. Farther back still, the entire 99th Infantry Division also was waiting in line to cross. It was obvious to all that the bridgehead could very well fail against a concerted German assault because we had fewer than three divisions—supported by few armored vehicles—facing five German divisions, of which two, plus one brigade, were tank-heavy panzer units. Moreover, the Germans continued to cling stubbornly to the dominant hills hemming in the bridgehead from which our efforts along the river could be observed.

By 1915 hours, our treadway bridge extended some three hundred feet out into the current. I had just overseen the removal of the last of the five damaged floats when Mike Popp ran up and breathlessly reported that two officers from 1st Army Headquarters had arrived at my CP and wanted to see me. I could not stifle the rather heated thought that I could not remember ever having had so much brass looking over my shoulder. But I calmed myself down by taking their view of the strategic importance of the mission.

My visitors were two old friends, Colonel Bill Carter, the 1st Army chief engineer, and Major Warren Pershing, the army engineering supply officer. The two, who had already helped themselves to hot coffee, shook hands and waited while I fixed myself a cup.

Francis Warren Pershing was the only son of General of the Armies John Pershing, the commander in chief of the American Expeditionary Force in World War I. He had not chosen to follow a military career, as his father had wished, but he had given up his career and his business to join the Army as a private soldier during the prewar expansion. I had first met Warren, as he preferred to be called, when I was an engineer training officer and he was a private in my platoon at Fort Belvoir. Later, he completed OSC and had been assigned as a platoon commander in my engineer training company. As I moved up in rank, Warren usually did also. Though Warren resembled his father in many ways—in his sharp features and solid bearing—he was a rather tall man with curly blond hair, easygoing, with a warm, affable manner.

I quickly briefed my two visitors, particularly on casualties, damage, and equipment losses, and gave them my thoughts on when the bridge might be completed—shortly after noon the next day, March 10. Colonel Carter told me that the 1st Army commander, Lieutenant General Courtney Hodges, was coming to visit Remagen. Then he explained that rumor or intelligence had it that the German high command had been caught flat-footed by our seizure of the Remagen bridge and that Field Marshal Walter Model, a Hitler favorite and commander in chief of the German Army Group B, had been assigned to overcome our troops on the east bank and destroy the Ludendorff. According to Colonel Carter, our intelligence organizations had already learned that the local German combat commander was Lieutenant General Fritz Bayerlein, commanding general of the 9th SS Panzer Lehr Division, a unit he had led with brutal distinction in Normandy and the Bulge. In addition to his own Panzer Lehr Division, Bayerlein had direct control over the 11th SS Panzer Division, the 106th Panzer Brigade, and assorted other units, which were still staging into the area. The word from my two visitors was that Bayerlein was preparing to mount an all-out dawn counterattack.

The news was by no means funny, but I could not help grinning. In response to the raised eyebrows on my visitors' faces, I explained that the information must be stale because I felt as if we had been standing in the face of an all-out effort most of the day. I also detailed the numerous air attacks and finished up with a detailed recounting of the V-2 detonation. "We've been under constant fire since eight this morning, but we're hanging in. God willing, we'll get this job done on time. Nobody else but God is going to stop us! We've taken everything they've thrown at us and the floats are still going out and across."

After straining to hear my every word against the rising crescendo of yet another artillery attack, Bill Carter gently patted me on the shoulder and replied, "Dave, I've ordered you to receive top priority. You're being sent everything Warren and I can think of, but we're here seeing, now, for the first time, what you're going through. Frankly, I've never seen anything like it. Is there any other way we can help that you can think of?"

I rubbed my chin while I thought through the implications of the colonel's once-in-a-lifetime offer. "Well," I finally said,

"More of the same, I guess. More equipment on standby, more replacement floats and saddles, more protection for the men I have doing the job out there, and replacements for the men who aren't making it. We've had more than our share of casualties you know, and I think we'll be having more."

Then, lest I seem too greedy or caught up in my own problems, "Colonel, from what I've seen, you've been doing your best. I feel good about that, but I think you realize now how bad things are around here, and how much worse they can get. Just keep it coming." And, finally, "Get me more floats!"

My two very important visitors left then, in the eerie glare of fires and shell bursts. Before jumping into the front seat of his command car, Colonel Carter firmly gripped my arm, looked me straight in the eye, and said in his usual sincere way, "Dave, we're really glad that you and the 291st are on this mission." He paused, looking like he was fumbling for words, but quickly ended with, "You know what I mean." Then he and Warren Pershing left.

No words, no gestures, could have done more to put me over the top of my wavering conviction. Like all good leaders, Bill Carter had inspired in me a desire to produce miracles just to please him.

Darkness and the renewed artillery attack further slowed progress at the bridge nose and around the worksites ashore. Our mess sergeant took advantage of the dark to set up an improvised chow line on the riverbank, and I circulated firm orders that everyone was to take a breather and get some hot food in rotation by squads and platoons. The darkness also shielded the platoon of the 299th Combat Engineers as it worked to replace the five damaged pontoons it had raised from the river bottom with five new ones.

As some of the troops ate, I made my way along the riverbank to deliver pep talks and admonishments to the platoon commanders, platoon sergeants, and squad leaders. I did not want anyone becoming complacent about the German artillery fire. We needed every available man working, not nursing wounds acquired through acts of bravado or stupidity.

I bumped into Staff Sergeant Melvin Champion, Lieutenant Bucky Walters's Company A platoon sergeant, as he came off the bridge for chow following hours of volunteer labor out on Suicide Point. When we met, Champion launched into what I thought might be a prepared speech: "Colonel, there should be a better way to get those connecting pins into the floats. It's really rough and takes a lot of time for each one. Some of the men were hit out there while they were sledging them in. It's almost impossible to do the job with those shells coming in all around us." Coming as it did from one of my best veteran troop leaders, a man who had solved countless little engineering problems with his straightforward practical view of the world, I became worried lest we were not trying hard enough to find a new and more useful way to breast the Rhine's current.

I joined the troops in the chow line and after getting my food joined Sergeant Frank Dolcha on the running board of one of the Brockway trucks. This was Frank's first break from helping navigate the utility boat out on the water. After we each ate a few mouthfuls of food in silence, this epitome of the reliable troop leader shook his head in wonder and ruminated for my benefit, "These guys are really something, Colonel. I don't know where they get the stuff that lets them stay out there and do that work." Then he named four junior troops who had been working out on Suicide Point since we floated the first pontoon. "They won't give an inch, Colonel."

Lieutenant Ralph McCarty, another stalwart who never gave an inch, walked up in time to hear the end of Sergant Dolcha's paean. "The sergeant is right, Colonel," Ralph broke in. "All our guys are taking a beating, but—wow!—I'll tell you, they're really sticking in there." Then, "Do you think there's anything we can do to get some more counterbattery fire? You can see where those Krauts are when they fire. Looks to me like they're not even worrying about hiding their positions."

I told McCarty and Dolcha that I had just conferred with Colonel Carter and that he had informed me that the III Corps had moved up and was emplacing the artillery and antiaircraft guns from five divisions. "That should get us by until our infantry on the other side gets up into hills to wipe out the German guns in the eastern hills. The 9th and 78th division troops are having a tough fight. You know, they're trying and dying. I don't guess any of us would want to trade places with them right now, even though it's no birthday party for us over here."

After a brief pause, McCarty reported that his platoon and Wade Colbeck's had just finished working with Captain Towner Webster's 988th Treadway Bridge Company to replace all the damaged equipment at the three assembly sites. As a special precaution to prevent fires, gasoline had been removed from all the equipment that did not absolutely need to be running. Ralph also told me that Captain Gene Hancock, of the 998th Treadway Bridge Company, was out on the span overseeing the work of the platoon from the 299th Combat Engineers.

As often occurred in the wake of such reports, I wondered if the 291st really needed a commanding officer. It seemed to run pretty well on its own.

From 2100 hours, March 9, until midnight, the German artillery zeroed in on the bridges, particularly our treadway bridge. This marked the beginning of the midnight counterattack by the 9th and 11th SS Panzer divisions Colonel Bill Carter had forecasted. At the stroke of midnight, the night skies were lit up by the heavy artillery fire put out by both sides, and we all were forced to halt work and take cover. Right at the start, Frank Rhea commented that it was the worst fire we had experienced in the war, even heavier than the barrage that had preceded Skorzeny's attack on Malmédy.

Direct hits struck the bridge and construction sites. Equipment was set ablaze and exploding fuel tanks marked a certain disaster where the men had been assembling treadway floats. The bridge itself was hopping up and down like a jackrabbit as pressurized pontoons were pierced by shell fragments.

There was nothing we could do. We would be powerless to act until the artillery attack let up.

CHAPTER 28

Lieutenant Colonel Harvey Fraser's heavily augmented 51st Engineer Combat Battalion had arrived in Kripp, its bridge site south of the Ludendorff, at around 1800, March 9. As Harvey was making his company assignments, he learned that the far side of the river, around Linz, was still in German hands. Harvey contacted his boss at the 1159th Engineer Group with news that it would not be practical to launch his heavy pontoon bridge until the opposite bank had been cleared. When Colonel Lyons, the III Corps chief engineer, heard the news, he directly ordered the 51st Combat Engineers to get started regardless of the situation across the river. Accordingly, though parts of Linz were in enemy hands and fighting raged throughout the town, a line platoon crossed by way of the Ludendorff Bridge and began preparing the east-bank approach. The engineers in Linz were terrorized by criss-crossing small-arms fire, but they got their work underway and fortunately sustained no casualties.

Later in the evening, Colonel Lyons relented and sent word to Linz that no more construction work was to be attempted until the Germans had been driven back from the town. The engineers immediately stopped work and set up a strongpoint around two .50-caliber machine guns at the edge of their worksite. Soon, an American infantry patrol supported by several tanks was ambushed and chased back toward the engineer strongpoint. The engineers helped stop the Germans with fire from their heavy machine guns and small arms.

The remainder of the 51st Engineer Combat Battalion was continually subjected to small-arms and mortar fire as it struggled with its work in Kripp, on the west bank. They took far more direct fire and about as much artillery fire as we had been taking during the day and evening, and Lieutenant Colonel Fra-

ser finally blew his top and demanded adequate artillery coverage of the enemy artillery positions in the hills and their mortar
and machine-gun emplacements in Linz that were firing on his
battalion main body. Even then, it took several hours for the
hard-pressed friendly artillery batteries to fire the missions.

When I began hearing the details of the 51st's ordeal less than
two miles from my own bridge site, I really became alarmed
over the possibility that the bridgehead might collapse. My real
concern was failing to get one or the other of the pontoon bridges
installed before the Ludendorff structure gave way and fell into
the river. Without at least one bridge in operation—the Ludendorff or a pontoon—there appeared to be no way to keep vitally
needed men and ammunition flowing to the east bank.

The German artillery fire around Remagen, which had been
unremitting if relatively inaccurate through the evening and after
midnight, abruptly ceased at about 0300 hours, March 10. Our
cynicism kept us rooted to our hiding places for five or ten
minutes after the shells stopped falling, then a few brave souls
warily stepped into the open to begin assessing the damage.
Moment by moment, our fears subsided and more of us stepped
out from behind our cover.

Five minutes into the lull, I was out on the bridge nose, inspecting what we had accomplished thus far. First Sergeant
Smith's team out on Suicide Point had advanced to about midstream, over six hundred feet from the riverfront. If anything,
they preferred working under the cloak of darkness. Just behind
the advancing bridge nose, Sergeant Sheldon Smith's squad of
Company C was also hard at work, fastening the kedge anchors
to ropes lashed to every other float. Each kedge anchor had to
be carried by the utility boats between 100 and 150 yards from
the upstream side of the bridge and dropped over the side. We
experienced few problems getting the anchors secured to the
bottom near the shore, but farther out in the stream the river bed
was composed largely of smooth stones, to which it was extremely difficult to get the kedge anchors to adhere. Despite the
extra work, however, this vital part of the job progressed more
or less at the same pace as the addition of new floats at the bridge
nose.

I left the bridge at about 0345 hours and walked over to Lieutenant Ralph McCarty's assembly area, and then on up to my
CP. As I neared the battered little building, I was overtaken by
a feeling of sheer exhaustion. I counted up the hours I had been

on the go and concluded that my last sleep had been a little catnap around 1600 hours, March 8—thirty-five hours ago. I sat down on my bedroll, thinking I would catch a few winks before the next crisis needed my attention. However, the harder I tried to sleep the more my mind churned up terrible images. I began dwelling on my ordeal at Malmédy, where I had gone virtually sleepless for three days. I was still far from slumber when the shelling began again, gradually at first but rising quickly to the old crescendo. I stood up to follow the fall of the German rounds and plainly saw direct hits on the Ludendorff.

The barrage reached an incredible zenith and held there for about thirty minutes. It seemed as though every big gun in Germany was pouring high explosives onto the big railroad bridge and our treadway. Though I could not see Harvey Fraser's upstream heavy pontoon site around an intervening curve, I imagined the 51st was getting hit, too.

At length, word arrived that our worksite had taken several substantial hits and that the troops out on the bridge had been ordered to shore. All our work ceased again. By then, many of us were beginning to feel that building a bridge on rubber floats was an impossibility. Thus far, our "Can Do" engineers had not been stopped, but the odds appeared to be going heavily against us.

When the firing abated around 0430, we decided to pull out all the stops and make up some of the lost time. After receiving damage reports from the company commanders, I rang up Colonel Lyons at the III Corps engineer forward CP and told him that twenty-six completely assembled floats, with treadways attached—312 feet of complete bridge—had been hit and would require removal from the water. My troops felt that most of the punctured floats could be patched and recycled, but I admitted to Colonel Lyons that we were going to miss my estimated completion time—1300 that afternoon—by at least five hours.

Colonel Lyons took the opportunity to update me on the condition of the Ludendorff and the progress of the 51st between Kripp and Linz. He also told me that the 164th Engineer Combat Battalion was getting ready to construct special booms above Linz to ensnare floating mines or frogmen the Germans might send down the river.

After speaking with Colonel Lyons, I told my company commanders to send as many men as they could spare to help the platoon of the 299th Combat Engineers in the removal and replacement job and then ordered the remaining engineers of Al

Edelstein's Suicide Point platoon to get some rest while volunteers from all three companies replaced them. Meantime, a scratch fire brigade from McCarty's and Colbeck's platoons of Company B did their best to restore the assembly sites, in which all other available engineers were at work assembling and reassembling floats.

We were well along in the cleanup when the Germans bracketed Suicide Point with several air bursts. Three Company B men were hit by the shrapnel. Though the Germans continued to fire the deadly air bursts, Captain Frank Watson, our new battalion surgeon, raced out along the exposed bridge to Suicide Point with a handful of his medics. Before the wounded had been treated and carried to shore, fresh volunteers were on the way to Suicide Point.

By sunrise, around 0600 hours, scratch teams directed by Captains Gamble, Rhea, and Hancock had removed thirteen of the damaged floats and, in the faint dawn light, I could see at last that the bridge was taking shape. Much of the damaged equipment had been removed from the three assembly sites by a ten-ton wrecker from the battalion motor pool. Lieutenants Kirkpatrick, Edelstein, and Colbeck were hard at work reorganizing the assembly sites and their troops were well along in making good the pontoon losses we had sustained during the night. In the brief lull that attended the new dawn, we could easily hear the pounding of the sledges and the attendant dainty language that seemed to be as necessary as the muscle work in driving home the four-foot connecting pins. As I looked and mused, I spotted several members of the original Company A team heading back out to Suicide Point to reassert their ownership. I doubted that First Sergeant Smith had even left the bridge nose for a meal—a correct surmise, as it turned out. Though I expected the German artillery onslaught to resume at any moment, I was absolutely certain—for the first time, if the truth is to be told—that the 291st would complete the job.

I held a command and staff conference at 0730 hours. We were disappointed and dismayed to learn how little overall progress we had made since dusk. The incessant shelling had wiped out the equivalent of eight hours of backbreaking labor, including the time required to build replacement floats. We had advanced the nose of the bridge well past the midstream point, but that did not account for the 312-foot gap of sunken floats that had been inflicted by the artillery.

* * *

The Luftwaffe made its biggest appearance thus far at 0645 hours. Streaking in at the forefront of the wild assemblage were a handful of the brand new Messerschmitt Me-262 jet fighter-bombers—a wonder none of us had seen before, or even heard of. I could not believe the swiftness of those little jets, and I had to admire German ingenuity even as they poured machine-gun and cannon rounds into the Ludendorff and around our own bridge. Not without good reason, the troops working the kedges and bridge nose rushed headlong for the shore, though the best they could manage were short spurts between strafing runs. Most of them spent most of their time lying inside the steel treadways, which provided ample protection so long as the pontoons beneath them were not punctured and sunk. As I watched in helpless awe and trepidation, the entire bridge buffeted and swayed like some lizardy monster whose head had been pinned to the ground.

Altogether, the German aircraft made ten separate bombing and strafing runs, but their aim was appreciably upset by the devastating and desperate fire of the many antiaircraft guns that had been set up on the heights on both sides of the river. Adding considerably if somewhat humorously to the antiaircraft array were the many thousands of bullets fired from rifles and even pistols in the hands of frustrated men throughout our section of the Rhine valley.

The air raid ended all thoughts I had of getting some sleep. I buckled on my web gear, grabbed my towel, washcloth, and soap, and trudged back down to the river in the hope of getting cleaned up a little. The Rhine water looked clear and clean, but to see that I had to overlook the rime of dead fish that was bobbing up and down beside the cobblestone revetment below the promenade. When I had finished washing, shaving, and changing into clean clothes, I faced the town and noticed for the first time how the many charming little tourist hotels along the promenade had borne the brunt of the German shellfire.

Following a restorative cup of hot black coffee at my CP, I went back to the bridge and struck up an idle conversation with Frank Rhea. We had just finished talking when I spotted Colonel Anderson sauntering toward us. As always, the Old Man was well groomed, calm, and collected. I was glad to see him, for he always treated me in a warm, avuncular manner.

I was a bit embarrassed because the bridge had fallen far behind schedule, but the colonel's darting eyes quickly took in the shambles of the assembly sites and the piles of deflated, damaged floats hauled up on the riverbank. He communicated his understanding of our plight with a few nods of his head and a few remarks, such as "Oh I see," or just "Hmmm." I told him of the exemplary response of the men to the many emergencies of the night and how we had gotten as far as we had only because they had thrown themselves wholeheartedly into their dangerous labors. As I continued my nervous recitation, he continued to take in the whole scene with his sharp, practiced eye. At last, he held up his hand to stop my yattering and asked the ultimate question—"Dave, when will the bridge reach the east bank?"

I thought for a moment. "Colonel Carter and Warren Pershing were here late yesterday and I told them I thought we'd have it in by around noon today. I had no idea then that we'd be stopped as often or as long as we were last night, or that we'd take the damage we took. I don't think we've been here twenty-four hours yet. Anyway, as I see it now, if we don't take any more direct hits or one of those V-2 things or something like that, I figure we should touch down at, say, early this evening." I shrugged and finished with a plaintive, "It all depends."

The colonel considered this answer and finally said, "That would be okay, Dave." He had a grave look on his face, but at least he now knew exactly what we were up against. "Under the circumstances, that's as much as I can possibly ask. If you think . . ."

Before the colonel could finish the sentence, a flight of German jets were on us. It was unbelievable how fast they flew.

Any weapon that could bear was fired as the string of jets swooped in. There was so much firing that the ground shuddered; it was awesome. The entire valley around Remagen became cloaked in smoke and dust before the Germans left—only three minutes after they first appeared.

Throughout, Colonel Anderson never wavered, never flinched. Though I was by then extremely gun shy, I felt obliged to stand up beside this straight-backed veteran of Black Jack Pershing's raid into Mexico and the trenches of France during what we used to call The Great War. If nothing else, Colonel Anderson certainly impressed and inspired the troops. Word of his unfazed stance in the face of the German jets passed through the battalion like wildfire.

As the colonel and I resumed our conversation, we watched an unusual movement directly across the river. At length, the scene resolved itself into a long line of German prisoners being herded through Erpel toward the Ludendorff Bridge. That stirred up some choice epithets from the troops while making the outcome of our sacrifices more tangible. As we eventually learned, those or other prisoners who were marched across later were taken during a daring dawn frontal attack in the hills east of Ohlenberg that eventually secured the Germans' best artillery observation position. The fall of that observation post might have been the reason the artillery fire had been less accurate, less devastating during the early daylight hours.

Not that the artillery fire ever quite abated! As Colonel Anderson and I watched the column of German prisoners recede, someone shouted, "Hit the dirt! Take cover!" And scores of recently inspired engineers raced in all directions to find cover. The colonel looked around at all the running and said, "I don't understand this. Why are they taking cover when there's no fire?"

Instantly, the first German rounds impacted next to the nearest assembly site. What the colonel and I had missed was the initial fall of rounds into the river and the progressive creep of the shell splashes from the southeast toward the assembly sites. What the colonel was asking about was an ample demonstration of how the 291st managed to weather intense fire with so few casualties.

The first rounds to impact on dry land did so only about twenty feet from where Colonel Anderson and I were standing. As I had minutes earlier, I continued to stand erect beside my superior. Lord knows, I wanted to run and hide, but I simply could not. Oh, how I wished he would break for cover! The troops who had gone to ground nearby were amazed. Finally, Sergeant Charlie Sweitzer, one of my leading demolitions men, crawled out and stood up beside us. A big, affable man who was as brave as anyone living, Sweitzer looked the colonel right in the eye and said, "Sir, you really ought not take chances. We'd feel better if you and Colonel Pergrin would jump into a hole or under something. We know when the Krauts are coming in with something, so, when we yell, would you mind taking cover?"

The old veteran looked back into Sweitzer's eyes and smiled. "Thanks, Sergeant, we'll take that under advisement. You men are doing a good job and I wouldn't want to do anything to take your mind off the work."

So there we were, exchanging pleasantries with the troops while German shells were falling in only yards away. And what was that the Old Man had said? *"Good job?"* What did he mean, good job? Couldn't he see they were performing a *superhuman* job? Good job, indeed! Later, in a saner moment, I realized that "good job" was about the highest praise the taciturn group commander had ever been heard to utter, the ultimate superlative in his limited lexicon of praise.

When the German shelling stopped, we were still standing in the open—the colonel, me, and Sergeant Sweitzer. Not then and not after would Colonel Anderson bow to the instincts of us mortals; no one ever saw him take cover in the face of German fire. For my part, I made it clear that the colonel's example was *not* to be emulated by the troops or officers of the 291st. We couldn't afford the possible losses.

By 1000 hours, the bridge nose stood nearly eight hundred feet out in the stream, about two thirds across to the west bank. However, minutes after the hour, we were again bombarded and five bays were knocked out by a direct hit. Our biggest fear by then was that one of the direct hits would sever a treadway and send a large portion of the floating bridge on an unstoppable downstream journey. The key thus far had been rapid replacement of the sunken floats, mainly by the special platoon of the 299th. Those men got each new emergency under control in constantly diminishing intervals. We would have been lost without them.

During the forenoon hour, a specially designated team from Warren Rombaugh's Company C completed and set up extra floats for the bridle cable. These five extra complete treadway floats were anchored about fifty feet upstream of the main span, ready to hold the bridle cable out of the water when it was run to the east bank after the bridge nose touched down on the eastern approach. Rope lines were cut so they could be run between the bridle cable and the span, thus providing extra support against the swift current, and to hold the main span in surer alignment. Other support lines were also prepared so they could be run out from each bank on both sides of the bridge. We were operating off the map of experience in that this was certainly the longest treadway pontoon bridge constructed in the European Theater. As far as I was concerned, no amount of strengthening or support could be viewed as being too much.

From noon until about 1245 hours, we bore the brunt of the heaviest artillery barrage of our two days on the job. Apparently, the Germans had gone out of their way to establish a new central artillery observation point in the eastern hills. All work ceased as the shells pounded in. My CP was struck, as were all the assembly sites. Thirteen floats were disabled or destroyed and another Brockway truck was smashed along with a dizzying variety of tools and equipment. When the shelling ceased, we decided to push the bridge all the way across to the west bank before we expended new floats on the replacement job, as we had until then. As far as we could tell, the treadway beam was still able to hold the whole structure together.

Worse than anything, the devastating noon barrage had inflicted about twenty casualties. Shortly, however, I saw most of the bandaged men return to work.

We had been experiencing an ongoing communications problem with the rear CP, so I decided to send word back to Rheinbach to displace the entire headquarters to Remagen. After dispatching a messenger, I sat down in my bedroll, back to the wall, and began devouring a K-ration meal. As soon as I finished eating, my head lolled to my chest and I was dreaming.

Barroom! My eyes opened and I jumped up, startled and wobbly. I looked at my watch and saw that it was 1345 hours. I had been out for about twenty minutes. As I looked out through the open wall of my CP, a string of jets streaked into view, diving to bomb and strafe the bridges. Then, as soon as the jets flew from sight, an absolutely monster explosion shook and rattled the walls of my CP and sent a thick cloud of dust and debris sailing through the air.

Struggling out through the noxious dust, I saw that the bridge was intact—no new gaps—and that there were no telltale fires at any of the worksites. Everyone I saw was looking around, seemingly as confused as me. I walked through the battalion area and found that the consensus was that we had been near-missed by another V-2 rocket. As Wade Colbeck observed, "If that had been any closer, good-bye 291st." In the wake of the Big Bang, we all sort of held our breaths waiting for the other shoe to drop, but nothing happened. Still scratching their heads, everyone got back to work.

I decided to walk down the river front to visit with Colonel Rusty Lyons, the III Corps chief engineer. He had set up a new forward CP in the deep cellar of a building overlooking the river and our bridge. We started off with some nervous chatter about the latest Big Bang and all the attention we were receiving from the German jets. Since the colonel had promised to keep me abreast of the situation in the bridgehead, I eventually led him around to that important subject.

As we stared at a large-scale topographical map the colonel's operations section was maintaining, the colonel launched into his brief. The bridgehead infantry line ran from Bad Honnef, directly on the Rhine in the north, to Dattenberg, also on the Rhine, in the south. The 78th Division's 311th Infantry Regiment was strung eastward from Bad Honnef, then the 9th Infantry Division's 39th Infantry Regiment was holding the line east of Rheinbreitbach. The 78th Division's 309th Infantry was in the center, facing east around Brüchhausen. Two battalions of the 310th Infantry were south of the 309th, and two battalions of the 9th Infantry Division's 47th Infantry Regiment were south of them, holding the key ridgeline east of Ohlenburg. East of Ockenfels were all three battalions of the 9th Infantry Division's 60th Infantry Regiment and, on their right flank, facing south, was the 1st Battalion, 310th Infantry, which had driven through Linz to Dattenberg. The western approach to the 51st Combat Engineers' bridge was thus just under a mile behind the friendly front.

Colonel Lyons and I were joined midway through the briefing by Lieutenant Colonel Robert Stann, the III Corps engineer operations officer. According to him, a great expanse of high ground needed to be seized from the Germans before my battalion's zone would be relieved of most, if not all, of the artillery fire.

The entire 78th Infantry Division had crossed the river and the 9th Armored Division's Combat Command B had been withdrawn to be refitted and placed in reserve in Remagen. The 9th Infantry Division was as yet incomplete and the 99th Infantry Division, which was en route, had yet to get one component across. According to Stann, the crack 1st Infantry Division was slated to follow the 99th Division across. In all so far, there were seventeen infantry battalions on the east bank, but the 78th and 9th division units were intermingled. According to Stann, the bridgehead continued to expand, but it would remain in jeopardy as long as the Germans remained in possession of the dominant hills and ridgelines. For the moment, the enemy outnumbered our troops on the east bank.

When he completed his part in the brief, Bob Stann looked me in the eye and echoed the message I had been hearing from every higher headquarters for two days running: "What we need,

Dave, is a treadway to get more people over there. What do you think you can do about it?''

I suppressed a groan and realized that Bob was sort of pulling my leg, but I also perceived the depth of his concern. "By damn," I replied, "I'll go back to my command post and see if I can buy you a bridge, Bob. Maybe I can get you one cheap." Then, as I grabbed my helmet and headed for the door, I closed with, "I'll send you gentlemen a bill in the morning."

Before I could get away, however, Colonel Lyons arrested my progress with a hand at my elbow. When I had turned in my tracks, he handed me a slip of message paper and smiled. "Circulate this, Colonel Pergrin. I know you fellows need a slap on the back, and you certainly deserve it for what you've been through trying to get that bridge over. Maybe it can buy us some quick time."

There were two messages on the sheet. When my eyes flicked to the signatures, I was stunned, and thrilled.

The whole Allied force is delighted to cheer the U.S. First Army whose speed and boldness have won the race to establish our first bridgehead over the Rhine. Please tell all ranks how proud I am.

EISENHOWER

To the men of the First Army who won this race I extend my congratulations. I share the pride of the Supreme Commander in your fine achievement.

LIEUTENANT GENERAL COURTNEY HODGES
Commander, First Army

CHAPTER 29

The riverfront was eerily still and quiet as I started back to my battalion's work areas from Colonel Lyons's CP. I glanced at my watch—it was about 1630 hours—and picked up my pace; the congratulatory dispatches were burning a hole in my pocket and I wanted to share them with the troops. I was in a sort of seventh heaven, but dodging around the big shell holes, noticing the devastated tourist homes along the promenade, and reentering the smoke and haze of an active battle site brought me back to earth with a dreadful thump of my heart.

Suddenly, as I got to the treadway approach, Jim Gamble and Bill McKinsey strode briskly toward me. I sensed by their purposeful manner that something was up, that some good news awaited me. "Come on, Colonel," the usually self-contained McKinsey bubbled while gesturing me forward, "Let's get out on the bridge. We've been trying to reach you at Colonel Lyons's command post and they told us you were on the way." Then, without even waiting for a response from their commanding officer, the two pivoted and started back out onto the bridge.

Though the two had communicated their excitement amply, I took only a few steps and then balked, "Whoa! Slow down! What's up?"

Gamble stopped and turned, a huge grin on his face, but he said nothing. Curious, I started forward again. When I was within a foot or two of Jim, his grin widened. "Colonel, we're about to touch down on the other side! We didn't want it to happen without your being there, but we aren't about to slow anything down. We knew you'd want us to go on with the work no matter what, so we didn't say anything. We just told the men over there to keep it going, but they haven't hit shore yet. Can

we get going, sir? I'd like to see the last bay put in. So would
McKinsey. And I *know* you do."

I felt uplifted; the days of worry and loss dissipated in that
moment. "Way to go! This is *great*! Let's get right over there."
And I surged ahead of the two captains.

We walked across the racing Rhine, across treadways that had
been put together with the blood, blisters, aching muscles, and
iron resolve of the men of the 291st, the 998th and 988th Treadway Bridge companies, and the platoon of the 299th Combat
Engineers. As I walked, I felt as if every shared experience from
Normandy on had been as training for this monumentally important assignment. And now we were only a few feet, a few
practiced acts, from becoming one of the great engineer units
in history.

Most of the men who had braved being out there, on Suicide
Point, for most of the past two days, were on hand for the touch-
down—First Sergeant Smith, Staff Sergeant Pigg, Sergeants
Geary, McDonald, and Billington, and Sergeant Dolcha in the
utility boat—all the battered survivors of Al Edelstein's platoon
and the score of volunteers who had regularly relieved them on
the bridge nose. All three company commanders, several of the
platoon commanders, and whoever else could get away from
pressing business were on hand, too. We made a frightfully large
target, so I decided to get the job completed and everyone dispersed in something approaching record time.

With practiced smoothness, the utility boat worked the last
pontoon in place, then the Suicide Point team drove in the last
connecting pin, placed the approach treadway over the abutment
sill, and put in the hook-end treadway wedge. It was done, but
there were no cheers, no shouts of joy. We were just a bunch of
professionals looking around to see if everything was in place
okay, checking to make sure nothing was missing.

It was somewhere between 1700 and 1730 hours—1710, officially—March 10, 1945. The Rhine barrier had been breached.

Minutes after the last link had been forged, no doubt on cue, a
great gaggle of news reporters and photographers arrived from
up one of Erpel's battered streets. Despite the moment-ago feelings of accomplishment and sense of pride, only then did I realize that my men and I had been the central figures in A Great
Moment in History. Battle-fatigued reporters from the *New York
Times*, the *Philadelphia Inquirer, Colliers*, the *Pittsburgh Press*,
Fox-Movietone News, and *Liberty* magazine, to name a few,

crowded around and among us, jotting down names and home-towns, getting impressions, shooting pictures which, if nothing else, would tell our loved ones that some of us were safe and well.

Amidst the bustle and shoving, big Bill Smith emerged from the pack and pushed his way to my side. The Company A first sergeant had on his face a grin that was a mile wide, a face that told volumes about relief. "Just think, Colonel," Bill said, sum-ming up the real experience of being there, "no more Suicide Point!"

The euphoria lasted only as long as it took the correspondents to get their stories and pictures and hightail it away from our high-exposure bridge as Luftwaffe jets streaked in to lay a deadly pattern of bombs between us and the Ludendorff. The Me-262s missed both bridges, but it was close. No doubt, the only thing that saved us was the intense fire of our antiaircraft guns.

When the air raid ended and I surveyed the treadway bridge, I plainly saw that there was yet much to be done before it could be put into service. First, eight damaged floats had to be re-placed, then the steel bridle cable had to be unreeled and placed aboard the four waiting cable floats, and four more floats had to be added against the current near the center of the bridge to help alleviate pressure on the treadway joints.

When I reached the western approach again, I confirmed that the bridge, which had taken just thirty hours to drive from bank to bank, was 1,032 feet in length. This was by a considerable margin the longest treadway bridge built to that time. Until then, there were many who doubted the efficacy of this type of bridge at that length, but the war would yet produce even longer tread-way bridges—thanks in part to some of our on-the-run innova-tions. However, our Remagen bridge remains the longest *tactical* bridge of its type ever built under enemy fire.

Though the treadway beam was at rest on the east bank, some of the men of the 291st and attached units faced a time when they would really be earning their pay. We now had to unreel and secure the bridle cable under what I was sure would be even heavier efforts by the Germans to blow us out of business.

Sergeants Ed Keoughan and Sheldon Smith asked for volun-teers to help with the cable. When I arrived on the scene, Keoughan was telling the men that the most important job now was to get the bridge anchored with the bridle cable supporting each float. Ed brought out clearly that the Germans would undoubtedly attempt to blast the bridge with their artillery, particularly since it was now all the way across to the east bank.

Despite Sergeant Keoughan's warning, volunteers quickly filled out the working party. In addition to Sergeants Keoughan and Smith, they were Sergeant Carl Russo, Corporal Peter Piar, Technician 4th Grade Fred Holzer, Corporal Ed Beaken, Technician 4th Grade Stuart Getz, Private First Class Charlie Bissell, and Private First Class Carl Petterson.

At first, Keoughan and his men attempted to right the extremely heavy ten-foot cable reel, which had been dropped off on its side on March 8. The idea was to roll the reel into the treadway channels and on across the river, unreeling the bridle cable as they went. When uprighting the reel proved to be impossible, the engineers put their heads together and came up with a reasonable solution. Sergeant Russo raced to his machine-gun position a half block from the reel and asked Technician 4th Grade John Andreatta if he would be willing to drive his bulldozer out onto the span and haul the cable end to the east bank. Andreatta agreed without a moment's hesitation and ran to crank up his bulldozer while Russo returned to the reel to help anchor the cable reel to a forty-eight-inch-diameter tree.

By the time Andreatta's bulldozer chugged to the west end of the bridge, the work party had fashioned a loop in the loose end of the cable and unwound thirty feet. The loop was affixed to the bulldozer and Andreatta proceeded toward the treadway. As he went, Sergeant Russo pulled a loop off the reel and all the others guided the cable into the channel of the south treadway. Ed Keoughan orchestrated progress by banging a large wrench on the bulldozer—two raps to proceed and one rap to stop. At Keoughan's order, Andreatta proceeded, then stopped while Russo threw a fresh loop from the reel. Initial progress was maintained at a rate of about five paces between stops.

Unreeling the first fifty feet of the cable was no problem because the first layer was rather loosely wound and Russo and Keoughan were within talking distance. However, by a hundred feet, the process had slowed to four-pace intervals because the second and succeeding layers of cable were very tightly wound and because Russo and Keoughan were no longer in direct contact because of the noise of the bulldozer engine and the start of a German artillery barrage. Also, it became increasingly difficult for the men guiding the growing length of cable between the reel and the bulldozer to keep it in the treadway channel. After awhile and further consultation, Russo and Keoughan de-

cided to maintain a steady rate of three-pace intervals. Among
other ensuing problems was the tendency of the increasingly
lighter cable reel to edge toward the water, but the forty-eight-
inch tree to which it was anchored fortunately held the strain,
or we would have had a real disaster on our hands. Also, the
shelling never abated. The workmen refused to react to anything
but the closest misses, which obliged them to lie down in the
treadway channel.

It took something over an hour for the bulldozer to reach the
eastern approach to the bridge. Keoughan guided Andreatta out
toward a river barge that had been sunk by artillery fire and
Russo, Holzer, and Beaken got to work transferring the cable
end from the bulldozer to this secure sea anchor. Next, Andreatta used the bulldozer to stretch the cable so it could be
aligned on the four barges that had been anchored at regular
intervals south of the bridge. Unfortunately, Ed Keoughan was
struck by the whip action of the cable as it was being stretched
and he required medical attention. By the time Keoughan returned from the battalion aid station, Sergeant Smith and Holzer, Beaken, Bissell, Piar, and Getz were completing the job of
tying down the ropes from the treadway floats to the bridle cable.

As the cable was being anchored, Lieutenant Tom Stack's
Company C platoon put the finishing touches on the eastern
approach and anchored three floats about thirty feet upstream
to further support the bridle cable. In addition to replacing a
number of damaged treadway floats, Lieutenant John Perkins's
platoon, also from Company C, bowed and aligned the bridge
by lashing manila hawsers from the bridle cable to each of the
eighty-eight floats comprising the 1,032-foot span.

After all the damaged pontoons had been pulled and replaced,
and after the support guy lines were checked and tightened,
several of my school-educated engineers and I inspected the
entire bridge to be sure that all was correct and secure. Then,
as the two approaches were tidied up, I walked up to my CP so
I could report our success to Colonel Anderson. I was only
halfway there when I turned impulsively to look at "my" bridge.
I felt tears welling up in my eyes, I was so proud! It was 1900
hours that gray, miserable March 10, and the bridge was done.
In our way, as combat engineers, the officers and men of the
291st Engineer Combat Battalion were truly the first across the
Rhine.

As I looked, the first customers were nosing onto the treadway span from the west bank. These jeeps, weapons carriers, and trucks bore the markings of the 99th Infantry Division. Beside the slowly moving vehicles were walking men—among them infantrymen of the 99th Division who had stood before the tanks of Dietrich's 6th Panzer Army squarely at the point of the Bulge's northern shoulder.

I thought of our Remagen treadway as being a toll bridge, for it had taken the heaviest toll of casualties the battalion had yet suffered in a single place—one dead and thirty wounded so far. We had also had destroyed three Quickway cranes, two Brockway trucks, two air compressors, three two-and-a-half-ton dump trucks, thirty-two floats, and considerable miscellaneous equipment and materials. The units directly supporting us had sustained additional losses.

The German fire never let up between 1900 and 2200 hours. Mortars firing from portions of the eastern riverbank not yet controlled by our infantry added considerably to the woes of the artillery fire, for it tended to be more accurate.

As the men and vehicles of the 99th Division poured across to Erpel and beyond, my troopers continued to put the finishing touches on our masterpiece. Capping everything was a pair of signs erected at either end of the span by Sergeants Charlie Sherman and Calvin Chapman, of Bill McKinsey's battalion intelligence section:

THE LONGEST TACTICAL BRIDGE BUILT
FIRST ACROSS THE RHINE
CONSTRUCTED BY
291ST ENGR C BN
988 TDWY CO
998 TDWY CO

That evening, also, I finally got around to sharing the congratulatory messages from our supreme commander and army commander. The words of Generals Eisenhower and Hodges were greeted with nods of approval and displays of satisfaction but with very little cheering and few words. As the men knew, we were still at the zenith of a battle that could go against us. Our accomplishment would do much to help our side, but we knew that it might prove to be too little too late, particularly if the teetering Ludendorff collapsed and the 51st Engineer's heavy pontoon span was long delayed or held from completion. To be sure, now that our bridge was in, there was no telling how much blood and effort we would be required to expend to keep it in. So, once the euphoria of the moment of completion dissipated, my veterans thought better of exhibiting more than a tentative, war-weary caution against the odds of the unknown. As they well knew by then, this was war, and anything was possible.

The III Corps commander, Major General John Millikin, had planned his attack across the Rhine in three phases. The first phase line was an arc reaching to about three miles north and south of the Ludendorff Bridge and about two miles into the hills directly to the east. The second phase line was open—however much ground to the east needed to be taken to prevent the river from being directly observed by German artillery spotters. Finally, in the third phase, the III Corps would attack toward Bonn and about ten miles eastward to the autobahn and south to Andernach to obviate shelling of all the bridges.

By March 10 the bridgehead had expanded beyond the first phase line but had not reached the last line of hills from which the river could be directly observed. By pure bad luck, many of the last Wehrmacht units to cross the Ludendorff before it fell to the 9th Armored Division—including the very last such—had been field artillery units, all of which were halted east of the river and set up to fire on the Ludendorff and, eventually, several engineer bridges. The Germans had brought in many additional artillery units in succeeding days.

General Millikin instinctively concentrated his efforts toward the east, to overcome the artillery. However, the 1st Army commander, General Hodges, had other thoughts. He wanted the bridgehead expanded northward to the vicinity of the Lahn River so engineers with the neighboring and idle VII Corps could begin throwing across even more bridges. Strangely, Hodges did not communicate his wishes to Millikin until March 10. Immediately grasping the strategic implications, Millikin began shifting the weight of his two-plus infantry divisions. The 78th Infantry Division was assigned a narrow corridor along the river and ordered to attack due north to uncover crossings for the VII Corps. The 9th Infantry Division was similarly ordered to reconcentrate and attack north beside the 78th. The fresh 99th Division was to assume control of the remainder of the bridgehead line and do what it could to obviate the artillery fire against the bridges.

The Germans had plans of their own. While the great shuffle

in the bridgehead was underway, General Bayerlein sent the 11th SS Panzer Division into the area north of the bridgehead to prepare to mount a fresh counterattack. Thus, March 10 ended with two of our divisions concentrating to deliver a strategically necessary attack through rough terrain that had been lightly held but was now covered by a crack unit quite capable of putting up a stubborn, inch-by-inch retrograde defense.

That night, at the 1st Army headquarters, Colonel Bill Carter briefed General Hodges on the engineer bridging plan. The 291st's floating treadway was in and in use and the 51st Engineer Battalion's heavy pontoon bridge was due for completion sometime the next day, March 11. In addition, Colonel Carter had ordered yet another engineer battalion to install a floating Bailey span several hundred yards north of our treadway. As soon as the second pontoon bridge was in, Colonel Carter averred, it would be possible to close the Ludendorff to traffic in order to effect the major repairs that had been put off in the face of the ongoing emergencies in the bridgehead.

Earlier that evening, when I had called Colonel Anderson to tell him our bridge was done, he told me about the plans for the floating Bailey span and had asked me to stand by to commit troops to that effort on an as-needed basis. I was a little taken aback by the request because, as Colonel Anderson well knew, all my troops had gone virtually without rest for over two days in order to fulfill our contract on the floating treadway span. But I could offer no excuses or alibis. We were needed, so I told the group commander that he only had to call and we would get our men on the way to the new bridge site.

The German commanders facing us well realized the strategic importance of our bridge. All they had to do was look at the completed floating treadway from the dominant heights still in their hands. What had been a tenuous two-division bridgehead was rapidly being strengthened by a fresh veteran infantry division crossing our span. No doubt, the effect of the entry of these fresh troops was felt almost immediately at the outer periphery of the bridgehead. If such was possible, the intense artillery barrages rose in power during the late evening of March 10.

The night was a mixed bag for me. After seeing MPs assigned to the bridge and the road net leading eastward from the bridge, I walked across the span to make a final inspection, posted an engineer guard detail, and saw to the assignment of an engineering detail to maintain the eastern approach in the face of the onslaught of traffic. I returned to the west bank through a misty, foggy rain, as depressing in its clinging closeness as it had been at the moment of our arrival in Remagen. Both depressing and uplifting was the inexorable low rumble of the endless stream of trucks, jeeps, ambulances, and weapons carriers crossing the steel-decked span in low gear. As I progressed from east to west, I had to shoulder my way past hundreds of young infantrymen whose lives would be on the line within the hour as they faced German shells and bullets in the dark craggy hills at my back. Indeed, the incessant fall of German artillery rounds placed those young lives—and mine—in jeopardy every moment we trudged across the exposed span. As it was, we all were spattered by droplets of water kicked up by the shell splashes. I have no doubts, also, that some young men I did not see were felled by shrapnel from near misses, right out on my bridge. I was inured to the crossing, but I am sure every one of those young soldiers would have preferred a safer last-mile walk into the jaws of death. For the beleaguered young men of the 9th and 78th Infantry divisions, I knew, any risk faced by the newcomers was worth the result. I am told that the men who had been battling in the hills for as many as four days cheered aloud when news of the completion of our bridge reached them.

CHAPTER 30

I walked out toward our treadway span at about 0700 hours, March 11, and saw that the special platoon of the 299th Engineers was continuing its labors by replacing floats that had been knocked out by shell fire during the night. Behind the screening promenade buildings, an immense pile-up of tanks, trucks, jeeps, ambulances, and troops were waiting for the repairs to be completed so they could cross to the bridgehead.

The situation at the bridge looked like it was under control, so I asked Jim Gamble to walk upstream (south) with me to inspect the Ludendorff Bridge, which the 276th Combat Engineers was battling to save. The walk was uneventful until we reached the abutment and approach road. Suddenly the whine and roar of German planes suffused the routine work noises and sent us scurrying for cover.

The raid did not last long; the German fighter-bombers and Stuka dive-bombers dared not make more than a quick pass apiece through the thundering salvos of our by-then immense antiaircraft umbrella.

When the air raid ended—within two or three minutes—Jim and I looked up from our vantage point to view the structural damage the failed German demolitions effort had inflicted on the Ludendorff. There was a large section of planking out near a heavily damaged panel point, but more striking to an engineer was a broken lower chord on the upstream arch truss. This obviously caused the downstream truss to carry the load and thus subjected the entire bridge to a twisting and warping effect for which the structure had not been designed. The dead load of the planking the Germans and our engineers had built over the railroad tracks—four-inch wooden flooring 15 feet wide and 515 feet long—added about fifty tons to the original weight of the straining structure.

"I can't understand what's holding this damn thing up," Lieutenant Colonel Clayton Rust offered as he joined Jim and me below the jagged steel framework. "The damage and extra weight is bad enough," the commander of the 276th Combat Engineers went on, "but the vibrations are killing it. I hate those German howitzers! So far, the main chords seem to be okay, and they haven't taken a direct hit. We're really glad you guys and the 51st Engineers are giving us the new bridges. As soon as the 51st's pontoon span is in, we're going to close this one up and really do a job fixing it. All we've been able to do since we got here is fix up shell damage and weld on some braces."

I asked Rust when he thought the second pontoon bridge would be completed and he said he had heard it would be in by that evening. "We only need to keep the Ludy busy for another day."

Jim Gamble, whose Company A would be responsible for maintaining the treadway, returned to our battalion area with me and went off to check with his troop leaders. I joined Colonel Anderson, whom I found standing on the west bank following his inspection of our handiwork. After speaking with the group commander, I decided to add Company B to the bridge-maintenance detail and, under orders, send Company C about 150 yards downstream (north) to help the 148th Engineer Combat Battalion install the newly prescribed Class 40 floating Bailey span.

As the colonel and I continued to chat, a German rocket unit located in Bellendoorn, Holland, fired off a salvo of eleven V-2 rockets at the Remagen bridges. Because the rockets descended from the stratosphere at speeds greater than the speed of sound, we saw, then felt, then heard the blasts. The closest hit was within three hundred yards of where Colonel Anderson and I stood, and its rather startling arrival was the only time I saw the Old Man flinch and hunch down.

Except for the V-2 salvo, March 11 was a blandly routine day. The movement of troops and vehicles over our treadway continued at a steady crawl through relentless artillery fire and an unending string of hit-and-run air raids by virtually every type of fighter and bomber remaining in the Luftwaffe's inventory. As we had feared, the completion of our bridge had heralded a general onslaught aimed directly at us. Bombing runs against our treadway became so frequent that several antiaircraft guns were set up directly beside the approaches on both banks. My lasting impression of the day is the constant *thump-thump-thump* of the automatic antiaircraft cannon.

My battalion rear headquarters was due to arrive in Remagen late on the afternoon of March 11 and set up in the Hotel Für-stenberg, along the promenade. The headquarters troops were to be billeted in the lower-level rooms of nearby back-street buildings to protect them from the incessant shelling, and the personnel manning my forward CP were to move in with them. However, as the German air and artillery attacks continued without abatement, I decided to put off the transplacement until March 15, by which time the matter would surely be settled. Thus, late in the afternoon, I returned to our little shell-battered forward CP in the side street overlooking the bridge. I intended to eat well and sleep long.

My sixty-plus hours in Remagen were beginning to have an effect on me. Short catnaps here and there, the highs and lows of the emotional setting, the weight of responsibility, the un-equal sustenance of C, K, and D rations, the unsettling loud noises, the unremitting fear for my own well-being and that of my men, my ongoing concern for the men across the river—it was all adding up.

Just as I got to the CP, a smiling Mike Popp drove up at the end of the latest of innumerable courier runs between Remagen and the rear CP. An especially large smile on Mike's face told me something was up, and I was opening my mouth to inquire when he handed me a letter from Peggy. I grabbed the envelope from my driver's hand and turned to find a private spot in which I could savor my wife's words.

"Wait a minute, Colonel," Mike called after me, "Don't you want the package?"

Minutes later, I salivated uncontrollably as cans of shrimp, chicken, and corned beef fell into my lap from the ripped end of the box from home.

I threw a little party on the veranda of the Hotel Fürstenberg late that afternoon. The honored guests were Messrs. Gamble, McCarty, McKinsey, and Hancock—the only officers I could spring from the ongoing busy labors at the bridge site. The menu was the delicious cuisine my thoughtful wife had provided, along with some of the delectable afternoon catch from the Rhine, prepared tastefully by one of the company mess sergeants. The delightful, civilized meal was complemented by a variety of excellent Rhine wines rifled from the hotel's cellar. Unbelievably, our German hosts must have caught the mood, for the artillery attack abated to silence.

After the leisurely meal, I repaired to an inside room to read Peggy's letter. She suggested that perhaps I was not being altogether honest in my descriptions of our rear-echelon jobs and asked if such work merited the flood of medals and honors from foreign governments the battalion and I had begun receiving for our work in the Bulge. (A week after this letter arrived, she watched the latest Fox-Movietone newsreel in a local theater and saw me and several officers and men she knew ceremonially driving in the sign at the western end of the Rhine treadway bridge. In fact, Peg and her sister sat through the entire show twice just to be sure Peg's eyes had not been deceiving her— and that I had.)

As soon as I checked on the situation around the Ludendorff on the morning of March 12, I learned that Lieutenant Colonel Harvey Fraser's 51st Engineer Combat Battalion had completed its reinforced heavy pontoon bridge at around 2200 hours the previous evening. The completion of the second engineer bridge across the Rhine immediately alleviated the congestion on the west bank and added immeasurably to the urgent build up on the embattled east bank. It also permitted the closing of the battered Ludendorff for repairs.

March 12 was an uncharacteristically routine day. The air and artillery attacks continued apace, but the addition of two new antiaircraft artillery battalions—bringing to thirteen the total of such units in our little stretch of the Rhine valley—helped account for a new high of twenty-six enemy planes blown out of the fifty-eight separate raids. The day also brought us news that, on March 8, Field Marshal Gerd von Runstedt had been replaced as Commander in Chief, West, by Field Marshal Albert Kesselring. The new adversary had waged a brilliant retrograde campaign in Italy since mid 1943 and was considered by Hitler to be Germany's last successful field marshal. Apparently, Runstedt had been sacked as a direct consequence of our seizure of the Rhine bridgehead.

I spent the entire night of March 12 and most of the following morning at my CP. I also gave all but one platoon the day off in the hope that the troops would get some needed rest. However, getting any sleep at all remained problematic because both sides had brought in so many fresh artillery units that the unremitting exchanges sounded at all hours like a continuous drum roll enhanced by wild crescendos at odd and lengthy intervals.

On March 13, the vanguard of the 1st Infantry Division arrived in the vicinity of Remagen and prepared to cross into the bridgehead. The three reinforced infantry and one armored divisions on the east bank continued to expand their holdings, but without strategic results.

On March 14, the 78th Infantry Division's 309th Infantry Regiment captured the heights overlooking the Ruhr-Frankfurt autobahn, seven miles due east of Erpel, and several combat patrols actually set foot in the vital German main supply route. Early on March 14, also, Bad Honnef finally fell to elements of the 78th Division, which then advanced into the high hills to the northeast. Daylong attacks by all three battalions of the 310th Infantry finally overran the best of the German artillery observation points overlooking the Ludendorff and the completed engineer bridges.

March 15 was yet another day of "routine" bloodletting east of the Rhine and incessant air and artillery attacks against the river bridges. A gang raid against the bridges by twenty-one fast bombers met such an intense antiaircraft response that the bridges were not even near-missed and sixteen of the bombers were downed. More V-2s were fired at us, and the 540mm railway mortar continued to shake the earth each time one of its immense shells detonated.

Most of my battalion rear command group left Heimerssheim at 1600 hours, March 15, and arrived in Remagen at 1730 hours. By the time I had gathered my gear from the former forward CP, the new headquarters had been quickly and efficiently set up on the ground floor of the Hotel Fürstenberg, directly opposite the float-assembly site occupied by Ralph McCarty's platoon. My first priorities were a bath, then digging through my spare gear for a change of clothes, then a hot meal.

Life had changed for the better during the day. We noticed that the German artillery fire was slackening off somewhat, the first such reversal since we had arrived. And the air raids were less powerful, less accurate, and less frequent. Nevertheless, the V-2s continued to fall, and the damnable 540mm railway mortar continued to scar our psyches. When my exec, Major Larry Moyer, saw the V-2 and 540mm shell craters for the first time that afternoon, he announced his opinion that even a near miss by either could bilge our bridge. Our evening bull session, which centered on the rockets and 540mm shells, was interrupted by grand news for a change. Lieutenant John Brenna, who was on duty in the CP, came in with two messages of interest that had been passed along by SHAEF to all 1st Army units. Both were commendations for the Remagen operation; one was from Secretary of the Navy James Forrestal and the other from Speaker of the House Sam Rayburn.

On March 14, during a ceremony at which Hitler awarded Colonel Otto Skorzeny and Lieutenant Colonel Joachim Peiper Knight's Crosses with Diamonds, the German Führer ordered Skorzeny to send underwater commandos to Remagen to blow up all our bridges. Skorzeny launched the underwater commando operation against the Rhine bridges on March 15. That evening, seven German Navy swimmers working under Skorzeny arrived at a point about ten miles south—upstream—of Remagen and entered the water in the hope of affixing demolitions packages to any or all of our bridges.

The German swimmers faced formidable odds. On March 8, Lieutenant Colonel Harry Cameron's 164th Engineer Combat Battalion had been detailed to erect several protective booms upstream of the bridge sites and to take other measures as proof against waterborne attacks of any sort. Construction of the first boom commenced on March 9.

The 164th Engineers installed three booms, each of a different type. The first was an impact-type boom which went in three hundred yards upstream of the Ludendorff Bridge. It was designed to stop heavy barges, wrecks, or other heavy objects sent floating down the river, inadvertently or otherwise. The second was a log boom designed to stop and collect debris or detonate floating mines. The third was a mine net used to screen and detonate floating mines or intercept swimmers.

In addition to the passive boom defense, the 164th Engineers developed an active screen of small boats from which twenty-five-pound depth charges were dropped at frequent intervals. High-powered thirteen-million candlepower searchlights kept the river approaches south of the bridges bathed in intense light at all hours, and machine guns emplaced all along both banks were constantly manned by vigilant crews.

The seven German swimmers donned their skintight rubberized suits, which had been specially treated with a chemical compound that gave off heat when immersed in water. Each man carried an oxygen tank to provide air for underwater breathing—then a super-secret device—and each carried four seven-pound packets of Plastit, a pliable plastic explosive compound. Each swimmer also carried cutters with which to breach the boom nets and a light with which he could signal his fellow swimmers.

When all was ready the seven German frogmen plunged into the Rhine and headed downstream. Fortunately for us, several of them encountered problems with their underwater breathing equipment, so the mission was aborted and rescheduled for the night of March 16.

March 16 was altogether different. As the infantry divisions in the bridgehead ground forward against weakening opposition, so too did the artillery fire continue to weaken. For the first time since March 9, we experienced gaps between the barrages of up to two hours. However, at 1730 hours, March 16, as everyone who was not working lined up for chow, all hell fell in on the battalion.

The Hotel Fürstenberg, beside which we were waiting for our food, suddenly shook and shed mortar and stucco. Choking, gagging dust instantly filled the air and the big cans holding hot soapy rinse water for our mess kits fell on their sides, releasing their contents over our feet. And *then* there was the thunderous clap of the V-2's descent.

Major Ed Lampp, Sergeant Clark Edwards, and Technician 5th Grade Curtis Ledet were just pulling into town to set up the battalion operations center when the thunderclap struck. All three men were thrown to the ground and badly bruised when the force of the blast spun the command car out of control and hurled it into a wall. When the dust settled, we found all three dazed men sitting amidst a pile of trash that had been Ed's neatly filed operations files. Fortunately, all three quickly recovered.

Most of the 291st had been within a matter of feet of being annihilated, but, fortunately, the falling debris and hot water caused no permanent damage to any of us. After getting myself calmed down, I sent firm orders to the company commanders regarding proper dispersal of the troops for as long as we remained in the bridgehead. The error had been mine, and I was determined that it never be made again.

Late that evening, Colonel Anderson called to schedule a noon meeting. He hinted broadly that the 291st was about to be handed a tough new assignment in support of a division scheduled to thrust its way out of the bridgehead.

Even later that night, the German frogmen prepared to swim downstream to the bridges. However, as they were donning their gear, their take-off site came under American artillery fire. The team commander decided to postpone again.

On March 17, elements of the 9th and 78th Infantry divisions crashed across the north-south Rhur-Frankfurt autobahn, thus achieving the III Corps' primary objective. In seven days of unremitting action against the German 3rd Parachute, and 272nd, 277th, and 326th Volksgrenadier divisions, the American infantry had advanced nearly seven miles into the teeth of one of the most intense artillery concentrations experienced by American forces in Western Europe. For all practical purposes, our infantry's final advance across the autobahn lifted the artillery threat against the Rhine bridges. Later in the day, the battered 78th Division was relieved in place by the leading regiments of the fresh 1st Infantry Division, which immediately resumed the attack to the east.

As promised, Colonel Anderson arrived at my command post shortly after noon on March 17 and we walked along the promenade past worksites manned by the platoons commanded by Lieutenants Arch Taylor, Wade Colbeck, and Ralph McCarty. The area had been policed of all varieties of damaged gear except for a great pile of deflated rubber pontoons. After inspecting several V-2 and 540mm shell craters and the visible results of bombing and strafing raids, the colonel asked about our casualties. I was glad to say and he was surprised to hear that we had taken only two casualties since March 10.

At about 1430 hours, we found ourselves standing beside the treadway bridge, across which the 1st Infantry Division troops and vehicles were still moving. The colonel stepped into the column of walking men and I darted in beside him. Along the way to the east bank, the group commander occasionally stepped aside to inspect the cable lashings or just to enjoy the scenery, which was breathtaking now that the shelling had all but ceased.

It was just coming up 1500 hours and the colonel and I were still on the treadway bridge when our attention was arrested by a loud, painful groaning from just to our south. As I instinctively glanced toward the source of the noise, I heard an even louder sound of simultaneous screeching, cracking, and splintering as steel rubbed against steel and wood. There, directly in front of me, the tired old Ludendorff Bridge was at last giving way. As the effects of the self-demolition progressed, the immense structure swayed and then caved in. It was like watching a slow-motion movie, the progressive action was so distinct.

The collapse of the Ludendorff Bridge set all available hands in the 291st to instant, instinctive rescue efforts and a frantic race to save our own span. Automatically, as soon as the big railroad bridge sounded its own death knell, my veteran engineers recovered from the shock and got to doing all the things that seemed to need doing.

In no time at all, all sorts of heavy debris was floating swiftly in the current toward our vulnerable treadway floats. As the infantrymen on the treadway span speeded up their pace from route march to every man for himself, my magnificent engineers appeared as if out of nowhere with cranes, powerboats, and other equipment that could be used to rescue swimmers and prevent fatal collisions between the debris and the floats. Scores of my men ran out from either bank armed with pikes, poles, or anything that came to hand that could be used to hold off debris and direct it between the pontoons. Max Schmidt and several others drove Quickway cranes out onto the bridge in order to lift the larger, heavier pieces of planking up and over our span. As efforts to save our bridge coalesced, many of my men worked their way out onto the saddles to help pull their comrades from the largely bilged 276th Engineers out of the dangerous current.

Most fortunately, several of our utility boats were on the water downstream of the treadway bridge when the Ludendorff collapsed. The crewmen of these and others arriving from the shore nosed against the imperiled treadway span, reinforcing it until the bulk of the floating debris had been poked through or lifted over to be swept away downstream.

We fished out eighteen survivors from the many members of the 276th I had seen scrambling for safety during the last moments of the Ludendorff's thundering, screeching demise. Among them was Lieutenant Colonel Clayton Rust, the battalion commander, who was picked up by a boat manned by Sergeant Frank Dolcha.

Severely shaken but unhurt, Rust eventually told us that he had been in about the center of the span when he heard several sharp reports, no doubt from rivets shearing off. He looked up in time to see a hanger break loose, and that caused the entire deck to tremble. Joining workmen who had by then dropped their tools and were scrambling to safety, Rust knew that the bridge was collapsing. He headed for the Remagen side but quickly encountered a literally uphill struggle as the center span gave way. The next thing Rust knew, he was pinned underwater. However, the debris shifted and he bobbed to the surface, grabbed some floating debris, and rode the current until he was dragged aboard Sergeant Dolcha's utility boat.

That was some of the good news. We eventually learned that the tally had mounted to twenty-eight killed or missing and ninety-three injured.

At about 1615 hours, while my troops were still clearing debris that had piled up against our floats, the Germans threw in a terrific artillery barrage. Most of their shells impacted around the treadway span and eleven of our men were wounded. As soon as our medics—Master Sergeant Doug Swift, Technician 3rd Grade Mack Barbour, and Technician 5th Grade Dave Fitzgerald—had seen to the evacuation of the wounded men from the bridge, I rushed to the aid station to see how everyone was doing. Captain Max Schmidt had been wounded so badly in the abdomen and chest that Dr. Watson had already had him evacuated to the nearest field hospital. I found Sergeant Joe Geary yelling up a storm of protests over his own impending evacuation, and my first instinct was to let him stay, but I quickly reversed myself when Dr. Watson told me that Joe's foot wounds were extremely serious and would probably cause him to be sent to the States. Jim Gamble had been struck also, but he refused evacuation and returned to work after having his wound dressed. I was glad for Jim, but I was devastated by the loss of my other fine leaders and their troops.

Things quieted down again by 1800 hours, so I ordered the cooks to serve everyone a hot meal. As the work crews came in off the bridge, I ordered the troop leaders to keep everyone well dispersed lest the Germans catch us with another V-2 or artillery attack. I saw on the men's faces the effects of the day's multiple blows. The conversation was somber and muted—a bad sign— and remained fixed on the loss of the Ludy and the casualties we had sustained. There was nothing I could think of that would lift the men from their funk, but things became gradually lighter as their resilient, youthful spirits inevitably rose. As we ate and talked, the troops and vehicles of the 1st Infantry Division resumed their crossing on our fully restored bridge.

Also as we ate and talked, the final chapter of the German underwater commando assault was played out. Quite simply, lookouts from the 164th Combat Engineers spotted the German frogmen about two miles south of Remagen. Instantly, the thirteen-million candlepower searchlights pinpointed the swimmers and streams of machine-gun bullets prodded them to shore. All seven Germans were captured long before they reached the first security boom.

By the morning of March 18, 1945, nearly two complete American infantry divisions had crossed into the Rhine bridgehead by means of our treadway bridge and the 51st Engineer Combat Battalion's heavy pontoon bridge. In all by then, four infantry divisions had crossed the Rhine at Remagen. Their doing so undoubtedly was the deciding factor in the end phase of the war in the West.

PART SIX

RACE TO THE DANUBE

CHAPTER 31

On the morning of March 18, 1945, the 291st Engineer Combat Battalion was reassigned to the 1159th Engineer Combat Group, which was headquartered in Linz, at the east end of the 51st Engineer Combat Battalion's heavy pontoon bridge. We were to move our CP to Linz that morning and immediately go to work in direct support of Major General Walter Lauer's 99th Infantry Division. Our new boss, the commander of the 1159th Group, was Colonel Kenneth Fields, who had graduated at the head of the West Point class of 1933 and was considered one of the very best engineers in the U.S. Army. According to my last briefing from Colonel Wallis Anderson, we faced an immense job of clearing mines and repairing and maintaining roads and bridges along the 99th Division's proposed route of attack out of the Rhine bridgehead.

While the rest of the battalion got moving, Ed Lampp and I drove into the bridgehead by way of the Kripp-Linz pontoon bridge and headed east along narrow roads in the trace of the 99th Division. As we had seen so often in our dash across France, Belgium, and the Roer region, the beauty of the countryside was marred by ruined villages, each with its battered church steeples. Tanks without treads or with turrets blown off lay askew in roadside ditches, waiting for the ordnance repair crews to arrive. Here and there, dead American and German soldiers and civilians remained uncollected by the overworked graves registration teams. Rotting horses and cows lay everywhere. Permeating the entire bridgehead was the overpowering smell of death and putrefaction.

When Ed and I arrived at the autobahn, we immediately faced several blown bridges and a roadway that was impaired by, among other things, an American tank that had been blown up

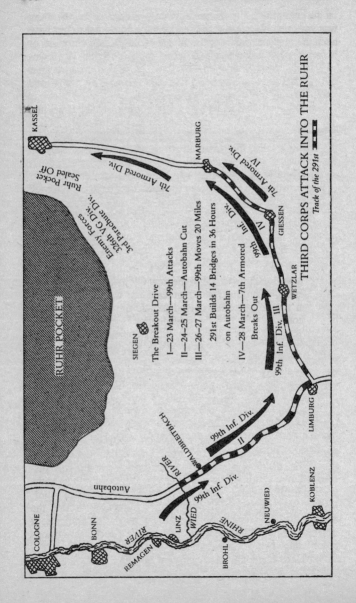

THIRD CORPS ATTACK INTO THE RUHR

Track of the 291st

The Breakout Drive

I—23 March—99th Attacks

II—24-25 March—Autobahn Cut

III—26-27 March—99th Moves 20 Miles

291st Builds 14 Bridges in 36 Hours on Autobahn

IV—28 March—7th Armored Breaks Out

RUHR POCKET

Ruhr Pocket Sealed Off

Enemy Forces
326th VG Div.
3rd Parachute Div.

KASSEL

7th Armored Div.

MARBURG

IV Armored Div.

IV 7th Armored Div.

IV 99th Inf. Div.

GIESSEN

WETZLAR

III 99th Inf. Div.

SIEGEN

LIMBURG

II 99th Inf. Div.

WALDBREITBACH

RIVER

I 99th Inf. Div.

Autobahn

COLOGNE

BONN

REMAGEN

LINZ

WIED

RIVER

BROHL

RHINE RIVER

NEUWIED

KOBLENZ

on the centerline. The former Luftwaffe airfield at Aegidienberg was wrecked, its runway pocked by huge holes that might have been the result of deliberate sabotage by the fleeing Germans or huge runway-busting bombs dropped by our air force. The towns of Kashbach and Honnegen looked like St.-Vith or Mortain after the last battles to claim them had died down; they lay in total ruin.

We followed a wide, sweeping route back toward Erpel and our own bridge and saw more of the same—more destruction everywhere we looked. Throughout, I was mindful that this was the enemy's land, that my concern should be focused only on the roadways, bridges, and other engineering chores, and not on the plight of the civilians, who were our sworn enemies.

We recrossed the Rhine at our own treadway bridge and turned north to check in with Company C. Captain Warren Rombaugh told us that the work on the floating Bailey bridge, which had been started the day before, was going well. It appeared to be about one third the way across the river. According to Warren, not one German shell had landed anywhere near the new bridge since Company C's arrival on the worksite.

When we finally returned to the new CP in Linz, Lieutenants Don Gerrity and John Brenna greeted me with news that the battalion was scheduled to stand parade on March 20 so the troops could be awarded the Presidential Unit Citation and an assortment of Silver Stars, Bronze Stars, and Purple Hearts. None of us was thrilled with the news because we all would have to spend the next two days polishing ourselves and our gear. On the other hand, we certainly would not be going back into the action until after the ceremony.

One of the many advantages we had in the combat engineers was the inclusion of a water purification unit in our equipment table. At least once a week in all but the direst circumstances, the platoon commanders were able to get their men on trucks for a ride to the battalion water point so all hands could shower, shave, and do their laundry. The men had become highly disciplined about taking what was offered to them, for regular baths prevented skin diseases and made everyone just plain feel better. Invariably, if there was a man prone to remaining in filth, the members of his squad took measures to ensure compliance. It was thus a relatively simple matter for me to direct all the troops to look their best at the ceremony.

Our H&S Company mess sergeant dug up a complete set of plates and silver from a shelled-out hotel and decided to make the ceremony complete with a full-course dinner under canvas. Among other things, the menu would include "Fish à la Rhein" and fawn from the forests. When he learned that the infantry units preceding us into the bridgehead had beaten him to the chicken coops, he added a festive but unappealing course of green powdered eggs.

Troops were detailed to build a reviewing stand and invitations were sent out by a courier to honored guests: Colonel Rusty Lyons, the III Corps chief engineer, Colonel Kenneth Fields, our new group boss, and Colonel Wallis Anderson, our former boss.

The troops turned out looking spiffy and clean, really quite sharp. As the color guard passed the reviewing stand, I heard our H&S Company clerk remark that this was the first parade in which Company A's Sergeant Joe Geary had not been a member of the guard. The comment brought a moment of sadness to offset the festive nature of the day, but it was a good reminder that we had not accomplished so much without a price. The mood carried over to the special dinner, during which I sat in virtual silence between Colonels Anderson and Lyons.

For all the good intentions of the cooks, the meal was a little on the somber side. Though abundant wine and champagne had been collected from the ruins of several riverside hotels, the troops were sparing in its use. No one even offered toasts in honor of the comrades we had lost, dead and wounded, in the Bulge, the assault into Germany, the Roer crossing, and the Rhine assault, but I knew that memories of those men were very much on everyone's mind.

That evening, after our guests had departed and the men returned to their billets, I sat down at my desk and began a long letter to Peggy. I was only about halfway through the job when Captain Bill McKinsey asked if I was ready to hear his reconnaissance report and assessment of the job facing the battalion. Bill's friendly grin snapped me out of my emotional funk and I told him to go ahead.

"You won't believe what we're facing, Colonel." Good old Bill; always getting right to the point. "All the bridges on the autobahn have been blown. In the 99th Division's zone of attack alone there are fourteen bridges that need to be rebuilt or replaced so that tanks can keep up with the infantry."

I told Bill that Ed Lampp and I had seen a short section of the autobahn, including several blown bridges, and then I complimented him on the thoroughness of his reconnaissance. However, after Remagen, I had one pressing question: "Were you fired on?"

"Not this time. I think the Krauts are too busy pulling back fast to do much rearguard shooting."

I told Bill to prepare to give a full-scale brief to the staff and company officers and turned back to my letter to Peggy. However, as I picked up my pen, I was aware that Bill had not moved. "Is there anything else, Bill?"

"Well, sir, as a matter of fact there is. We all feel you should take a break. You haven't missed a battle or a bridge under fire since December 17. You look like hell frozen over. You used to be a husky Penn State football player, but you look kind of skinny now, sir. You have two big black circles around your eyes. So, we're giving you a one-week pass to the Riviera—courtesy of the staff, the company commanders, and Colonel Carter's 1st Army Engineer Section. You're flying down on Colonel Carter's plane. Hotel costs, meals, and all the trimmings will be taken care of."

I was sure I had tears in my eyes by the time Bill stopped talking. "Bill, I really appreciate the thought and all the trouble you've gone to, but I can't leave now that we're about to jump off in a major assault. I thank you all for your concern, but I'm not leaving."

Bill nodded his acceptance of my decision but insisted upon having the last word: "Colonel, we're going to force your hand on this after the 99th Division breaks out of the bridgehead."

We held our staff and command meeting later that night, March 20. Captain Lloyd Sheetz had just returned from meeting with the 99th Division chief engineer, so I asked him to relate the division's plan of attack. "They're going to jump off at a minute after midnight, March 23, with a surprise attack under cover of darkness. Crossing sites have been selected, routes fully agreed to, and precise objectives set for each combat unit. Our part of the mission is to open the autobahn by replacing bridges so the 7th Armored Division can get its tanks into the assault."

Next, Ed Lampp laid out an intricate plan in which the battalion would replace all fourteen blown bridges along the autobahn in forty-eight hours with new Bailey spans. I listened and became certain that my staff was pulling my leg, for I had not been privy to the planning. "You guys have to be joking. I don't think 1159th Group can provide us with enough bridging equipment fast enough to do a job like that."

Jim Gamble spoke up, as if ready for my incredulous reaction. "Colonel, if this battalion could build an eleven-hundred-foot floating treadway under fire in thirty-two hours, we can sure get this little bitty job done—especially when McKinsey says the Jerries are turning tail and running."

Lloyd Sheetz had some background to add. "Colonel, the 99th Division is a crack unit. This afternoon, their division engineer led some infantry across the Wied River by taking off his coat and wading out into the stream while the enemy shot at him and the infantrymen he was trying to lead just stood and gaped at him. The troops sort of expect big things from engineers."

I rose to the many implied challenges set forth by my officers and approved the plan. The 291st would try to set an all-time record for the most assault bridges constructed in the least amount of time.

The battalion was all set to go early on the evening of March 22, so I drove up to the 99th Division CP to meet with the staff and follow the jump-off from the division operations center. Though I still hated to be away from the 1111th Group, I was completely at ease with our assignment to the 99th Division. This unit had been the rock upon which the entire north shoulder defense of the Bulge had been built. It was indeed a crack unit, thoroughly competent and coldly efficient.

Precisely on time, at 0001, March 23, 1945, the 393rd and 395th Infantry regiments slid down from their positions in the hills overlooking the Wied River, waded across the stream, and started climbing the hills on the far side. As hoped, the troops took the Germans completely by surprise, driving forward to the first dominant ridgeline and then on into the hills toward Kurtscheid. Advancing far ahead of schedule throughout the day, the infantrymen quickly overran Rossbach and continued to rush ahead through one German town after another. The few Germans who attempted to stand and fight were rooted out by combat troops coldly impervious to enemy fire, a trait they had acquired at the point of the Bulge's northern shoulder. Altogether on March 23, the two regiments the 99th Division had on line swept four thousand yards deeper into Germany.

Throughout the first day of the breakout, line platoons from the 291st drove forward in the immediate wake of the assault, removing roadblocks and sweeping for mines. Directly to our rear was a full combat command of the 7th Armored Division, its tanks ready to sweep forward as soon as the roads had been swept and the blown bridges replaced.

On March 24, the infantry advanced an additional fifty-five hundred yards across the hill country, firmly securing a great length of the north-south Ruhr-Frankfurt autobahn in the direction of the Lahn River. During an inspection tour of the front, Ed Lampp, Bill McKinsey, and I marveled at the tenacity of this relatively new division, which had arrived in Belgium only a short time before the Ardennes Offensive erupted.

Our job now was the replacement of the fourteen road bridges. After assuring me that all the bridging materials had been lined up by Captain Jim Walton, who had returned to Supply after Max Schmidt had been wounded out on the Rhine treadway bridge, Ed added, "Colonel, if I were a betting man, I would place some money on the battalion getting all the bridges in within forty-eight hours. The troops are *ready* for this job!" Word around the battalion was that Frank Rhea's Company B had directly challenged Jim Gamble's Company A to see which was the best in the battalion. When Warren Rombaugh's Company C troops heard, they had challenged the winner for top honors. There was no question, as Ed pointed out, that the troops were in top form. Bill McKinsey added that he was afraid that his intelligence chief would not be able to get enough signs built and painted in time to tell the world who had built so many bridges so fast.

Our zero hour was a minute after midnight, March 26. Lieutenant Arch Taylor's Company A platoon started the first Bailey bridge precisely on time and completed it in the dark at 0530 hours.

I spent the entire night on the road with Mike Popp, visiting each bridge site in turn. The troops were more motivated and animated than I had ever seen them. As far as they were concerned, this was the olympiad of bridge building; everything they had accomplished until then had been training and confidence building. To me, the regimented lifting and piecing together at each site looked like a champion rowing crew in action—the unity of purpose and action was that perfect. Every line platoon in the battalion built at least one bridge and several of the early starters built two. The last of the fourteen bridges was completed at 1645 hours, March 28, by Lieutenant Tom Stack's Company C platoon. We did it without sustaining a single casualty or suffering a single injury.

Damned if we didn't do it all in under thirty-seven hours—

eleven hours and fifteen minutes ahead of our outrageous schedule. Damned if we really weren't the best engineer combat battalion in the world!

The completion of the fourteenth autobahn bridge allowed the 7th Armored Division to enter the fight in direct support of the 99th Infantry Division. The added weight of the crack armored battalions carried the III Corps assault well beyond the region of the autobahn and on toward the Lahn River and the big city of Giessen. The 99th Division forward CP displaced to Kurtscheid, and our battalion forward CP closed up on it in its fifth move since leaving Remagen on March 18.

The 99th Division's drive into the heavily wooded mountainous region east of the autobahn carried it through Neder Reden and Hardet. The fleeing Germans left behind many abatis roadblocks consisting of felled trees interspersed with mines and booby traps, so my line squads had to remain close behind the advance to open roads for tanks and other supporting vehicles and, sadly, the ubiquitous ambulances. Next behind the infantry were the line platoons charged with repairing the roadway and installing new bridges so that the 7th Armored's tanks could keep more or less apace with the infantry.

Suddenly, in true blitzkrieg fashion, the 7th Armored Division passed through the 99th Infantry Division's front and slashed ahead thirty miles through three weakened and confused volksgrenadier divisions. For two days, the unsupported armor was able to roam the enemy countryside at will while the troops of the 99th Division mopped up pockets of resistance and accepted the uncontested surrender of thousands of demoralized German soldiers. For two days, we experienced lightning warfare as we never had before. The Germans had had no time to blow bridges or block roads, so we became little more than ad hoc provost marshals, storming into one town after another to root out burgomasters and demand that the citizens turn in cameras and all types of weapons. We often found ourselves ahead of the infantry and within sight of the advancing armor.

Our battalion vanguard pulled into Giessen on April 1 and went to work convoying many hundreds of German prisoners back to camps in the rear. I was stunned to see the state of the vaunted Wehrmacht, for the majority of the prisoners clearly appeared to be middle-aged men and boys under the age of sixteen, all dressed in ragged makeshift uniforms. News that evening from Captain Lloyd Sheetz, our liaison officer at the

99th Division CP, indicated that the 7th Armored Division had reached Paderborn and had thus sewn up the so-called Ruhr Pocket. However, by then, according to Lloyd, the pocket was breaking up and scores of thousands of unarmed German soldiers trying to surrender and uncountable liberated slave laborers were clogging the III Corps main supply routes.

Bill McKinsey brought up some statistics at our evening bull session: Since jumping off on March 23, eight days before, the 99th Infantry Division had conquered 495 square miles of enemy territory, taken over 200 towns and villages, and captured 8,542 prisoners, of whom the bulk had been processed and transported by the 291st. The creation and imminent collapse of the Ruhr Pocket by the 1st Army's III, V, and VII corps had deprived the Nazi regime of its industrial heartland and had taken as many as four hundred thousand German soldiers and airmen out of the war. By all appearances, Germany stood on the brink of collapse.

CHAPTER 32

The Germans quit the Ruhr region altogether on Sunday, April 15, 1945, three days after we were rocked by the news of the death of President Franklin Roosevelt. By then, all of our prisoner-of-war camps were filled beyond capacity by fit German soldiers who were clearly placing their lives and futures ahead of any remaining loyalty to the Nazi regime. Only the most rabid Nazis were still putting up appreciable resistance.

As the Allied armies in the West converged along a narrowing front and the Ruhr became a backwater, I took the opportunity of our relative inactivity to institute a major program of rest and recreation for my men. Every man we could spare from routine road and bridge maintenance duties was given an opportunity to wash, shave, and trade in worn clothing and shoes. Everyone who wanted to go was sent on fishing expeditions in the clear streams and lakes that dotted our operational zone. We played hard at a wide variety of sports. As the transportation system sorted itself out, long leaves in Paris and Brussels became available on a limited basis.

The moment things settled into a routine, Bill McKinsey was back with his ''order'' that I leave for my vacation on the Riviera. By then, even I felt the need to take a break, so I acceded and joined a fellow lieutenant colonel from the 1st Army Engineer Section for the flight to Cannes. The week passed in a blur of unwarlike activity. On the way back to the Ruhr, the pilot of our C-47 transport plane dipped low over Remagen so I could see the 291st's handiwork. It was satisfying to see that the treadway pontoon bridge was as busy with traffic as it had been on its first day of business.

I was met at the airfield at Scheinfeld by good old Mike Popp. As I greeted my driver, however, I was struck by the look of despair on his face. Instantly, the positive effects of a week away from the grind dissipated in a shudder of fear. I knew instinctively that someone close to me had died. As I climbed into the command car for the drive to my new CP, in Klein, I asked the inevitable question, "Who was it, Mike?"

"You won't believe it, Colonel. It's your chess-playing buddy."

"Not Kamen!" I felt dizzy as the face of Dr. Paul Kamen, the battalion dentist, flashed before my eyes. "How did our medics get involved in a shootout?"

"We were in convoy, keeping up with the 99th Division on the way south. On April 20, the Krauts dive-bombed our column near a place called Kitzingen, south of Frankfurt."

I wanted more details; I wanted to know how Paul Kamen, the hero medico of Malmédy, had died. Mike took a deep breath and laid it out. "We were in a motorcade, meeting no resistance, when we heard the Kraut jets coming down on us. All the trucks stopped and everyone hit the ditch. It was routine stuff, Colonel. We'd done it a hundred times since we crossed into Germany. Anyway, I was at the front of the column and the medical section was all the way in the rear. According to the guys who were back there, the medics never got out of their trucks. The jets hit them too fast. Doctor Kamen's truck took a direct hit. He was killed instantly. They also got Doug Swift. We got Doug out, but he died in the hospital. Mack Barbour was with him when he died."

I was dumbfounded, too overcome by grief to speak, so we finished the drive to the CP in silence. When we got there, Lieutenant Don Gerrity came out to greet me with what he hoped would be better news. "Five men from H&S Company were wounded in the jet attack, Colonel, but," and he held up his hand before I went crazy, "they've all been returned to duty. Nothing serious." After Don told me who the wounded men were, I asked where I could find Technician 3rd Grade Mack Barbour. Don said that he would get Mack for me.

As soon as Mack walked into the CP, I asked how Paul Kamen had died. "He went right away, sir, as soon as the bomb got the weapons carrier. We were stopped before the bomb hit, but we didn't have a chance to get out. I wasn't touched. I checked his vital signs right away, but he was gone. Sir, there wasn't a mark on him. It could have been a concussion or it could be his heart stopped from the shock of the explosion. We got him to the evac hospital and the doctors confirmed that he was gone.

"Master Sergeant Swift had pretty nasty abdominal wounds, but it looked like he was going to make it. I thought he'd make it, but he died during the same evening."

While I had been waiting to return to the battalion by air that morning, I had learned that we had been attached to Lieutenant General George Patton's 3rd Army. The jet attack and deaths had occurred as the battalion column was moving on roads in the 3rd Army zone. As soon as Mack Barbour left the CP, I asked my assembled staffers—Majors Moyer and Lampp and Captains McKinsey and Sheetz—to tell me what was going on.

Larry Moyer spoke up in his clear, unruffled manner: "Patton needed some crack troops to strike at the Hitler Redoubt, so he talked Bradley into transferring the entire III Corps to Third Army. We're going to put the finishing touches on the Nazis." That made sense; Major General James Van Fleet, the new III Corps commanding general, was a 1915 West Point classmate of Eisenhower's and Bradley's. Storming into the so-called Hitler Redoubt, the mountainous area near Berchtesgaden, Austria, in which the last of the Nazi true believers were reportedly preparing to make their last stand, would certainly add luster to his career.

After giving the complete rundown, Larry noted that the battalion had received a letter of commendation directly from General Eisenhower—and enthusiastically endorsed by Lieutenant General Courtney Hodges—for the job we had done at Remagen. In a separate letter, General Van Fleet also commended us for our virtuoso performances at Remagen and during the 99th Infantry Division's breakout. Lloyd Sheetz, our liaison with the 1159th Group, told me then that the group commander, Colonel Kenneth Fields, had ordered a parade formation to honor us the next day with medals earned in Remagen. Colonel Rusty Lyons, the III Corps chief engineer, also would be attending.

I next asked for a tactical appraisal, which brought Ed Lampp and Bill McKinsey into the conversation. We were still operating in direct support of Major General Walter Lauer's 99th Infantry Division. The III Corps, attacking with three divisions abreast since April 19, was on the 3rd Army's right flank, tied in with Lieutenant General Alexander Patch's 7th U.S. Army, a component of the 6th Army Group. Our mission was to support the 99th Division's rapid drive to the Danube River near Ingolstadt,

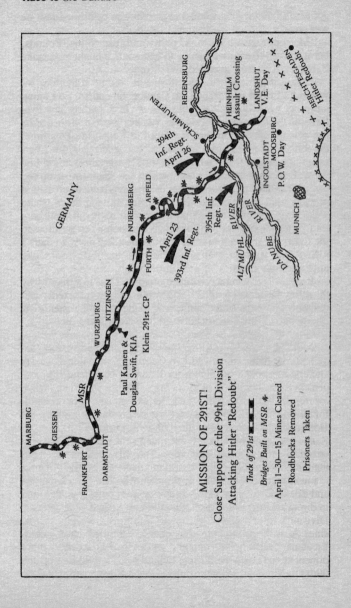

GERMANY

MARBURG

GIESSEN

FRANKFURT

DARMSTADT

MSR

WURZBURG

KITZINGEN

Paul Kamen &
Douglas Swift, KIA

Klein 291st CP

FURTH

NUREMBERG

April 23

393rd Inf. Regt.

ARFELD

394th
Inf. Regt.
April 26

SCHAMHAUPTEN

REGENSBURG

ALTMÜHL RIVER

395th Inf
Regt.

DANUBE RIVER

HEINHELM
Assault Crossing

LANDSHUT
V.E. Day

INGOLSTADT

MOOSBURG

P.O.W. Day

MUNICH

BERCHTESGADEN
Hitler "Redoubt"

MISSION OF 291ST!
Close Support of the 99th Division
Attacking Hitler "Redoubt"

Track of 291st
Bridges Built on MSR
April 1–30—15 Mines Cleared
Roadblocks Removed
Prisoners Taken

doing all the odd jobs we had been doing since Normandy. As soon as we reached the Danube, the 291st was to construct an assault bridge across the mighty river and support the III Corps drive across the Munich plain and on into the mountains around Berchtesgaden, the so-called Hitler Redoubt.

I asked if anyone had any information on the conditions we would find when we reached the Danube. Of course, Ed Lampp had it all worked out. "It looks like we'll be putting in a five-hundred-foot treadway bridge in a heavy current with maybe less enemy opposition than we faced at Remagen. This time, the 99th is going to cross in assault boats and the 324th Engineers is going to try to build a footbridge right behind the first wave. Our job is to get our treadway in fast so the 7th Armored can get its tanks up. Word is that the first regiment to cross will hook around to cover the second regiment, and that's where we'll build the bridge—behind the second regiment. It'll be a lot like the support we gave the 78th Division when we crossed the Roer, but it's been raining a lot the past few days, so there's lots of mud and the water will be high and fast. Looks like another soupy mess."

As usual following a command briefing, I had to wonder why the 291st needed a commander. My officers' recent activity and my recent absence added some sting to the traditional postbriefing thought. Now I *really* believed they didn't need me!

We did our second big spruce-up in a month and stood parade on a soccer field "somewhere in Germany" so Colonels Fields and Lyons could read aloud our letters of commendation and present a new pocketful of Silver Stars, Bronze Stars, and Purple Hearts. Only the recipients and H&S Company were on hand, for all our line platoons had work to do, replacing bridges and repairing roads throughout the 99th Division zone.

The speeches were gratifying, but I kept seeing the faces of our dead and evacuated comrades. The only comfort I took beyond that of recognizing deserving individuals was when I scanned the faces of many of the men who had been wounded and returned to duty. The ceremony was quickly ended and everyone scattered to get on with the next assault.

As soon as the award ceremony ended, I climbed into my command car beside Mike Popp and set out to inspect every one of the battalion's many worksites. Behind me, I left Ed Lampp and our supply officer, Captain Jim Walton, hard at work arranging to have all the bridging materials and equipment we would need on site as soon as we closed on the mighty Danube.

At the Bailey bridge construction site at Arfeld, Sergeants Ed Keoughan and Sheldon Smith marked my return from leave by offering me a rack stick—the two-man implement used to lift and move Bailey bridge panels—and guiding me to a choice spot with their squads. I was tempted to pitch in, for their Company C platoon was faced with deploying a 190-foot double-triple span in virtually record time. An all-hands effort eventually saw the bridge to completion in a very respectable twenty-seven hours. Other works in progress I saw that evening were a sixty-foot double-single Bailey built by Lieutenant Arch Taylor's Company A platoon at Giessen; a fifty-foot double-single completed in two and a quarter hours by Lieutenant Al Edelstein's Company A platoon at Berghausen; and a ninety-foot triple-single Bailey completed by Lieutenant Ralph McCarty's Company B platoon in three and three quarters hours at Markhausen.

Following a brief stop-off at the battalion CP around midnight to bolt down a quick meal and read our mail, Mike and I headed to Megen to see how Lieutenant John Kirkpatrick's Company B platoon was progressing on a seventy-foot double-single Bailey span. We arrived just as the platoon was finishing the three-hour task. When I commented on the speed, John allowed as he and Lieutenant Wade Colbeck had some money riding on the outcome. Thus, when I set off for Colbeck's worksite—an eighty-foot double-single bridge replacement directly on the Reich's autobahn—I expected to find a nest of frenetic activity. Nothing of the sort. I was greeted by the wide-grinning platoon commander and informed that the bridge would be completed in a matter of minutes, only two and a half hours after the job was started. As Wade led me around the job site, he pointed out Sergeant Charlie Dishaw, one of my Malmédy roadblock commanders. Charlie had been wounded on March 28, but was now supervising the work at the end of the bridge even though his bandage-swathed arm still was in a sling. Next, Mike drove me to two more bridge sites manned by Company C platoons—a 120-foot triple-single that was emplaced at Grevenbruck in seventeen hours and an eighty-foot double-single that went in at Fürth in three and a half hours. Rounding out the list Ed Lampp had given me, I had Mike drive me to bridges that had been completed at Harrbach, Altenfeld, and Richelsdorf during the last days of my leave. All along the roads to the bridges and on back to the CP was evidence of the massive mine clearing and road repair effort the battalion had undertaken in the past few days. Here and there, massive piles of felled trees attested to the talk I had heard about intricate abatis roadblocks built up by the fleeing Germans throughout the region.

After seeing to the road net behind the III Corps, the entire 291st joined in the final push on the Danube.

In the southern sector of the 99th Infantry Division's zone of operations, the 395th Infantry Regiment reached the Altmühl River late in the evening of April 24, 1945, and, next morning, advanced into a strongpoint held by elements of the 17th SS Panzergrenadier Division near the town of Kinding. While its two sister battalions engaged the strongpoint, the 2nd Battalion, 395th, attacked Kinding and, in two hours of vicious action, broke through into the town and thus obliged the SS troopers holding it to retreat across the Altmühl. The fall of Kinding allowed the 324th Combat Engineers to throw several bridges across the Altmühl so the entire 395th Infantry could advance under cover of darkness. From there, the dryshod infantry drove straight toward the Danube, about sixteen miles farther on.

Early on the morning of April 25, the 99th Infantry Division's 394th Infantry Regiment raced into Mittle Franken, in the north portion of the divisional zone, and then pushed on through moderate opposition into Dietfurt. In the afternoon, two battalions of the 394th Infantry attacked abreast to the Altmühl River after pushing through the remnants of the 17th SS Panzergrenadier Division. After briefly stopping his troops at the river so the 324th Engineers could build bridges, the commander of the 394th decided to continue his attack in darkness against what he sensed was crumbling opposition. The regimental vanguard crossed the river at 0130 hours, April 26, and smashed forward nearly fifteen miles, to a line of dominant low hills within a thousand yards of the banks of the Blue Danube. There, under the fall of mortar and artillery shells from beyond the regiment's right flank, intelligence scouts from the 99th Division's 324th Combat Engineers crept forward to the river to locate and reconnoiter crossings and bridge sites.

During the wee hours of April 26, the Waffen SS troopers screening the river had fired intermittently and then retreated to the other side. As they did, the 393rd Infantry Regiment passed through the 394th's lines and advanced to the riverbank. By 0600 hours, April 26, the entire 393rd and 394th Infantry regiments were arrayed on the banks of the Danube. The 395th

Infantry began arriving near the proposed crossing sites that evening, following which the 324th Engineers conducted site selections along its portion of the river.

Around dawn on April 26, the 291st vanguard arrived at Schamhaupten, ten miles behind the Danube barrier, following a twenty-mile drive on April 24 and a twenty-three-mile drive on April 25 and on into the predawn hours of April 26. Though we had troops and equipment strung out all along the line of march—building and repairing, as usual—our superb communications discipline and earlier experience in the drive across France and Belgium stood us in typical good stead.

We had only just arrived at the new CP site when Bill McKinsey roared in with the news that the 99th Division had reached the Danube. Minutes later, Lloyd Sheetz arrived from the 1159th Group CP with similar news and a firm order directing us to build a treadway pontoon bridge at a site selected by the 324th Engineers' reconnaissance team. According to Lloyd, this was at a boat landing near the village of Heinheim.

After hearing what Captain Sheetz had to report, I turned to McKinsey and told him to reconnoiter the site and report his findings to Ed Lampp. I then sent Sheetz to the 99th Division CP to learn what General Lauer's troops would be doing, so we could coordinate our plans with theirs. Then I told Lieutenants Don Gerrity and John Brenna to pack up the CP and move it forward to a safe spot within five hundred yards of the new bridge site.

I spent the day attending to a thousand details and then drove over to speak with Colonel Fields at the 1159th Group command post. There, the colonel gave me the entire detailed operations plan for the 99th Division's assault crossing. It was impressive. The 324th Engineer Combat Battalion was assigning a complete company to each of the two infantry assault regiments to man a total of 136 assault boats. The third engineer company was to handle a variety of ferries and rafts as well as construct an engineers footbridge as soon as the lead wave of infantry had crossed. The 291st was to build the treadway from the boat landing near Heinheim. We were also to help man the ferries and rafts *and* send troops across to help clear mines.

After following the group commander's explanation on the map, I suggested that we both go down to the river to take a look. As I had feared, we found the bridge site in the midst of a rather muddy area, the result of heavy rain and light flooding during the past week. After assessing the problem and discussing options with the colonel, I left to join my brain trust at our new CP, which was just being set up.

As soon as Mike Popp dropped me off at the top of the hill on which our tents were being erected, I joined Ed Lampp and Bill McKinsey. Bill was grinning over an incident attending his recent reconnaissance of Heinheim, our immediate objective. "At least we'll have the nuns in the Catholic church praying for us on this one, Colonel," Bill began. "When we saw the church steeple near the bridge site, we went in and the nuns took us up to the tower to observe. Then they fed us cookies." According to Bill's interpreter, Sergeant Charlie Sherman, the nuns had been buzzing with glee over the imminent end of the war. Bill reported that he had not been fired on at all while reconnoitering the village or its environs.

Not surprisingly, Bill and Ed Lampp already had a plan worked out. Jim Gamble's Company A was to fabricate the treadway floats, Warren Rombaugh's Company C was to build the bridge, and Frank Rhea's Company B was to work the powerboats and ferry rafts, set the cable, and help clear mines behind the infantry.

When I asked Bill McKinsey what he thought of the bridge site, the slim Black Irishman laughed and allowed as we were facing "the muddiest assault in history. That bottom ground down there would be difficult for pigs to assault through!" Lloyd Sheetz cautioned that we better rustle up some plank tread for the roadway approach, and Mac added that there had to be enough for about two hundred yards of roadway. With that, I noted that it was after midnight and suggested that everyone turn in right away.

Early on the morning of April 27, I joined Colonel Fields for a walking inspection of the cobbled roadway leading to the bridge site through Heinheim. The roadway was in decent shape in the village, but the cobbled surface was poorly maintained as it curved away to the southeast from the edge of town and descended about six hundred yards to the boat landing.

Heading toward the river, I called the colonel's attention to activity I could see on the far side. "You can see some German soldiers milling around over there."

"They don't seem to care," the colonel commented and then returned his attention to the roadway.

"I don't think it will hold many tanks and halftracks," I observed.

"We have no other choice, Dave. We'll have to use the extra treads the bridge company has with it."

"If worse comes to worst, Colonel, we can plank-tread the road approach. That's a long way down to the river, but we'll do our best."

With that, Colonel Fields pointed across the river. "I think the Germans have seen us, and I think we've seen enough for now." He turned and briskly led me back up the hill toward the village.

As we neared the spot at which we had left our command cars and drivers, Colonel Fields turned aside toward a mortar crew that had set up its weapon since we had passed in the opposite direction. We learned that this and many other mortars had been emplaced to support the river assault with indirect fire against Germans like the ones the colonel and I had seen during our stroll. As we were preparing to leave, a German on a motorcycle appeared on the far bank, racing from north to south. With an insouciant shrug, the gunner called his crew to order and the begrimed dogfaces popped off a single round. Seconds later, the rapidly moving motorcycle flew one way and its incautious driver flew the other. I stared at the fallen German until I was sure he would never move again, then I turned to the colonel and said in a low voice, "I've seen so much killing and dead bodies in this war. I hope this is a quiet crossing and that the Germans give it up soon." The group commander, a professional soldier, simply nodded.

The first of the 99th Infantry Division's two assault regiments—the 393rd—jumped off on schedule at 1100 hours, March 27, but things started going wrong almost immediately. The 1st Battalion, 393rd, crossed the Danube without opposition well south of Heinhelm, but it immediately became bogged down on the muddy south bank. As a result, though the Germans never seriously threatened it, the battalion was unable to swing aside to cover the portions of the south bank that other battalions were to assault. In fact, the mud was so bad that the 1st Battalion, 393rd, could not get itself reorganized until after 1700 hours.

When it became clear that the 393rd's crossing was impeded by the mud, the division CP ordered the left-flank battalion to cross onto what was hoped would be firmer ground. Company F of the 2nd Battalion, 395th Infantry, got across the stream in good order but ran headlong into extremely intense small-arms fire and a brutal artillery barrage that pinned it to the south bank.

At the same time, extremely well-planned fire from German small arms, mortars, artillery, and 88mm flak guns pinned the rest of the 2nd Battalion on the north bank, preventing the follow-on companies from moving, much less crossing. Assault boats that had to be hauled across a dike on the north bank were stopped before they could be brought forward, and many were splintered by German shrapnel. Several further attempts to push more troops across in the face of the exceptionally well-emplaced Germans resulted in no progress and heavy casualties. Within the half hour, the division CP called off the 395th Infantry's assault crossing and ordered the 393rd to resume its effort from south of Heinhelm.

The 2nd Battalion, 393rd Infantry, moved to the riverbank while the reserve 394th Infantry fired over the heads of the advancing troops to keep the Germans down. Then, following a brief artillery preparation, the 2nd Battalion crossed south of Heinheim at 1330 hours against zero opposition. However, as the virtually dryshod troops of the 2nd Battalion, 393rd, moved forward, they were all but stopped cold by extremely heavy infantry fire from around Eining. Slow gains through the afternoon eventually forced the Germans from Eining at about 1630 hours.

We had been hoping to begin work on our treadway bridge at about 1900 hours, but by then the infantry was not even close to securing the far shore. I thus spent the entire night of April 27 with Colonel Fields at the 393rd Infantry CP, waiting for word that we could begin. Nothing of the sort happened, so I returned to my own CP at around 0100 hours, April 28, to get some sleep.

The next thing I knew, Colonel Fields was shaking me awake. It was 0630 hours and time to start work. I treated the colonel to a cup of coffee and then we headed out to the bridge site through a heavy downpour. At about the time the colonel and I jumped aboard our command cars, German artillery fire landed in the Company A assembly site, killing Private Arnold Hall and wounding two other engineers. It also killed and wounded a handful of tankers who happened to be standing around.

As planned, as soon as we received clearance to begin, Captain Frank Rhea detailed Lieutenant Wade Colbeck's platoon to build several treadway rafts, complete with outboard motors, so we could begin ferrying tanks and troops to the south bank. On one of the first ferry runs, Frank and Sergeant Joe Conners crossed

the river and advanced to the infantry lines. Finding the infantrymen pinned down, our West Point professional bullied his
way onto the artillery net and called down a barrage on German
positions only a hundred yards in front of where he lay. Relying
on Frank's pinpoint calls, the big guns pulverized the German
fortifications. The infantrymen around Frank launched an immediate assault and quickly overran the dazed German survivors. As soon as the infantry assault got going, Frank and
Sergeant Conners organized the wounded Americans and shep-
herded them to the ferry site with an assist from several Germans
who gave themselves up. The wounded Americans were sent to
the nearest aid station and the German prisoners were put to
work building the treadway bridge approach over the muddy
road from Heinheim.

The pontoon treadway bridge at Heinhelm was to be 450 feet
long. In normal circumstances, we could have completed the
job at a rate of fifty feet per hour, but the site had to be approached through watery mud that sucked in our heavy Brockway trucks and Quickway cranes long before they reached the
water. It took the constant attention of our tireless, skilled bulldozer operators to drag the heavy vehicles—and each other—
out of the mud. Work parties from Company A and Company
B quickly used up all the treads we had allotted to the road
surface, but to little avail. We even had to have jeeps pulled
from the slop.

Incoming fire impeded progress until the troops acquired a
to-hell-with-it attitude and simply concentrated on the job. We
never broke our impasse with the mud, but sheer determination
eventually saw the first section of the bridge take shape. As the
bridge nose slowly progressed across the water, Company B's
ferrymen carried infantrymen and equipment across and brought
scores of virtually unsupervised German prisoners back. Nearly
to a man, the prisoners looked relieved to have survived the
waning war.

At 1830 hours, March 27—twelve hours after starting the
bridge and three hours later than anticipated—Sergeant Ed
Keoughan tied down the last float. Within minutes, an unremitting flow of men and vehicles began debouching into the 99th
Infantry Division's Danube bridgehead.

The wheels and treads of trucks, jeeps, tanks, and halftracks
quickly churned the fragile approach roadway to a foaming
muck, obliging us to leave four bulldozers on permanent duty

to pull mired vehicles free with their winches. Shortly, my troops began waylaying German prisoners who, much to my amazement, went to work shouldering vehicles out of the mud with remarkable willingness. Meantime, I ordered up truckfuls of twenty-two-foot by one-foot by three-inch wooden planks, which Captain Jim Gamble's Company A used to build a plank-tread roadway *around* most of the muddy area.

As I stood in an out-of-the-way spot wondering what we would do if the bypass failed, a jeep bearing a two-star flag pulled up in front of the bridge. Out stepped Major General Walter Lauer, the 99th Division commanding general. Before I could gasp a protest, the general bounded from the vehicle and trudged through the mud to lend his shoulder to efforts to free a stalled truck. Then, as I waded through the mud to join him, the general smiled, patted a few of the more than two hundred workers on the back, and climbed back aboard the jeep. He sped off before I could thank him or report.

We worked long into the night, unloading stone and gravel onto the mud road, adding it on until it settled to the bottom of the quagmire and thickened it into a surface that could support our heaviest vehicles. Next, we brought logs up from the nearby forest and built a corduroy roadway over the sinkholes. Finally, we lined up a number of our vehicles and turned on their headlights to prevent any of the passing tanks or trucks from straying off the roadway and into the mud during the dark hours. At the end of three backbreaking hours, Lieutenants Arch Taylor and Al Edelstein reported the roadway job done and signaled the head of the stalled column to advance to the bridge. Even the German prisoners cheered enthusiastically as the first laden truck negotiated the approach roadway without incident.

The rain never quite abated, but the artillery fire that had killed Private Hall and wounded two other engineers at the outset of the job ended completely within an hour and never started up again. I cannot imagine how much harder the effort would have been had we faced anything approaching the ferocity of the artillery and air attacks we had experienced at the Rhine.

As the first vehicles of the restored column reached the far bank of the Danube, I passed orders to the troop leaders to begin sending the troops back to get some sleep. All hands had been continuously on the job and without rest for thirty-six hours.

CHAPTER 33

The entire 99th Infantry Division was across our treadway pontoon bridge at Heinhelm, on the Danube, by the night of April 29. By then, the 393rd and 395th Infantry regiments had advanced against meager opposition to the Isar River, captured the town of Moosburg, and began crossing on a span erected by the 324th Combat Engineers. In its eighteen-mile plunge from the Danube to the Isar, the 99th Division captured 3,128 German soldiers, an ordnance warehouse, and several ammunition dumps. When the 395th Infantry arrived in Moosburg, it found there a prison camp chock full with thousands of our countrymen and British and Commonwealth airmen and soldiers. Shortly after his liberation from the Moosburg camp, the brother of our own H&S Company's Sergeant Pete Landrum arrived in Heinheim for a surprise reunion.

The city of Landshut fell to the 99th Division on May 1, yielding another six hundred German prisoners of war. The word was that pockets of resistance were drying up and disappearing all across the III Corps front. Munich, the despised birthplace and symbolic home of the Nazi party, fell to the 7th Army's XV Corps. On May 2 the 99th Division crossed the Inn River on an intact bridge. Salzburg and Berchtesgaden fell to the 7th Army's XV Corps on May 4. By then, it had become obvious that the Hitler Redoubt was another fabulous Nazi myth, that little or nothing stood in our way in the mountains behind Munich.

Hitler and Goebbels committed suicide in their Berlin bunker on May 3. Immediately, Hitler's successor, Grand Admiral Karl Doenitz, ordered all German forces everywhere to surrender to the nearest army of any *Western* ally—something short of a full-scale capitulation in that the war against Russian forces was to continue for as long as possible so the bulk of German servicemen and civilians could reach the West. On May 4 all the German forces in northwest Germany surrendered to Field Marshal Montgomery's 21st Army Group. On May 5 all the German commanders in Italy surrendered to the U.S. 5th and British 8th armies. By then, all the forces under General Eisenhower's SHAEF command had been ordered to halt in place while the situation crystallized.

As German intentions became increasingly obvious, General Eisenhower warned Admiral Doenitz that the Western armies would jump off again unless he agreed to an immediate and unconditional surrender to the entire alliance, including the Soviet Union. Doenitz dithered for one more day, but then General Alfred Jodl, the chief of the German General Staff, decided to surrender the Wehrmacht. Admiral Friedburg, who had succeeded Doenitz as the German Navy commander, joined Jodl. At 0241, May 7, Jodl signed the article of surrender. The war in Europe was to end at midnight, May 8, 1945.

We had been sitting around in Landshut for five days when, at 0630 hours, May 7, Captain Lloyd Sheetz ran into the CP with the stunning news that it was as good as over. There was a moment of silence, and then pandemonium struck. Young and middle-aged men all over the battalion area were breaking into tears while they and others ran about shouting gleefully and slapping one another on the back. Ed Lampp and Bill McKinsey broke into an impromptu Irish jig while a stunned and somber Larry Moyer just kept repeating, "It's over." My thoughts went first to the eight members of the battalion who had given their lives for this moment, and to the nearly one hundred others who had shed blood and survived.

The celebration ended in due course and, on May 10 we found ourselves bound rearward, for Hammelburg. The road took us through familiar countryside, for we had fought our way in the opposite direction for most of the preceding month. I was shown the spot at which Paul Kamen and Doug Swift had been killed, and I recited a brief, silent prayer for their souls. On May 14 we again followed the 99th Infantry Division to the rear, into Brückenau, 262 road miles from Landshut. Once there, we got to work helping the infantry restore order by processing prisoners and improving the road net. As soon as we reached Brückenau and located billets, I ordered everyone to clean up and don new uniforms. As soon as possible, we began sending all the troops we could spare on local passes and long leaves throughout France, Belgium, and Bavaria.

On one grisly drive, I arrived at the Dachau death camp with several of my headquarters troopers. No words can possibly describe the barbaric horrors we witnessed, for the place was well short of being rid of its great mounds of withered murdered corpses. There, for the first time really, I realized what the bloodshed had been about. Until I saw Dachau—and despite vivid memories of the Malmédy killing field—I could only just imagine a world in which the Nazi scourge remained afoot. After Dachau, I knew that our war had been a just war, and that all the deaths had been for a glorious, human cause.

We continued to do odd jobs in the 99th Division zone, but the main effort was placed in restoring our bodies and minds. We organized an immense sports meet on June 2 and celebrated the first anniversary of D-Day on June 6. There was not enough to do and, by then, all hands were wondering what we would do next—would we be sent to fight the Japanese or sent home?

Finally, on July 7, I was called to the 3rd Army headquarters and informed that the officers and men with the most time overseas were to be processed and returned to the United States. All others—the bulk of us who did not qualify—were to be given a choice: Either volunteer for service in the Pacific with the 112th Engineer Combat Battalion, a move that would involve virtually immediate home leave, or remain indefinitely in Europe with the 291st. Since I did not qualify for going home, I was offered command of the 112th Engineers, whose own commander was to be sent home. For all practical purposes, then, the 291st and 112th were being consolidated so the 112th could be sent to help lead the invasion of Japan.

I asked the 3rd Army chief engineer why, of all the engineer combat battalions in Europe, we were among the very few being singled out for continued combat duty. He replied that the 112th, which had led off on D-Day, and the 291st, had been specifically requested by the Pacific commanders. More to the point, I was told, Colonel Bill Carter, the 1st Army chief engineer, had been reassigned to the Pacific and *he* had insisted on taking the 291st with him. In the end, enormous personnel problems brought on by the point system had resulted in the decision to offer the consolidation plan.

The impact of the point system on the 291st was that we were about to lose the bulk of our senior sergeants, professional soldiers who had been on active duty far longer than the rest of us. However, I was certain that the bulk of my stalwart troops would follow me to the 112th, if not out of loyalty to me then out of a desire to visit home sooner rather than later.

As expected, almost everyone who qualified volunteered to transfer to the 112th. On July 12 I turned over command of the 291st Engineer Combat Battalion to Major Ed Lampp and left Brückenau with a convoy that included most of the men I had commanded since our arrival in Europe. We had only just reorganized and were beginning to train in Reims, France—the promise of quick home leave conveniently forgotten—when news reached us that the atomic bomb had been dropped on Hiroshima. We knew instinctively that the whole bloody war was about to end.

The 291st Engineer Combat Battalion, Major Ed Lampp commanding, was deactivated on October 20, 1945, at Camp Patrick Henry, Virginia. The 112th Engineer Combat Battalion, incorporating most of the men who had fought across Western Europe under my command, was deactivated on November 12, 1945, also at Camp Patrick Henry.

EPILOGUE

The 291st Engineer Combat Battalion Association continues to hold annual reunions. In 1988 there are 365 active corresponding members, including widows, who attend on a regular basis. Since the end of the war, we have learned of the passing of over one hundred of our comrades and have been unable to locate 267 of the men who served with us in Europe.

Among us are physicians, educators, statesmen, oilmen, farmers, accountants, engineers, ministers, salesmen, contractors, scientists, mechanics, railroaders, executives—a true cross-section of our society, thanks in part to the educational benefits many of us enjoyed under the GI Bill. Many remained on active duty in the Army or served in the National Guard or U.S. Army Reserve, and, now that old age has overtaken us all, many of us continue to serve our nation and our communities in a stunning variety of volunteer activities.

Here is a sampling of what became of some of the men who served their country in the 291st:

Chuck Hensel, now retired, lives in Gasport, New York, spending much of his time communicating with members of the squad he led with such distinction.

Al Edelstein, still an active civil engineer, lives in Virginia, Minnesota.

Ed and Peggy Lampp live in retirement in Pensacola, Florida, where Ed was a consulting engineer and educator.

Tom Stack lives in Boynton Beach, Florida. He is a retired AT&T executive.

Larry Moyer, who retired to Tampa, Florida, passed away in 1987.

Ralph McCarty, who farmed and was a public servant in Turon, Kansas, passed away in 1988.

Jim Gamble went to medical school on the GI Bill and practiced in Lovingston, Virginia, until his death in 1988.

John Perkins lives in Louisville, Kentucky, where he is still working as a civil engineer.

Joe Conners, now retired in Buffalo, New York, was known to millions of wrestling fans over the decades as the Masked Marvel.

Wade Colbeck worked as a civil engineer in Freeland, Michigan, until he passed away in 1986.

John Conlin fully recovered from the serious wounds he sustained on Christmas Eve 1944 in Malmédy and became a railroad executive and raised a large family before he passed away in 1985.

Big Max Schmidt also recovered from his wounds and went on to become a lumber industry executive. He is now retired and lives in Shelton, Washington.

Frank Rhea stayed in the Army Corps of Engineers and retired with the rank of colonel following an immensely distinguished career. He now lives in Golden, Colorado.

Jim Walton also stayed in the Army and also retired as a colonel before moving to Albuquerque, New Mexico.

Mack Barbour was commissioned after the war and also rose to the rank of colonel in the Army Medical Corps. He makes his home in Norman, Oklahoma.

Bill McKinsey lives in retirement in Fresno, California, following a career as a certified public accountant and running his own business.

Bucky Walters, a retired engineer, lives in Edmonds, Washington.

William Miller served as an engineer and missionary in Africa for many years.

Charles Sweitzer recently retired after many years service as an Army Corps of Engineers civilian architect at Fort Belvoir.

I cannot help but think as I read over this short list that our wartime accomplishments as a unit were ensured by the terrific human substance we brought with us as individuals. Who we were helped us succeed in battle, and what we became in the war helped us succeed as individuals, as productive citizens of a nation whose greatness we helped preserve and whose thankful bounty helped us reach our full potential as citizens, as fathers, as husbands, and as men.

ACKNOWLEDGMENTS

This book was compiled with the enthusiastic support of many of the men, some now deceased, who served with the 291st Engineer Combat "Damned Engineers" Battalion in Europe. Those of our immediate comrades who helped are listed in the bibliography.

"Outsiders" who provided material help or assistance are Colonel Ron Damon, my first battalion commander; Brigadier General Harvey Fraser; Major General William Carter; Lieutenant General E. R. Heiberg, chief of the U.S. Army Corps of Engineers, and his excellent staff of historians—Dr. John Greenwood, Dr. Barry Fowle, and Dr. Charles Hendrix; Dr. Charles B. MacDonald; Charles Hammer, 285th Field Artillery Observation Battalion Association; Jürgen Raths, West German Ministry of Defense; Morton Tuftedahl, 99th Infantry Battalion (Separate) Association; Robert Culver; Adolph Walsavage; Major General Mike Reynolds, former British commander of NATO Mobile Ground Forces and Kampfgruppe Peiper scholar; the staff of the U.S. Army Military History Institute at Carlisle Barracks, Pennsylvania; François de Harrene, the mayor of Malmédy; Hans Peter Kurten, mayor of Remagen; Emile Lecroix, creator of the Lienne Creek monument; Clyde Taylor, our literary agent; and Tom Stewart and Erika Goldman, our editors.

My fellow engineer and old friend Tom McKinney rates a special mention for assistance and acts of friendship too numerous to mention, not the least of which was moral support.

All of the photos appearing in *First Across the Rhine* are official U.S. Signal Corps photos. The majority of them were taken by my colleague, Sergeant Calvin Chapman of the 291st Engineer Combat Battalion.

In closing, I offer a special thanks to Mrs. Marietta Anderson

for providing a great deal of material about her late husband,
the redoubtable Brigadier General Harry Wallis Anderson, USA
(Ret).

DAVID E. PERGRIN
Wallingford, Pennsylvania
July 1988

APPENDIX A

Staff and Command Roster
291st Engineer Combat Battalion
December 15, 1944

Commanding Officer	LtCol David Pergrin
Executive Officer	(vacant)
S-1	1stLt Donald Gerrity
Asst	WO John Brenna
S-2	Capt William McKinsey
Asst	1stLt Leroy Joehnck
S-3	Maj Edward Lampp
Asst	1stLt Thomas Stack
S-4	Capt James Walton
Asst	WO Coye Self
Liaison Officer	Capt Lloyd Sheetz
H&S Company	Capt Max Schmidt
Medical Officer	Capt Walter Kaplita
Dental Officer	Capt Paul Kamen
Motor Officer	Capt William Smith
Asst	1stLt Clifford Wilson
	WO Robert Bryant
Company A	Capt James Gamble
Executive Officer	1stLt Frank Hayes
1st Platoon	1stLt Albert Walters
2nd Platoon	1stLt Alvin Edelstein
3rd Platoon	1stLt Archibald Taylor

Company B	Capt John Conlin
Executive Officer	2ndLt Robert Marshall
1st Platoon	1stLt Wade Colbeck
2nd Platoon	1stLt John Kirkpatrick
3rd Platoon	1stLt Frank Rhea
Company C	Capt Lawrence Moyer
Executive Officer	1stLt Martin Tintari
1st Platoon	1stLt Donald Davis
2nd Platoon	1stLt Warren Rombaugh
3rd Platoon	1stLt John Perkins

APPENDIX B

**Staff and Command Roster
291st Engineer Combat Battalion
January 15, 1945**

Commanding Officer	LtCol David Pergrin
Executive Officer	Maj Lawrence Moyer
S-1	1stLt Donald Gerrity
Asst	2ndLt John Brenna
S-2	Capt William McKinsey
Asst	1stLt Leroy Joehnck
S-3	Maj Edward Lampp
S-4	Capt Max Schmidt
Asst	2ndLt Coye Self
Liaison Officer	Capt Lloyd Sheetz
H&S Company	Capt James Walton
Medical Officer	Capt Frank Watson
Dental Officer	Capt Paul Kamen
Motor Officer	Capt William Smith
Asst	1stLt Clifford Wilson
	2ndLt Robert Bryant
Company A	Capt James Gamble
Executive Officer	1stLt Frank Hayes
1st Platoon	1stLt Albert Walters
2nd Platoon	1stLt Alvin Edelstein
3rd Platoon	1stLt Archibald Taylor
Company B	Capt Frank Rhea
Executive Officer	2ndLt Robert Marshall

1st Platoon	1stLt Wade Colbeck
2nd Platoon	1stLt John Kirkpatrick
3rd Platoon	2ndLt Ralph McCarty

Company C	Capt Warren Rombaugh
Executive Officer	1stLt Martin Tintari
1st Platoon	1stLt Donald Davis
2nd Platoon	1stLt Thomas Stack
3rd Platoon	1stLt John Perkins

APPENDIX C

The Bailey Bridge

The Bailey Bridge, invented by Sir Donald Bailey, is an engineering marvel that is built by hoisting various scientifically determined combinations of prefabricated five-by-ten-foot vertical "panels," each weighing five hundred pounds, into position across an obstacle such as a stream or a ravine and then installing a tank-bearing roadway. Sir Donald's concept was so perfect that, virtually unchanged in a half century, the Bailey bridge is still an engineering mainstay in Western armies in the late 1980s.

The first step to installing a Bailey bridge is to make a reconnaissance of the proposed bridge site. Those making the reconnaissance use a steel rule to determine the length of the bridge, from abutment to abutment, and the grade, if any, by using a level.

Once the length has been determined it is simply a matter of looking up the construction requirements on a chart. If the length is ninety feet, for example, the chart will indicate a "double-single" bridge. That is, the completed girder (or bay) will be two panels wide on each side and one panel high so the bridge will be able to bear a forty-ton load, the weight of the heaviest tanks we had in Europe in 1944. The greater the length of the span, the more girder strength is required to bring the bridge up to the then-required forty-ton capacity.

Bailey bridges can be built to a maximum length of 180 feet, which requires a "double-triple"—a bridge two panels wide by three panels high. Other bridge lengths would yield other combinations—single-single, single-double, double-single, triple-single, and so forth.

Once the length and girder-construction panel combinations are determined, the necessary parts are ordered from a bridging company that is part of the engineer combat battalion's own engineer combat group. The bridging companies act as both depot and delivery units, and the men in them are trained to assist in the building of the bridge if the situation is particularly pressing.

If an entire engineer combat platoon is to build the bridge, it moves into the bridge site and, as soon as the bridge parts arrive, sets steel base plates on either abutment equidistant to a center-line string that is extended across the obstacle. Rollers are emplaced on the base plates so they will be beneath each girder.

Next, a single-single "nose" panel is fabricated. This temporary assembly will be used to balance the progressively heavier load of the progressively longer bridge and to complete a landing on the far side of the obstacle.

The prefabricated five-hundred-pound panels are emplaced by an eight-man team using rack sticks and bolted into position. While one squad is hoisting the panels into position and installing pins to form the girder span on either side of the bridge, another squad clamps I-beam lateral transoms to the girders. The third squad, which assists the others during the heavy construction, will place the flooring longitudinally on top of the transoms and bolt the curbing in place when the entire bridge structure is fully emplaced.

As each bay is completed, the platoon moves the entire bridge out over the ravine on the rollers and then begins work on the next bay. Once the nose of the bridge is landed on the far side of the obstacle, the nose panels are removed and the bridge is removed from the rollers by means of hydraulic jacks. Then the flooring is installed, as are the end ramps and bracing to stabilize the structure. Finally, signs are placed facing traffic at either end of the bridge indicating that it is a Class 40 bridge, which means that vehicles may not exceed a single-load limit of forty tons.

Even in training in England, our fastest platoon was able to install a ninety-foot double-single Bailey span in only four and a half hours, a very good time.

BIBLIOGRAPHY

BOOKS

Beck, Alfred M., et al. *The Corps of Engineers: The War Against Germany.* Washington: U.S. Army Center of Military History, 1988.

Bergen, Howard R. *History of the 99th Infantry (Norwegian) Battalion.* Oslo: Emil Mostue, 1972.

Blair, Clay. *Ridgway's Paratroopers.* Garden City: Doubleday & Co. and The Dial Press, 1985.

Bradley, General Omar N. *A Soldier's Story.* New York: Henry Holt & Co., 1951.

Eisenhower, David. *Eisenhower at War, 1943–1945.* New York: Random House, 1986.

Eisenhower, General Dwight D. *Crusade in Europe.* Norwalk: The Easton Press, 1948.

Esposito, Brigadier General Vincent J., ed. *The West Point Atlas of American Wars*, Vol. II, 1900–1953. New York: Frederick A. Praeger, 1959.

Gallagher, Richard. *Malmédy Massacre.* New York: Paperback Library, 1964.

Gavin, James M. *On to Berlin.* New York: The Viking Press, 1978.

Giles, Janice Holt. *The Damned Engineers.* New York: Houghton Mifflin Company, 1970.

———, Ed. *The G.I. Journal of Sergeant Giles.* New York: Houghton Mifflin Company, 1965.

Hammer, Charles A. *History of the 285th Field Artillery Observation Battalion.* 285th Field Artillery Observation Battalion Association, 1978.

Hechler, Ken. *The Bridge at Remagen.* New York: Ballantine Books, 1957.

Hewitt, Robert L. *The Story of the 30th Infantry Division.* Washington: Infantry Journal Press, 1946.

Lauer, Major General Walter E. *99th Division Battle Babies.* Indiana, PA: A. G. Halldin Publishing, Co., 1951.

Leinbaugh, Harold P. and John D. Campbell. *The Men of Company "K"*. New York: William Morrow & Co., 1985.

MacDonald, Charles B. *A Time for Trumpets: The Untold Story of the Battle of the Bulge*. New York: William Morrow & Co., 1985.

McKinsey, William L. *History of the 291st Engineer Combat Battalion*. Privately published by Edward R. Lampp, Jr., 1946.

Plonski, Edward. *Rhine Journey: The 78th Infantry Division*. 78th Infantry Division Association, undated.

Sayer, Ian, and Douglas Botting. *Nazi Gold*. New York: Congdon & Weed, 1984.

Weigley, Russell F. *Eisenhower's Lieutenants*. Bloomington, IN: Indiana University Press, 1981.

Whiting, Charles. *Skorzeny and the Massacre at Malmédy*. New York: Stein and Day, 1972.

SPECIAL STUDIES

Gregoire, Gerard. "Fue-Fire-Feuer-Vuur (Dessinateur Emile Lacroix)," 1982.

_____"Decembre, 44 Les Panzer de Peiper Faces à' US Army, 1976."

DOCUMENTS

After-action reports and unit journals of the following units: 291st Engineer Combat Battalion, 51st Engineer Combat Battalion, 1111th Engineer Combat Group, 1159th Engineer Combat Group, 105th Engineer Combat Battalion, 303rd Engineer Combat Battalion, 202nd Engineer Combat Battalion.

MISCELLANEOUS

Private papers, tapes, and other documents used in completing this study were provided by Brigadier General Carroll Dunne, Brigadier General H. Wallis Anderson, Major General William Carter, Major General Mike Reynolds, Colonel Edward Lampp, Lieutenant Colonel Lawrence Moyer, Colonel Frank Rhea, William McKinsey, Ralph McCarty, Bernard Koenig, Joseph Geary, Joseph Connors, Hon. Ken Hechler, Sheldon Smith, Oran Nunemaker, Albert Walters, Lee Van Lew, Jim Coupe, Virgil Lary, Joseph Masurkeiwicz, Max Schmidt, Edward Woertz, Harold Burnap, Fred Holtzer, Leroy Joehnck, Charles Sweitzer, Francis Simington, Louis Dymond, Ed Keoughan, Peter Piar, Carl Russo, Stuart Getz, Glen Salsburg, Charles Bissell, John Scanlan, Vincent Corcoran, Raymond Nice, Bernard Goldstein, and John Williams. Additional documentation pertaining to the Malmédy Massacre was kindly provided by John M. Bauserman.

INDEX

ABOUT THE AUTHOR

COLONEL DAVID E. PERGRIN graduated from Penn State University in civil engineering. He commanded the legendary 291st Engineer Combat Battalion in World War II, called the "Damned Engineers" by Colonel Joachim Peiper, when they slowed and finally halted the Panzer "Blitzkrieg" thirty-eight miles inside the American lines. He has since become a historian of the 291st, and lectures frequently on the subject. The men of his battalion are role models for the Corps of Engineers. He has served as a consultant to NATO and in 1988 he received Penn State University's Outstanding Engineer Award.

ERIC HAMMEL is a professional military historian with a dozen books to his credit, including *The Duel for Golan*, *Ace!* and *A Marine Night-Fighter Pilot in World War II*. He and his family live near San Francisco.